JOHN

C000066295

# 'MANN' AND MANNERS

### AT THE

## COURT OF FLORENCE

### 1740-1786

*FOUNDED ON THE LETTERS OF HORACE MANN*
*TO HORACE WALPOLE*

### VOLUME II

Elibron Classics
www.elibron.com

# 'MANN' AND MANNERS

AT THE

## COURT OF FLORENCE,

1740—1786.

*FOUNDED ON THE LETTERS OF HORACE MANN
TO HORACE WALPOLE.*

BY

## DR. DORAN, F.S.A.,

AUTHOR OF

'LIVES OF THE QUEENS OF ENGLAND OF THE HOUSE OF HANOVER ETC.

*IN TWO VOLUMES.*
VOL. II.

LONDON:
## RICHARD BENTLEY AND SON,

Publishers in Ordinary to Her Majesty.

1876.

LONDON :

PRINTED BY WILLIAM CLOWES AND SONS,
STAMFORD STREET AND CHARING CROSS.

# CONTENTS OF VOL. II.

## CHAPTER IV.

### 1761, 1762.

## CHAPTER V.

### 1763, 1764.

## CHAPTER VI.

### 1765.

## CHAPTER VII.

### 1766.

## CHAPTER VIII.

### 1767, 1768.

## CHAPTER IX.

### 1769, 1771.

## CHAPTER XVII.

### 1781, 1782.

## CHAPTER XVIII.

### 1783, 1784.

## CHAPTER XIX.

### 1785, 1786.

# 'MANN' AND MANNERS

AT THE

## COURT OF FLORENCE.

## CHAPTER I.

### 1758.

In the January letters of this year, Mann deals largely in matters of small importance. On February 11th, he writes :—

'We have been a fortnight in weepers for the good Princess Caroline,' (third daughter of George II.) 'I am vastly concerned for every accident that may give affliction to the King, who has too many motives of a publick nature to be unhappy; domestick concerns are frequently the most sensibly felt.'

As Sir John Gray (whose father was said to have been a groom) was not sent to Madrid, but was left at Naples, with the Order of the Bath to console him, Mann was left at Florence. In a letter of February 11th, he writes :—'Lord Bristol expects it' (the post at Madrid) 'and should he succeed I shall have no ambition to supply his place at Turin. The climate,

the court which occasions so great expences, and the
example of such a predecessor, are sufficient objections.
Lord Bristol gives 500*l.* a year for his house, and has
everything in it equal to that expense. What could
anyone do who has only his appointments to live
upon ? . . . I am a good deal surprized to see Lord
Huntingdon in the list of those who wish to go to
Spain. He must have altered his mind strangely, or
have had occasions to convince him that a Court life
meets with more rubs than when he was determined
to accept only of preferment there.' Lord Bristol
went as Minister Plenipotentiary to Spain, and he was
subsequently Lord Lieutenant of Ireland.

Mann occasionally writes at great length concerning the progress of what came to be called 'the
Seven Years' War,' but it is for the most part a mere
reporting or denying the assertions in the foreign
gazettes. One incident alone in these dull details is
worth extracting. It refers to the war being carried
on in the winter. 'The French,' he says, 'suffer extremely, and are quite disgusted of fighting in fur,'
and again, 'The Court of France seems displeased
with its favourite hero, Richelieu, as he most heartily
is with the rough Germans who make him fight in
cold weather.' But these matters, gossiped about in
Florence, and concerning nations, were as nothing
compared with circumstances concerning the personal
welfare of Walpole. Mann closes his letter of the
above date with these words :—' I am extremely glad
to hear that your eyes are better ; but still beg most
earnestly that you will spare them. Reflect only on
the general preference that all deaf people give to

their sight, and don't risk the loss of so precious a
faculty. Sir William Stanhope assured me, when he
was in Florence, that if he could only recover from
his deafness, or rather thickness of hearing, that he
would, that instant, willingly become blind. No one,
I think, can understand this, but the fact is that deaf
people are always melancholy, and blind commonly
gay. I am desired to tell you that when you dip
your head into cold water, that you should stop your
ears with cotton. I can't bear the thought of either
faculty being weakened . . .' This message sent by
desire from Florence is as important to bathers as ever
it was, and will be.

And now the time, dreaded by some, hailed by a
few, arrived when the Grand Duchy of Tuscany,
supposed to be neutral, was called upon as an imperial fief to send a contingent to the army of the
Empire, in aid of Francis and Maria Theresa against
the King of Prussia. On the 4th of March, Sir
Horace writes :—' You can't think what a military air
everything has had here for the fortnight past, nor
will believe the feats that these troops promise to do ;
there is not a Cadet or an Ensign who will not take
the King of Prussia and carry him, dead or alive, to
the Empress Queen. I don't joke. One has heard
of twenty of their schemes ;—to dress themselves in
the Prussian uniform to get access to him, for that
purpose. The common men, I believe, will not make
so much ceremony of it, but will go over to him in
their own cloaths in great numbers. The publicity
with which they talk of deserting is uncommon ; but
this has put the young officers upon exercising their

four or five facchin (?) horses, (which were only meant
to march) to make an attempt to run after them.'

' One has seen troops of these boys, especially on
holy days, on the publick Corso, forcing through the
rank of coaches as fast as their nags would go, to
show the Ladies what exploits they will do in the
field.   This has afforded some disorder and much
mirth ; but what has been very solemn is a review
of each division, by Marshall Botta, the day before
its departure, in Via Longa.   So new was this
spectacle that many preferred it to their dinner.   The
Marshal is never visible to the ladies but in the
streets, in his fine Equipage, commonly of six horses,
and his Ecuyer on a white one ; a sight we had not
been used to since your old Princess Craon who, to
make her visits about the town, used to go out of one
gate, to come in at another, for the sake of the
*Appanage.'*

Voltaire has been called the most French of all
Frenchmen, the truth being that he had nothing at
all in him of the Frenchman, except those two qualities which he found in himself—combinations of the
tiger and the monkey—combinations which he therefore affected to find in all his countrymen as personal
and national characteristics.   He covered with his
abomination the noblest woman of his country that
ever lived—Joan of Arc ; and he had the incon-
ceivable baseness to compliment the King of Prussia
on gaining the victory of Rosbach over the French.
Mann sends this example of Voltaire's homage to the
King of Prussia,—a sample which moved even easy
Florence to indignation :—

' De petits rois, de grands exploits,
    Frederic ! la moitié suffit pour votre gloire.
Vous êtes le model et la terreur des rois ;
    Chacun de vos instants est compté dans l'histoire ;
        Vos ennemis, au Temple de Mémoire,
            Gravent eux-mêmes votre nom,
        Et l'univers doute qu'une victoire
            Vous content plus qu'une chanson.'


'. . . Did you ever hear the answer the King of Prussia made to a crowd of French officers, prisoners, who were presented to him after his victory at Rosbach ?—who complained of the straightness of the Quarters that had been allotted to them ?—"Vous avez raison, Messieurs, mais je ne m'attendais pas à si grande compagnie ! "

'I forgot to tell you that the 3000 Tuscans are to take their oath to the Empress-Queen, at Lintz, and to enter into her pay and service.'

Walpole was, however, instructed in other matters than those referring to Frederick and Maria Theresa ; among others, to the medals in the Stosch collection, concerning which, Mann (May 13th) mentions as some of the most curious :—' 1st. Paul 3rd, with the Ganymede on the reverse.   It is of bronze doré of the same coin as that in silver, for which, in silver, Stosch demands 20 zecchins ; that in bronze costs a trifle. . . Neither is very rare.   2nd. Julius 3rd, with the reverse : *Anglia, resurges.*   3rd. Innocent 10th, with the reverse : the Capitol.   4th. Gregory 13th, with the reverse : *Hugonotorum Strages.*   This medal becomes very rare from the pains that the Court of

Rome takes to buy them and destroy them. 5th. The mezzo piastro fiorentino, with the reverse, *Jesus Rex noster et Deus noster*, which was struck in Savannerola's (*sic*) time, when, by his advice, this State was put under the protection of Jesus ;—this is very rare. . . . I have of my own a medallion of the Empress Queen when she was friend to England, and when our Fleet protected her ; which is expressed on the reverse, among other figures, by Neptune, with the motto : *Securitas Augustæ;* also a smaller medal of the Emperor and Empress, struck by Cardinal Albani, on the birth of the second Arch-Duke, whose head, opposite to his brother's, is engraved on the reverse, with *Æternitas Imperii* . . . and also a most ridiculous vulgar brass medal struck by some Irish priest at Rome. On one side is a figure with a halter, by which the Devil is leading it to hell ; with the words, " Make room for Sir Robert ! " and at the bottom, " No Excise ! " On the other side is a figure in robes and in armour, with " The Generouse Duke of Argyle," and at bottom, " No Petitioners ! " Your friend, Mr. Deimer, whose title I have forgot, wanted much to have it, as a monument of the vulgar animosity of the times. I had almost forgot an insolent medal of the Pretender. . . . Stosch holds his obscene drawings and prints, both Chinese and others, at a vast price, and has views of being able at some time or other to dispose of them to the King of Prussia.'

'. . . Lord Bristol is making vast dispositions for going to Spain. . . . Twelve men out of livery ; thirty in livery ; and six pages ; by which you may judge of the rest.'

But by far the most important news that Sir Horace had to communicate at this time, was that of the death of Prospero Lambertini, the learned, amiable, and gently-joking Pope, Benedict XIV. *May 6th.*— ' Five couriers passed by yesterday, directed to the different Courts, with an account of it, some of whom go so near England, that it will soon get there. It is thought that there will not be much caballing at Rome for the new Election. The Cardinals will endeavour to be inspired before the heats come on, as they are so dangerous in that part of Rome. The Conclave will soon be ready, as everything has been so often prepared for it.'

*June 3rd.*—' You was at Rome the last Sedia Vacante, and know what a tedious piece of business the Cardinals made of it, and that, even at last, the factions could only agree in choosing a man who was incapable of offending either, for neither the Corsinis nor the Aquavivas meant to do so well as choose Lambertini. The Albani party, in defiance of the French King's message to the Colledge to stay for the arrival of his Cardinals, was near abridging the whole ceremony, in favour of Cardinal Mosca, but the attempt failed, and probably will exclude him for the future : so that I can't possibly tell you who will be Pope.

' . . . There has been a fracas in the Conclave between the Turinice Cardinal de Lanze and Cardinal York. The latter went to compliment him upon his arrival, but observed that during the whole visit, he never once pronounced the word *Altezza* or joyned anything royal to *Eminenza.* Cardinal York stifled all his resentment at the time, but resolved to be even

with him, and waited for the return of the visit, the
hour of which having been asked and granted, Cardinal de Lanze proceeded with ceremony, but found
the door of York's Cell shut, and was refused admittance.  This affront caused a complaint to the Cardinals who are called *Capi d' Ordine*; to whom
Cardinal York pretends to justify his behaviour, by
alledging that he was the first offended by the refusal
of the title which all the other Cardinals gave him.
Cardinal de Lanze states that he could not deviate
from the rules of his Court, and so this important
affair is like to remain undecided.'

'Cardinal de Lanze has some tincture of royal
blood on him.  His father, who was called Comte
de Sales, was bastard uncle to the present King of
Sardinia.'

*July 6th.*—'. . . The Holy Ghost gave the Pope
a successor in the last week, and settled so long on
Cardinal Cavalchini that the Inspiration was not in
the least equivocal.  Thirty-four votes were resolute
for about 24 hours, and in spite of all that the french
Cardinals could do to engage them to suspend their
decision till the arrival of Cardinal de Rodt, the
German Cardinal who, it is supposed, brings the
Secret of the Court of Vienna,—that is the term ;
*such a one has the Secret of such a Court ;*—but in
vain, and they were determined to proceed on the
next morning to the liberation of their own Idol,
when Lo ! ! Cardinal de Luynes produced the french
King's exclusion.  This struck amazement in the
whole Conclave, whilst Cavalchini was reposing in his
Cell, and pleasing himself with his future grandeur ;

which reflections and golden dreams which the Time
might well produce, nobody would interrupt that
night.  It was agreed that his great friend, Cardinal
Lanti (?) should the next morning announce to him
the fatal stroke.  *Fatal*, for though by the answer
which was given out in his name, he was supposed to
have received the news without any emotion, yet it is
said that the disappointment will kill him.'  The
answer made public was :—'. . . That he desired that
his most humble thanks might be made acceptable to
the King of France, for having eased him of so great
a burden as that of being *Vicario di Cristo in terra!*'

' The motive for the exclusion is, for being a subject of the King of Sardinia, but his voluntary (*sic*)
crime in the eyes of France is his being a declared
friend of the Jesuits, and having wrote strenuously
for promoting the Canonization of Cardinal Bellarmine,
—which proves sentiments which might be dangerous
in the present religious fermentations in France.  A
courier was immediately despatched thither with the
news.

' It is said that Cardinal Durini too was to have
been excluded by the same Court, had he come up
first.  His crime is, the having, when Nuncio, refused
to make a visit to Madame Pompadour.  But, as
France has made use of its exclusive faculty, if it
should persist to forbid the elevation of Durini, which
they now say is very likely to happen, France must
borrow an Exclusion from the Empress-Queen, or some
other Court.

' Archiuto too is in great *predicamento ;* he has
no other objection (*sic*) but his great youth, for he is

but 60 years old ; an age which is subject to many inconveniences, particularly that of living too long, which the Cardinals more, ripe in years would be much offended at.   Rome has abounded with Satyrs (*sic*) from the beginning of the Conclave, but none good. This event may, perhaps, produce something either in a satyrical, political, or perhaps in a tragical way that may be worth attending to, as the Jesuits,—who have had so many mortifications of late in Portugal, and, since the Pope's death, by a Bull he left signed ; and now, by the exclusion of a Pope on a suspicion of his being their friend,—have on slighter occasions, shewn strong resentments.'

'The Pretender was, the last week, in the greatest danger.   His health has been, long, much impaired ; and though he was better when the last accounts came from Albano, it was the general opinion that he can't live long,—having some organick disorder in his stomack.   The Cardinals offered Cardinal York leave to go to attend his father ; but his religion teaches him, that he must reject the ties of blood and humanity to attend to the duties or rather cabals of the Conclave.   Cardinal Bardi has, however, left it on account of his own health.'

*July 7th.*—'. . . I announce a Pope to you, in the person of Cardinal Rezzonico, a Venetian of 65 years old.   The cabals that have brought about this event are not yet known, but it rather looks as if it had been done to exclude others ; but it is odd ; had the Holy See itself had any influence, it would not probably have disposed of itself to the subject of a State' (Venice) 'that was on the point of Excommunication, for disobedience to the Church. This will probably heal all soars, and make the Republick as obedient a Daughter as any. I even foresee the end of exile and return into favour of your old pretty acquaintance, Madame Capello. In short it must have many whimsical consequences. Great is the disappointment of others who have failed, and of those who could not succeed for their friends.'

'Cardinal York, whom Pasquin has made cry: "Ha! ha! ha! Nescio, Domine, loqui!" has offended the Court of France beyond all reconciliation. His father was already on that foot. The french Cardinals could not believe that he would persist for Cavalchini, when reminded by them of the great benefices he has in France, and that they desired him to desist; but that argument has always had little weight with Churchmen. They then addressed themselves to his sick father at Albano, believing that filial duty might have some weight. So it had,—to add to his obstinacy. Cardinal York's answer to his father, the Pretender, was, that he had rather loose (*sic*) his head than do anything against his conscience. Cardinal Lanti was in the same case, having lately had great benefices from the Court of France. He therefore persisted in favour of Cavalchini; both out of friendship, and a promise of being his Secretary of State. The French have discovered that they have neither interest at Rome, nor must expect gratitude in the Sacred Colledge.'

While the papal election was thus being carried out to completion, Mann's items of news and notes of passing events were of various sorts. Marshal

Botta he found to be as poor a politician as he was a general. 'The Great Duke (and Emperor) Francis, entreated him, as Vice Great Duke of Tuscany, to draw up the credentials of the new Tuscan Envoy to England, Pucci.' They were expressed in such transcendental haughtiness that our Government did not know what to make of them. 'There is a hitch,' says Mann, in the fixing Mon$^{sr}$ Pucci in England, Marshal Botta attempted a piece of grandeur with regard to his credentials that did not succeed, and he must correct them.'

Next, Mann sends to Walpole a copy of King Richard's Provençal Poetry; transcribed by young Cocchi, who succeeded to his father's appointments. The professorship of anatomy brought him 100 crowns a year, that 'of Antiquarian,' 180 crowns. 'He has copied it with the utmost attention. The first was made in much hurry, but he thinks he can answer for every letter of this being exactly as the original; he thinks too that he understood more parts of it; and, had he time, he would have made a little dissertation upon it, though even St. Palais, who has taken the most pains to interpret the old Provençal language, is uncertain in many cases.'

Turning from poetry to Stosch's collection of intaglios, Mann writes:—'Old Stosch was the first who had the idea of making a suite of them as of Medals. The number of Intaglii, set in gold, as rings, is upwards of eight hundred, and near fifteen hundred unset. His own method was to set two in gold and four in silver every week. The latter was purely such as served for history . . . The Cammei are not

very numerous . . . The medals are, and supposed
to be fine in many branches.   He was in treaty for
some time with the Pope, for his collection of maps,
which is prodigious, and for which Cardinal Valenti
had offered thirty thousand crowns to the late Baron ;
a price which he himself owned to be extravagant, but
which did not however tempt him to sell.    His
nephew, the present possessor, hoped for some time
that the Pope would have given him 20,000, in order
to make a present of the collection to the Institute
at Bologna ; but the treaty seems to have been broken
off.    Stosch's library too is very considerable.   He
has great offers from France, where he has already sent
all his Cammei.    Mme. Pompadour, who engraves
herself, has put this branch of virtú into fashion.'

Florence, according as it sided with French or
English interests, was divided into parties on the
question of a naval engagement, of which Mann gives
this account :—

'Our little engagement off Carthagina will do the
greatest honour to the two ships that engaged the
French, who surely will be ashamed, for the future, to
make use of an impertinent expression which they
were said to, in speaking of the Dutch ships, with
regard to their own of equal force: " Nous nous battrons;" and of the English, "Nous les battrons." Monsieur Du Quesne, I hear, is more modest, and does his
antagonists more justice.    There is no instance, they
tell me, of a 64 gunship fighting for three-quarters
of an hour with one of 84, at the distance of a pistol
shot, and making her strike, for though another ship
was come up within Gunshot, none fired on the

Foudroyant but the Monmouth. Mons. Du Quesne was put on board the Hampton Court, Capt. Hervey, whose politeness is of their own sort, and whose magnificence probably exceeds anything they have on board a ship.'

'Count Lorenzi' (French Ambassador) 'will not allow this little victory, having heard from Barcelona that the Foudroyant was got safe into Malaga, nor will admit that the distance between these two ports is sufficient to invalidate the authority of his correspondent, so that really on that alone, many wagers are still depending.' Of the modern Tuscan bravery, Mann says:—'The Tuscan troops that went from hence, are not to be trusted in the field, but are to remain in Garrison at Vienna. This is doing them justice which they will probably take for a compliment.'

'The King of Prussia is inimitable. . . On hearing that the Tuscan troops had arrived, he said haranguing his men, "Mes enfants, il est toujours inglorieux de tourner le dos, mais à present il seroit dangereux aussi."'

Next, on matters of art, Mann says:—'I have lately had a commission from Mr. Hoare, to buy the Carlo Cigniani and the Carlo Maratti, in which is the portrait of the Marquis of Pallavicini and the painter himself, out of the Arnoldi Collection here, but the former was bought about a fortnight before by order of Hamilton the Painter, of Rome, for 500 Pistoles; which I suppose must be a secret in England. It is said to be for Lord Litchfield. The picture was always kept up to 2000 crowns, or £500; but the

present possessor being conscious that it is much
damaged and decaying very fast, was glad to get that
price for it. The Carlo Maratti I have secured for—
which must be a secret too—900 crowns, though the
old folks always insisted on 2000. I only wait to
their getting a licence to send it away, for Richecourt
made a law some years ago, to prohibit the exportation
of any valuable things of this nature, or in sculpture ;
just as if the country was rich enough to prefer them
to money.'

As agent for the purchase of pictures,—the cheap
rates at which they were bought being supposed to be
kept secret,—Mann received handsome commissions
from some of his principals. 'I have received the
magnificent present which Lord Northumberland has
made me ; a prodigious fine snuff-box which must have
cost a great deal—a sumptuous token of his Lordship's generosity.' When Mann speaks of 'Hamilton
the Painter, of Rome,' he refers to Gavin Hamilton
who, if not the first of British artists who had settled
in Italy, was perhaps the best known. He was a
Scotsman of ancient lineage, and he inherited an
estate in that country, but he spent nearly the whole
of his artistic life in Rome ; painting pictures or
successfully bringing to light some of the buried art-
glories of the old Roman Empire. Gavin Hamil-
ton's ' line ' was severely classical. *Jupiter* Carlyle of
Musselburgh obtained that pre-name from his sitting to
Hamilton as a model for the King of Gods and Men.
His picture of the dead Hector, dragged at the chariot
foot of Achilles round the walls of Troy, was bought
by the Duke of Bedford ; but the Duke sold it soon

after the death of his son, the Marquis of Tavistock, who was killed by a fall from his horse and being dragged in the stirrup. Hamilton died in Rome in 1797. He was so good an Italian that, it is said, grief at the entry of the French into Rome, killed him.

*July 29th.*—'I can learn nothing of the Pope worth sending you. He has made a piteous regulation about the dress of Canonici and Abbés, by which they are forbid to wear powder or ruffles, flowered silks, or pockets to their coats;—and are not to frequent the Assemblies. Some, to excuse him, say that it is a thing of form; and quote the late good Pope who, at the beginning of his reign, to a numerous audience, recommended modesty in dress and behaviour; but concluded by singling out a Monsignore Frescobaldi, an old fellow remarkable for his slovenliness: "A voi parlo, particolaramente Monsignore Frescobaldi, e dico che non voliamo Ganimedi," upon which the whole Assembly burst into laughter.

'The present Pope, however, has shewn some resolution, in persisting to give the important post of Datario to Cardinal Cavalchini, notwithstanding the opposition of the French Cardinals, who, not content with having excluded him from being Pope, forbid all the subjects and dependants of their Court to address themselves to him.—The Pope, nevertheless, has fixed him in it, and they despatched an Express to Versailles, to complain to the King.'

'. . . Our friend, Captain Hervey, has done a good deed in destroying lately a mischievous-doing ship, called La Rose, of 36 guns and 300 men. He drove her a shoar (*sic*) at Malta, and the French, to prevent her falling into his hands, set fire to her. The Maltese exclaim at this insult to their coasts; but as they fired 200 shot at our ships without hurting them, Captain Hervey, in his turn, sent to complain of the insult done to the King's colours. He had promised me a visit of two or three days, but Lord Bristol hurries to Genoa, whence he is to carry him to Alicant.'

This Captain Hervey was one of the four sons of 'Molly Lepel,' the charming wife of John, Lord Hervey. Three of those sons became successively Earls of Bristol. Captain Hervey, at this time, had been privately married to the famous Miss Chudleigh, since 1744. A quarter of a century later, this lady married the Duke of Kingston; which marriage was declared illegal by the House of Lords.

*August* 19*th.*—'. . . I am endeavouring to hear something of the new Pope, by which you may judge of his character; but I think he has none. The first thing he did was to lop off the superfluous parts of the Abbés' dress and locks. He never goes out but in publick which puts all Rome in a bustle, from the vast ceremony it is attended with. He is a sayer of sentences, but very different from the facetious ones of his predecessor. When the General of the Jesuits went to complain of the persecution which his order was under, the Pope replied: " Ci volevano tre cose, Tempo, Silenzio ed Orazione." When the Venetian ambassador told him what honour the Republic had conferred upon his family, he said, " It was greater than they had deserved, but that they had done nothing as yet, for *him!* meaning the repeal of the decree which has been the subject of their quarrel

with Rome. This is a point which will decide his
character.'

The news of the triumph of the English at Louisbourg was received at Florence, by the English party,
with great satisfaction, but with such caution that
they only whispered their congratulations in Mann's
ear. ' The consternation of the French party,' Mann
writes, September 9th, ' is greater than I can describe.
It was in proportion to the hopes they had conceived
of a quite contrary event. . . . Monsieur Chavigny
assured Count Lorenzi, by letter, that the English
would soon be obliged to raise the siege, at the very
instant that I received mine with the account of the
surrender. Both which letters, going about the town
at the same time, met and made the most ridiculous
contrast that can be imagined, till I appeared at
Marshal Botta's and declared the victory.'

' We were alone for some time, and I could
perceive it did not cause the same sensation as it
probably did at Vienna and Paris. The Nuncio came
in, and as a few days before, and in the same place,
I had some warm disputes with him on the subject,
I had a pleasure in repeating all the circumstances
which I had communicated to the Marshal, tho' the
latter, out of eagerness, frequently took the words
out of my mouth. Count Lorenzi hopped in, in the
evening. . . . . "This America," said an ignorant
Cavalier, " has it anything to do with Vienna ? "
Thinking that the taking Louisburg opened a direct
passage thither. Another said at Botta's table :
"Truly, the loss of Louisburg is a disgrace ; but we
must wait to see the issue of the siege of Cape

Breton"!! In France, public rejoicings were made, by order, for the alleged raising of the siege of Louisbourg.

'The Pope has been so much abused for his simple Letter to the Senate of Venice, and for giving up the rights of his Church to his native country, that he fell ill upon it. He so far mistook the matter, however, that, in his answer, he thanks the Republick for yielding to him as Sons to a Father; and tells them that he cried for joy. They laugh from the same motive.'

*September 16th.*—'Our passions are strangely and very differently agitated of late. We were still rejoycing for Louisburg . . . when the melancholy account of the repulse at Ticonderoga' (unsuccessfully besieged by Abercromby in July) 'came in and struck such a damp on the whole company that was accidentally with me at table, that would be difficult to describe. . . . There was a letter under my cover for Stosch, who was present, containing an account of the King of Prussia's victory at Zorndorf, on the 25th. Joy got the better again, and we triumphed for a day or two. . . . Marshal Botta supports the vulgar opinion that the King of Prussia was obliged to cross the Oder with a loss that he will never recover. . . . The Marshal had the weakness to say that the pomp of sending an officer (with news of a victory) to Berlin, preceded by so many postillions, might be to deceive Berlin, and to prevent the ill consequences of a popular alarm on his defeat.' Zorndorf, however, was a fairly won victory. The Czarina's army lost, in killed and wounded, nearly 22,000 men; the Prussians lost about half that number.

'The Abbé Bernis is to be made a Cardinal, soon, which will make him perter than ever. Mons. de Stainville, le fils, is to be made Duc et Pair. These are evidences of the Pompadour's power. They have both wit, which is all. The latter has lately wrote, "qu'il est fatigant d'être français à Vienne," where it will be long ere we desire him to be anglois.'

*October* 21*st*.—'We are told here that an expensive firework is to be played off at Paris, for the victory gained over the English at Ticonderoga; for the defeat of the English troops and the complete victory of the French at St. Malo. One would believe from such instances, that the French think it necessary to sing *Te Deum* whenever their troops will fight and are not beaten. The Parisians probably are not such dupes, however necessary their Ministry may think it to amuse the people with such shows whilst they are loading them with unheard of taxes. It is quite the fashion to make free with *Te Deums*. The Austrians and Muscovites have sung them for the latter's supposed victory at Zorndorf, whilst the King of Prussia has done the same; and to convince the world that his was the only good one, he has drove the rest of the Muscovites into Pomerania, and a large garrison which they had left at Louisberg, to deceive him, into Poland.'

'Count Woronzow, who is the soul of the Russian Ministry, such a soul! a very little more animated than an oyster, was here in your friend, the Princess's time. She, unluckily, was not quite dazzled the first time Madame Woronzow went to visit her. No case was ever more embarrassing. It was impossible to

admit a very fine—great—young woman to the mis-
teries of a worn out Toilette, and it was as improper
to make a relation of the Zarına wait.    In this
dilemma there was only the choice of faults.    The
Russian grandeur must suffer ; but such a resentment
was prepared as showed what impression the affront
had made.    An opportunity soon offered at a great
dinner to which many ladies were invited.    Madame
Woronzow made them wait full two hours, telling
people who pressed her to go, that it was too soon, and
that the Princess would not be drest ; then went
herself in an undress, accompanied by her husband
*in his boots and spurs !*    The Princess, either to do
the honours of the table, or for fear of being spurred,
put herself at the head of it, so distant from either
of the Woronzows, that she must have had a speaking
trumpet to hold any conversation with them ;—
another affront which they resented *sur le champ ;*
for Madame Woronzow, pretending to have the tooth-
ache, ordered a Couch to be got ready, and went from
table before the Dessert was brought on.'

    ' I had the honour to be on the Princess's right
hand during this whole scene.    Nothing went right
that day.    The dinner was bad.    The servants served
ill, and I remember that at the second course they put
a row of flasks on both sides of the table, like a
rifettorio di Frati.    The Princess stared, and turning
to me, asked " pourquoy tant de flasques ?    Est ce que
l'on fait ça chez vous ?    Il me semble que cela desorne
furieusement ! "    " Effectivement," said I,    " Ce n'est
pas beau." '

    ' The Count kept no company at Florence but the

Post-master, with whom he was always galloping through the streets, to see the Gallery and the curiosities of the town. I never saw the Princess better pleased than when they went away.'

'We are impatient to see whether our fleets will return to sea, and upon what expedition. This of the Mediterranean has had no luck of late. There are, however, three French men-of-war out, and some of ours are in quest of them. Admiral Brodrick goes ten times a day up to Mr. Dicks' tower in hopes of seeing them brought in; but the time is past and we begin to despair. I have escaped making the fleet a visit this time at Leghorn; reciprocal invitations have passed between Admiral Brodrick and me, et voila tout.'

It was about this time that the French were said to be preparing to 'return our visits' to their coast.

'There are even rumours,' says Walpole to Mann, 'of some stirring among your little neighbours at Albano,—keep your eyes on them; — if you could discover anything in time, it would do you great credit." With this warning, the eyes of Sir Horace were inquisitively directed towards the house of the old and young Chevalier, but he could discover nothing. À propos to the hint relating to the folks at Albano, Mann writes, November 18th:—'I cannot think there can be anything going forward there. The old man is decaying so fast, that he cannot hold out long. It is much doubted whether he knows anything of his son, who most likely would not consult him, even if anything was in agitation, as he

could not in the least contribute to it.   However,
pray let me know what you hear on this subject in
England.'

Mann's last letter of the year ends with a pleasant anecdote, told in return for details sent by
Walpole, and told in his letters, of the delicate
generosity of the Duke d'Aiguillon to the English
prisoners, taken in an abortive attempt on the French
coasts.   ' I am charmed with the humanity and good
breeding of the Duc d'Aiguillon to our prisoners.   I
believe that our people have behaved generously, at
least in similar cases.   Captain Stanhope, to whom
Mons$^r$ Du Quesne struck, received him and most of
his officers on board his ship, and treated them for
thirty-two days with the greatest hospitality and
attention.   His generosity particularly appears in
restoring to his prisoners everything that was personal.
Mons$^r$ Du Quesne had on board a set of plate, some
jewels and toys, to the value of 1500*l*.   I much
question, notwithstanding their great politeness, if the
French would have pushed this generosity so far.
Fighting will soon become a very polite occupation.
It is the Muscovites only who retain their ancient
savageness.   Their Empress' (Elizabeth, daughter of
Peter the Great) ' drinks destruction to the Prussians
in every dram, and her soldiers confirm it with *an
oath upon their sabres*.   It is certain that they would
neither accept nor give quarter at Zorndorf.'

Mann was in a position to tell the Florentines
that the French pushed their generosity to the same
extent as the generous Captain Stanhope.   Walpole
had informed him some months previously that, in

the hurry of the retreat from St. Malo, the Duke of Marlborough (grandson of the great Duke, and descendant of Waller's Sacharissa) left his silver spoons behind. As he had generously sent back an old woman's finger and gold ring, which one of our soldiers had cut off, the Duc d'Aiguillon sent a cartel ship with the prisoner spoons; and, in October, Walpole wrote to Mann:—" You yourself, the pattern of attentions and tenderness, could not refine on what he has done, both in good nature and good breeding; he even forbad any ringing of bells and rejoicings, wherever they (the English prisoners) passed.'

# CHAPTER II.

## 1759.

THE amenities of war receive a fresh illustration in Sir Horace Mann's first letter of 1759, dated January 20th:—' The French are making great preparations and threaten us with an invasion, or a surprize on Gibraltar. . . . They are, with four or five ships only, already masters of this part of the Mediterranean. They have actually blocked up the Gibraltar, man-of-war, at Villa Franca; and two days ago, one of the privateers took a merchant vessel in sight of Leghorn. It belonged to an old Quaker, who would not trust to his prohibition to the Captain to shed blood, but allowed him neither cannon nor any arms to make the least resistance.'

In November of the preceding year, an attempt was made to assassinate Joseph I., King of Portugal ; who narrowly escaped death.    Under the idea that the attempt was the result of a wide-spread conspiracy, many noble Portuguese were killed under torture, and their names declared infamous.    The Jesuits were expelled the country.    In reference to these events, Mann writes : —' We have received the

first accounts, but not the particulars, of the conspiracy in Portugal. . . . I must tell you that the
Nuncio, who in the beginning not only wrote positively that the King's hurt proceeded from a fall, but
forbade his friends giving any credit to the report
*they would soon hear*, that His Majesty was wounded,
now writes that he had his reasons for telling such a
Lye. The Portuguese ministers might have had good
reasons for concealing the truth. Their conduct in
this affair, till the King's danger was over, and the
making all secure before they published the discovery,
does them great honour.'

The account of the cruel executions which
followed the discovery, sent a shudder through usually
indifferent Florence. In a later letter, Mann writes :
' We are expecting a whole detail of the conspiracy,
and of the method of executing it, which is printing
at Rome, where nobody attempts to conceal the part
which the Jesuits had in it. The Nuncio at Lisbon
persisted to the last in his assertion that the King had
not been assaulted, but had only hurt himself by a
fall downstairs. He now says that he had his reasons
for persisting in that story. Monsignore justifies Sir
Henry Wootton's definition of a publick minister :
"Legatus est vir bonus peregre missus ad menticudum
Reipublicæ causâ," which he himself translated thus :
" An Ambassador is a good man sent to lye abroad
for the good of his country." The Nuncio was as
ready to do it for another. The whole management
of the affair since, does great honour to Mons^r Car-
valho, the Portuguese Minister ; but Marshal Botta
attributes the King's escape alone to the visible care

which God takes of those he has appointed to govern
the world.   This, he says, nobody can dispute.'

On the subject of divine intercession, Mann
adds :—' Our weather this winter has been just
such as you describe, the merit of which is totally
attributed to the Madonna dell' (*illegible*), whom, you
may remember, was brought down to Florence, after
the Inundation, when you were here.   The whole
Town went to her on the late one, to ask for a cessa-
tion of rain and for fine weather,—and obtained it.
This neither can anybody dispute ;—and, if you won't
believe it, ask Marshal Botta.'

The following lines were now circulating in
Florence, and Mann thinks them witty enough to
send a copy to Walpole :—

> ' Nos Rivaux triomphants,
>      Notre Gloire flétrie,
>      Notre Marine anéantie,
>      Nos Isles sans defense,
>      Nos Ports saccagés,
>      Le Credit epuisé,
>      Le Peuple surchargé ;—
> Voila ! le digne fruit de vos conseils sublimes,
>      Trois cent mille hommes egorgés !
> Bernis ! est ce assez de victoires ?
> Et le mépris d'un Roy pour vos petites rîmes,
>      Vous semble-t-il assez vengé ? '

De Bernis, that particular and witty favourite of
Madame de Pompadour, was at this time nine and thirty
years of age.   He had been for ten years a member
of the French Academy.   His gracefully licentious

verses justified M. de Mirepoix in refusing to confer
any ecclesiastical benefices on this vivacious abbé;
but on the fall of that minister, Louis XV. presented
him to the Benedictine Abbey of Saint Arnault, Metz,
a benefice worth 30,000 francs a year. In 1752, De
Bernis was sent as French ambassador to Venice, but
he was thought too young and too low in the ranks
of the Church to sustain that dignity; therefore, the
King of France raised him in this year, 1759, to the
dignity of Archbishop of Alby; and he subsequently
attained a higher elevation.

'. . . Our ships have taken some liberties of late
with ships under Tuscan colours, and carried them
into Gibraltar, which has gone further, and condemned
them as lawful prizes; but, by lucky discoveries that
I have made, I have proved that those ships had
nothing Tuscan about them, but their colours and
their false bills of lading, in the names of some
Tuscan merchants, solely with a view of covering
them against the French; but that both belonged to
Irish merchants at Leghorn and Cales, who never
dreamt that they had anything to fear, in this clan-
destine trade with French effects, from their own men-
of-war. The Marshal's dignity is greatly hurt by not
being able to support that of the Emperor's *Pavillon;*
and when I tell him that he must be indifferent about
the event of these disputes at Gibraltar, as Tuscan
subjects have really no concern in them, he talks of
the letter of Treaties and of Neutralities. I object
the abuse of them; so that we never agree.'

*June 26th.*—' On our great festival of St. John,
(the 24th) Marshal Botta was acting the Great Duke,

and receiving homage for him, with the addition of all
the Imperial dignity.' (The French were then threaten-
ing to invade England).  'The Marshal has hitherto
frightened me by telling me how easily we may be
conquered.  I am now prepared to tell him that we
wish to have such an opportunity to demolish the
naval force of France.  That which is at Toulon
seems to keep itself as a corps de reserve, though they
had fixed the 16th to send it out to drive Admiral
Boscawen from their coasts ; but in the mean time,
he sent three of his stout ships close in to the shore,
to demolish two frigates that had crept in unseen.
Our brave captains, unlike some of those in the East
Indies, in spite of several batteries that played continually upon them, drove those ships ashore, and
dismantled one of the batteries, at Cape Sicie.  The
Culloden was so much hurt, that she only escaped by
being towed off by all the boats of the Fleet.  The
French were astonished at the bravery of this action,
which will probably deter them from engaging with
fifteen more such brave fellows.'

The above incident occurred at nearly the close
of the life of this fighting Admiral,—who died in
January, 1761, after fifty years of hard work.  Lord
Chatham did Boscawen full justice, in these words :
'When I apply to any other officers respecting an
expedition I may chance to project, they always raise
difficulties ; Boscawen always finds expedients.'

Among the popular Englishmen at Florence was
Lord Northampton.  'He seems' said Walpole of him,
'to have too much of the coldness and dignity of the
Comptons.'  Walpole announced Lord Northampton's

approaching marriage with Lady Anne Somerset,
sister of the Duke of Beaufort; to which Mann
replied:—'The news that he is going to be married will
displease here ; as it will destroy the hopes which he
has constantly cultivated since his arrival in England,
that he would be back again here, in September next ;
but for three posts he has been silent.   It is awkward
writing to an old Love, when a new one has taken its
place.'   To this Walpole rejoined, in August:—' Lord
Northampton has not acted a much more gallant part
by his new mistress than by his fair one at Florence.
When it was all agreed, he refused to marry unless she
had eighteen thousand pounds.   Eight were wanting.
It looked as if he were more attached to his old flame
than to his new one; but her uncle, Norborne Berkeley,
has nobly made up the deficiency.'

Among the unpopular English travellers who
sojourned at Florence, was a Mr. Dering.   Mann
barely names him, but Walpole shows what advantages this young gentleman had derived from his
foreign experiences :— ' There is a dreadful Mr. Dering
come over, who to show that he has not been spoiled
by his travels, got drunk the first day he appeared,
and put me dreadfully out of countenance about
my correspondence with you;—for mercy's sake, take
care how you communicate my letters to such cubs.
I will send you no more invasions, if you send
them to bears and bear leaders.'   In the meantime,
interests more important were at stake.   ' A letter was
read a few days ago at Marshal Botta's, in my presence,
giving an account of the notification which Monsieur
D'Afrij is supposed to have made to the States General,

of his Master's intention to make a descent in England, with the young Pretender at the head of it ; and lest that circumstance should make the Dutch suppose that by their Treaties they would have to furnish 12,000 men, the French Monarch assured them that as England had very unjustly begun this war, so they (the Dutch) were discharged from that obligation. This was really the sence of it, and I should not wonder if it was the literal speech of Mons<sup>r</sup> D'Affrij, and that the Dutch were convinced by force of his eloquence.'

*June* 30*th.*—' We have just received notice of the death of Cardinal Borghesa. This makes the 22nd vacancy. The Pope has almost promised to fill them up the 16th of next month, the anniversary of his own promotion. Such sort of reasons have great weight with him in every thing. Never was any Successor of St. Peter more generally and more publickly despised. Your late old friend did not want such a foil, but it makes his character appear more amiable in every respect.'

*July* 21*st.*—' The King of Portugal ' (Joseph I.) ' has referred (in some measure only) the affair of his Jesuits to the Pope, who being one of the best friends they have, has chosen a number out of the Colledge, as partial as himself, to study the affair and advise him what to do. The Empress would have gone very differently for the Jesuits, had your old friend Lambertini lived, who most undoubtedly would have erased St. Ignatius from the Calendar, and annulled the Order. . . .'

The project of invading England with a French force, headed by the young Pretender, was still a source of uneasiness to Mann, who relates the following curious incident in connection therewith.

'. . . Marshal Botta, who says he knows those things very well, literally told me t'other day, that nothing was so easy, though the enterprize was very hazardous. I attributed my not understanding the distinction to my ignorance in military affairs, and in order to confirm the latter part of his sentence, I enumerated the considerable Fleet we had before Brest and on our Coasts ; with the troops, both regular and new-raised Militia, that we had to prevent their landing ; but, as a Marshal, I found he had but a mean opinion of the latter, being persuaded that a handfull of regular troops would put thousands of them to flight. I must however do him justice, that he is not partial ; nay, it is plain, as M. de Stainville said at Vienna, that he finds it bien fatiguant d'être Français. He provoked me, however, in the sequel of his discourse, upon my telling him that Admiral Boscawen's Fleet was gone towards Gibraltar, to get water and provisions, by insinuating that it was to avoid fighting the French who were certainly coming out to attack him ; and that he probably would not give the French the advantage of fighting so near their own Ports. This is the turn that, I see, everybody will give it ; though our people are persuaded that the French would never have come out so long as the English were waiting for them ; and this is a point that the partizans of each will positively decide as their inclinations lead them.' Nothing could be more absurd than the insinuation made by Marshal Botta. A reluctance to fight the French at any odds was a thing utterly unknown to him. Once, at night, in the single ship then under his command, he was aroused from sleep by his first Lieutenant, who announced that there were three French ships near; and who asked what, in such circumstances, he should do ? " Do ? " exclaimed Boscawen, jumping up : " Do? damn 'em; fight 'em ! " '

*July* 28*th.*—' Count Lorenzi and all his colleagues abroad have received orders to declare that his Master, the King of France, has resolved to invade England, in spite of all the precautions and numerous fleets to defend our coasts. I was much diverted by an article in the common newspaper here, relating to the method of Admiral Rodney's proceedings—summoning the Governor of Havre de Grace to deliver up to him the flat-bottomed boats, but that the Governor's refusal to comply with that reasonable request, obliged Rodney to set to work and do all the mischief he could. . . . I am sorry for this sort of war, not only for the sufferers, but for the consequences. . . . The animosity in the lower people is reciprocal, and as great as possible, and would always produce cruel effects, if not restrained by their superiors.'

' I cannot have the least fear that the French will interrupt your building ; the addition which you are about to make to your castle will make it big enough, in case of need, to confine many of them in your round Tower.'

' Your sister-in-law is going to build here. She has taken a fancy to a small house and gardens in the skirts of the town, belonging to the Salviati family. The reparations that are absolutely necessary to make the house habitable will, according to the plan that has been sent to Rome, for Duke Salviati's approbation, cost 2000 crowns, or 500*l*., which it is probable he will give her leave to spend, and promise to let her enjoy as long as she pleases, for an easy rent. . . . The weather is hotter here than for many summers past; but I love the heat so much, that I do not even complain when it arrives to excess.'

*August* 25*th.*—'An Express, the arrival of which I always dread, brought the first news to Marshal Botta, of the advantage which the Muscovites gained over the King of Prussia, twelve days after the victory of Prince Ferdinand over the French, which prevented the latter from taking possession of the whole Electorate of Hanover. . . . Marshal Botta so far immediately announced it to the publick as to make his own French Horns play for some hours in his courtyard ; but he does not dare yet continue to sing a Te Deum, for fear it should turn out a victory on the other side, like that at Zorndorf. I dare not, however, flatter myself that the King of Prussia will be able to extricate himself from the many dangers that surround him.'

'. . . The month of August in which the French threatened to invade us, is near over, and the season will soon increase the difficulties and dangers of executing it. Most sensible people in France look upon this enterprize as the dotage of an old Land officer who knows nothing of sea-expeditions.'

'. . . We are persuaded here that the King of Spain is dead. Three couriers passed by very lately, within a few hours of each other, and neither would give himself the time to speak a word but to hasten the saddling of his horses.   The King of Naples (now, King of Spain) will surely go by sea, to avoid an interview of which the French have renewed the report, just as if they did not know that it would be the most disagreeable thing to the King of Naples, in the world.'

*September* 8*th.*—' A Courier from Naples passed by, a few days ago, for England, by whom you will have heard of the new King of Spain's intention to set aside his eldest son, as an Imbecile, to declare his second son Prince of Asturias, and the third (Ferdinand) King of Naples. This has been notified at Naples, by a despatch or order to each of the people who are to examine the unhappy young Prince, for form's sake. This sets aside the Treaty of Aix, and the dispositions of so many Courts, none of which seems at present in a condition to oppose it, though the pretensions of either of them would have been sufficient in any other conjuncture to have kindled a war in Italy ; perhaps, indeed, it may only be deferred till they are more at leisure to support them.'

' France will lose something of its dignity on this occasion by abandoning the interests of her son-in-law. She has been a little out in her politicks too, by making herself so principal a party in the match between the Archduke and the Princess of Parma, a preference which the new King of Spain thinks his daughter had a right to.   Such accidents may long contribute to confirm the new King of Spain in our interest, and in all probability, we shall not neglect the opportunity to make a merit of being the first to acknowledge the dispositions with which he begins his reign.'

'A Spanish Fleet is on its way to Naples, where orders have been given that everything be embarked the 20th of this month; and the Court proposes to depart the 10th of the next, on which day little Prince Ferdinand is to be declared King.'

*September 15th.*—'The new King of Spain sent his order to all his Counsellors, Physicians, etc., to examine the state of mind of his eldest son, not doubting that they would unanimously agree about his imbecility; upon which all his Majesty's other dispositions depend, but that does not go on so smoothly as was expected. Dr. Sarreo, one of their most accredited physicians, differs from the rest, they have called in the surgeons, and in many meetings were come to no resolution, though at first the whole was looked upon as a piece of formality only. Maturity, they say, may produce a great change in the young Prince's constitution; and after all, as a Commander-in-Chief who, in the height of the confusion at Genoa, would not stir an inch before he had heard his Mass, said to me, that God might work a miracle; if the majority of Counsellors should be of this devout opinion, one might naturally suppose that they do not look upon Imbecility to be any impediment to Government.'

'There are other seeds of disturbance. The people are clamorous against Tannucci and Gregori. The first is a very honest and learned man who, though he has long enjoyed the King of Naples' confidence, has too much sense not to see that neither in the King's absence he could maintain his credit, or could support it among the Grandees at Madrid. Marquis Gregori,

who is confidant of the Queen but not of the people,
has, by their clamours, been called upon to give an
account of all the money raised or disposed of during
his Administration.'

'The city too have desired a conference with the
King in secret which, after many day's refusal, has
been granted. All this portends some domestick disturbances. At the same time it is said that the
courts interested in the execution of the Treaty of Aix,
will at least protest against the nomination of a King
of the Two Sicilies, which they had destined for Don
Phillip.'

'The Florentine Government is under great consternation by the notice they have received, that a
Prussian Privateer (which they call an English vessel
under Prussian colours, and on that account take it
very ill of us) had seized a Tuscan vessel in those seas,
and carried it into Cagliari. This is the first instance
of hostilities being committed against the Tuscan
colours by the above new flag, which will find a good
harvest for some time. Our governors here are too
much alarmed to be able yet to take any resolution,
though they are continually consulting about it.'

*September* 29*th.*—'His Prussian Majesty never
shines so great as in his resources after a defeat, and
he now seems again in a condition to act offensively.
It is true that he was obliged to abandon Dresden
after he had lost all the rest of Saxony, but is it not
strange that the inhabitants of the capital received their
deliverers with the utmost coolness, so that it is not
thought safe to let the troops of the Empire remain
there. Both the Empresses' (of Russia and Germany)

' are ruining themselves in presents to their armies,
though neither has gained an inch of ground by their
valour that day; it is highly probable that this campaign will finish like the last, when each party will
content itself with the hopes of doing great matters in
the Spring. The King of Prussia has still 160,000
men on foot. The desertion of any one of his enemies
would give him a superiority that would make the
rest tremble; and really one cannot account for the
perseverance of the French in Germany, which
exhausts them of money and reputation at the time
that their affairs go so ill everywhere else.'

'I return by this post my compliments of congratulation for Admiral Boscawen's victory at sea; for
the defeat of the army that was to have saved
Niagara; and for the taking of that place, Ticonderoga, and Crown Point. How will you contrive to
crowd all this into one Te Deum? It must be like a
Mass that they say at Vienna for the souls of all who
have died in a whole campaign.'

' At Naples, things take a more peaceable turn than
was expected. No one has objected to the decision of
the Imbecility of the young Prince, nor seems to have
thought of our good Marshal's confidence, that God
would work a miracle for him. The report, a most
confused performance, has been made, wherein they
applaud the King's profound sagacity in perceiving
that his son was past all hopes of recovery.'

' Part of the Spanish Fleet has arrived at Naples,
and they are hastening the disposition for the King's
departure. France will be beforehand with us, in
approving everything that the new monarch pleases

to do, and in acknowledging the young King' (of the
Two Sicilies) 'whom he designs to declare.   A French
Courier passed by last week with everything that
could be wished on that subject, though we hear
nothing of the Courier that was sent to England.'

'On the 20th, the Pope made 22 new Cardinals
and twice as many enemies by excluding the Governor of Rome, Caprera (?), and the Secretario della
Consulta, Cenci, whose employments give them a right
that has never hitherto been set aside.   The first was
too gallant with the woemen, and the latter wears too
spruce a wig ; crimes unpardonable with him.'

*October* 12*th.*—' I want strength and patience to
support the reproaches that are made us here, for
violating the Law of Nations, and the respect due to a
neutral state by destroying the French ships on the
coasts of Portugal.   I don't know whether the French
themselves are weak enough to object to the legality
of Admiral Boscawen's victory over them, but their
partizans here are very clamorous.'   When a French
snow captured an English brig, under the cannon of
Leghorn, Mann claimed that the brig should be given
up ; but Lorenzi, the French Ambassador in Tuscany, opposed this, on the ground that an enemy may
continue his pursuit into limits within the jurisdiction
of a neutral state.   On the present occasion, Mann an-
ticipated that Lorenzi would abandon his old argument
and deny the legality of Boscawen's victory.   Captain
Hervey agreed with the Count's earlier reasoning —
'when he, not long ago, pursued and destroyed the
Rose, a French 20 Gun ship, under the cannon of
Malta.   The Grand Master endeavoured to prevent it,

but I never heard that he complained or declared war
with us for it.    The Tuscans are almost inclined to do
it, for lending our Privateers to the King of Prussia.
They are gone towards the Levant, where they may
have a great harvest.'

'The new King of Spain is gone peaceably to take
possession of his new kingdom; and has given his old
one to his third son; to which nobody has raised the
least objection.    He will, however, send a body of 12
thousand Spaniards to defend this young king against
his domestick and foreign enemies.    The latter will
probably discover themselves when they are more at
leisure.'

'It is no wonder that Kings and Empresses are
the principal subjects of our letters, since the welfare
of mankind so much depends upon them, especially
now that they choose to be at variance.    Can one be
indifferent to the vast preparations that the Monarch
of France is making to conquer the Three Kingdoms,
at the time that we are endeavouring to exclude him
from a greater extent of country in America?    These
are interesting objects.    The success of the latter
depends upon Quebec, which I hope to hear of by the
next post, since you could not send it to me by the
last.'

*November 3rd.*—'I announce to you the arrival
here of a devout Catholic Lord, Arundel, with his
Jesuit Governor, Booth; whose devotion would not
permit them to continue their journey yesterday, out
of respect to All Souls. . . Count Firmian here has a
regular correspondence with a bookseller (Dodsley, I
believe) who sends him everything that comes out,

so that his collection of English books is remarkably great. . . . I lent him, when he went to Naples, Middleton's works, to read here and on the road, and they prolonged his journey. They became his own too, and I have since had them again from England.'

'I am impatient to inform you of the arrival of one hundred and thirty-three Jesuits at Civita Vecchia, a present which the King of Portugal has made to Pope Clement, who very unlike his amiable predecessor, cherishes that turbulent sect; but has, on their account and on his unpardonable recommendation of them to the Prince they would have assassinated, met with the greatest mortifications.   His Brief, or Publick Letter to the King, who knew the contents of it, was detained a long time, and then sent back unopened. His Nuncio despatched it by his own valet de chambre, en courier extraordinaire, with the notice at the same time that the Jesuits were embarked the same day, and that this pestiferous merchandize was to be landed in the Pope's State!   This was done a few days ago; so soon as they are all safe (I mean except the three Arch-wicked) they no doubt will begin to write and perplex the most clear cases with their lies, to defend themselves and to justify the tenets of their Order.'

'A foolish thing of this kind came out some time ago, in which the attempt to naturalize the Jews in England is made the ground-work of the whole.   It is said, they had already given thirteen millions sterling to the Parliament, which was one hundred and twenty millions in debt, and resolving not to restore that sum to the Jews on the (*illegible*) of the

Bill, cast about how to indemnify them, and luckily thought of recommending them to Portugal, to engross all the trade and set on foot at the same time the exchange of some territories in Paraguay, between Spain and Portugal, and then, to clinch the ascendant which England attempted to have over the Kingdom of Portugal, the Duke of Cumberland was to marry the Princess of Beira,—twenty more absurdities like this which, however great, meet with their protectors, so as to draw one plump consequence—that the whole report of the attempted assassination of the King of Portugal is an invention, without foundation, to put the Jesuits into an odious light, and if the King was really wounded, which many of the partizans doubt, it was done by the Queen Consort, to lay the odium upon them.'

The news of the great victory won by Wolfe and his gallant soldiers at Quebec highly elated the English Colony in Florence ; but the French and Italian Gazettes, having their own idea as to how history should be written, exhibited the character and quality of the idea, by Paris furnishing, and Italy adopting, the following version :—' The Court has just received· by a small vessel which has arrived at Bordeaux, from North America, the confirmation of the victory gained by the Marquises of Vaudreuil and Moncalm over the English who threatened to besiege Quebec. A furious tempest destroyed the greater part of their squadron on the river St. Laurence.   The French have captured five of their line of battle ships, and made 2,500 of their regular troops prisoners. This loss will render it impossible for the English to undertake anything, for a long time, in that quarter. In the meantime, M. de Moncalm will profit by his advantage to recapture the Forts which had fallen into the hands of the Enemy.'

The above is a translation of a cutting from a French Gazette, which Mann sent, and which still lies loose in his letter of November 10th, 1759, to Walpole. Sir Horace truly adds, of such an impudent attempt to write contemporary history, that 'what heightened the ridicule of it is, that in the Supplement of the Gazette to which this scrap belongs, there was a translation of the Articles of the Capitulation!'

Speaking of an antique column which Mann had despatched to Strawberry, he says:—'You will be as much surprized as I was about a month ago on hearing that that column was buryed six feet underground, to be out of the way! I can't tell how I came not to hear of it sooner, for the burial was performed two years ago. I accidentally asked after it, at Marshal Botta's, on recollecting I had not seen it, and he told me of its fate. "Buryed!" said I, "'tis the first that was ever hidden in such a manner. It has had the fate of its pedestal, which was made use of as rubbish for the foundation of Viviani's lying Arch, and both to be out of the way." The Marshal seemed struck with the reproach (though it was not his doing) when I observed to him what pains and expenses people were at at Naples, Rome, and all other classic ground, to bring such things to light; and that the Goths themselves had never taken the pains to bury them.'

*November* 17th.—' All the news that Italy affords

this week, consists in the arrival at Genoa, of 122
more Jesuits from Portugal; who were not permitted to land but were to proceed to Civita Vecchia
with the first fair wind. Their brethren have been
placed at Frascati. The Pope begins to see the
necessity of appearing to repent of his behaviour to
the Court of Portugal on this very delicate occasion;
and it is said that his Secretary of State, Cardinal
Torreggiani, will make himself a voluntary victim, to
atone for it, in hopes of appeasing his Portuguese
Majesty, not to put his fidelity to stronger trial than
perhaps it would endure; for though this age is
certainly not fanatick enough to totally throw off one
religion for another, yet their Patriarch might go great
lengths in curtailing the power of Rome to please the
King and people; and were they only to follow the
example of Spain in buying off, by force, the nomination to benefices, at a million and a half, Rome
would be a bankrupt many years sooner. . . . '

'. . . A few days ago, the Emperor of Germany's
two small ships of war, commanded by English men,
retook a Tuscan prize from a Prussian privateer,
commanded likewise by an Englishman; and what
perplexes the matter still more is, that the prize itself,
though under Tuscan colours, belonged to an Englishman. This (Great-ducal) Government, never having
had the honour before of being at war, except with
Barbary, is now in the prosecution of it, and has
begun to treat their prisoners, consisting of one
English officer and five sailors, two Swedes, one
Dutch, and one Frenchman, with too much rigour; by
sending them from the prize, in irons, to prison.

They have been surprized to find, by a copy of the officer's Prussian Commission, that the French were not counted among their enemies, but that, on the contrary, the privateer had recommendations for Marseilles, in case he had chosen to carry his prize there. This vexes the more, as it destroys the opinion that they wanted to inculcate, that these privateers were English in disguise.'

Although the French authorities described our victory at Quebec as a defeat, but in a supplement to the Gazette in which they thus wrote history upside down, printed the articles of their own capitulation, they did not attempt to deny the defeat of their gallant Admiral Conflans by our equally gallant Hawke.   On December 15th, Sir Horace says :—' Count Lorenzi has announced it to us, by the authority of his own Court. . . . . In M. de Conflan's own words, he complains bitterly of all his Captains.   Their confusion was so great, he says, that it was a *Vraye Billebode,* a term we did not know here, but very properly made use of, they say, to give the King of France a just notion of it, as it is a term of *chasse,* when all the dogs have lost scent, and run different ways or over each other.   De Conflans says that they (his captains) crowded so much upon him that he had not room to move (except to run away), that one of their ships was sunk by leaving the Port-holes open when they turned her about, and in short that he was forced to run his own ship ashore to prevent it falling into the hands of his enemy; and that another followed his example; but he hoped at least to save their guns.   He concludes by saying, that he knew nothing of the rest of his fleet. Of this rest, I would demand an account of Admiral Hawke . . . . What a fine opportunity to renew Queen Elizabeth's Medal on the defeat and flight of the Spanish Armada, " Maturate fugam," etc. Had the French taken even a frigate on this occasion, and returned safe into Brest, we should have had medals with Louis XV. on the right hand of Neptune triumphing over the whole ocean.'

## 1760.

*January 12th.*—' I pitied Marshal Conflans who was obliged to obey the orders he had received, to set forth in such a season to collect their ships and transports from their different ports, in sight, one may say, of an enemy so much superior in number and courage, who was waiting for them. I think that instead of De Conflans' head, which he voluntarily offered as an atonement, if his Master should have thought him answerable for the event of that day Bellisle would have been a more just sacrifice, for planning and pushing on an enterprize that carried with it so little probability of success. However, their Admiral, it seems, has accused five of his Captains ; and they must bear all the blame.'

The climate of Italy is discussed in the same letter with as much earnestness as Hawke's victory.

' I have been prevented writing, by a rheumatick disorder that has been very general, and is attributed to the extraordinary wet season. It has rained, without an intermission of three days together, for near

three months, and may probably continue.  All the
common devotions seem ineffectual; and it is too
expensive to have recourse to the Madonna dell'
(*illegible*) as last year.  We are seriously alarmed by
the notice of a sort of an Epidemical disease in the
Romagna, the effect likewise of the weather.  The
Pope must take care of that, and the Florentines hope
to. ward against it, by promoting the circulation of
their humours, by the diversions of the Carnival.'

The bad weather was not confined to Italy.  On
the 16th of February, Sir Horace wrote:—I thought
we should never have got any more letters from England.  Six Posts, that is to say, three weeks' letters,
were due, and came in together on Wednesday.  I
was afraid that the Postillion had been frozen and
all his letters lost in the snow, for one hears of nothing
but strange accidents occasioned by the rigour of the
season.  I hope however, tho' the Sentinels in Germany, and the Couriers who are sent from them to
St. Petersburg, to encourage the Zarina to persist
in her animosity against the King of Prussia, lose their
limbs by the cold, that you will save your gold fish
and orange trees.  The former thrive wonderfully
here, and require no other care than to break the ice.
Those which the Marquis Gionori has at his China
Fabrick are larger, I am told, than any in England.'

'. . . I have studied my head-aches very seriously,
but have never been able to fix any constant cause
for them, excepting one of a late date, which is the
Marshal's close room, heated with a German stove to
a degree that would produce Pine apples.  It was a
long while before I could perswade myself it was

that; though during the whole last winter, I literally
escaped but once having a most severe head-ache when
I awaked the next morning.    I now am more careful,
go seldom, and at an hour before he retires into that
furness (*sic*); but then how can one account for them
in the summer?    I believe the head-aches are con-
stitutional.    Dr. Cocchi once thought them periodical
too, but that I have not observed.    I think them
nervous; therefore, must have patience, as it is too
late in life to hope to correct the most nerveless constitution imaginable.'

'Did I ever acquaint you that Sir John Gray, in
his new credentials to little King Ferdinand, had
obtained the additional title to his Envoyship, of
Plenipotentiary, with an encrease of 3*l.* per day.    I
rejoyce in his good fortune; it is all luck.    He had
solicited it for some time, and pleaded long services
as a pretence.    If that alone be a title, his neighbour'
(Mann) 'has a better right; but I believe that sometimes importunity stands in lieu of it.    He has been
promised the Bath ribband too, in the above promotion.    I lost above a thousand pounds' appointments
as *Chargé des affaires,* from an ill-judged modesty in
not asking the payment in time, and I see no probability of any other notice or advancement.'

## CHAPTER III.

### 1760.

AMONG the further records of this year, the most interesting refer to the political situation of the Pope, and the physical condition of the Pretender. It was Sir Horace Mann's especial business to inform his Government of every detail he could learn concerning the life of the Stuart Prince. Accordingly Mann sent his information to 'the Office,' and, having enlightened Mr. Pitt, Sir Horace hastened to inform Walpole by private letter as to the intelligence he had officially communicated to the Minister. On the 26th of April he says :—

'I have written twice a week of late to Mr. Pitt, to inform him of the dangerous state of health of the Pretender. On the 16th, the Cardinal, his son, who is never so happy as when he is acting the Priest, had the consolation of administering the Viaticum to him, with all the ceremony and solemnity that such a function is capable of. The last accounts were, though I am hourly expecting fresher, that, having sent for the Pope's Benediction, *in articulo mortis*, the Pope carried it to him in person, and sat by his bed-

side near half an hour, but it was still thought the
Pretender would make that blessing useless (for they
don't keep long) by holding out some time.   Nothing,
most assuredly, of consequence passed between them,
for want of something better to ask (*sic*) (for it is some
time since the present Pope confirmed the late Pope's
settlement of the Pretender's pension on the Cardinal,
his son).   The Pretender desired that the Pope would
promise him that no funeral Oration should be made
for him.   The Pope repeated the whole discourse on
this subject, as an instance of the other's great
humility, and he applauds himself for not letting
himself be persuaded to grant the request, though
it would have saved an expence to the Chamber of
eight or ten thousand crowns.   Princess Sobieska's
funeral, exclusive of the Mausoleum in St. Peter's,
cost six thousand.   They must add something to this,
were it only to amuse the Cardinal.'

'I should, however, have told you that the old
Man recommended his two sons to the Pope, in the
most tender manner; on which occasion, as your late
friend, Pope Benedict, said, when he had assisted
Aquaviva, *si fece un bel piangere*—there was a fine
bout of weeping!   So, then, the eldest son is still
alive!   I always thought so, and I was tired of writing
home, that his father, on such and such a day, received
a letter from him, without either date or place, though
it was positively and literally true.'

'. . . This instant, I receive an Express . . . to
inform me that on the 23rd, at noon, the Extreme
Unction was administered to the Pretender, and that
it was believed he expired a few hours after.   But

that was not, nor could be, positively known at the
departure of my letter' (from Rome), 'for very few
people were admitted into the house, and nobody into
the room but the Priests, who had been appointed to
attend on that occasion,—who continue their functions
sometimes after, as well as before the patient expires.
But, if art is used, the death may be concealed long.
In the meantime, his Courtiers may prepare their
mourning.'

On May 3rd, Mann writes:—' When the last
letter came from Rome, the Pretender was still alive,
though he had had the Extreme Unction and a second
blessing from the Pope, in *articulo mortis.*  The
Cardinal, his son, would be inconsolable, if the satisfaction which he has in all holy functions did not
take off his attention from his father.  The *Catafalco*
was making in the Church of Santi Apostoli, where
more his body is to lay in state for some days, till
the magnificent preparations are made at St. Peter's.
This and the exposition of their Sacraments in several
Churches amuse the Romans, at present, for the
devout are convinced they shall never have such
another King of England.  " Who," they ask, " will
cure the King's Evil for the English ? "  They would
not dispute the descent of that right to his son, but
they doubt his virtue.  I believe Cardinal York, who
has got his father's pension, will put in for his
attributes likewise.'

On the 17th May, Mann states that, ' When the
last letters came from Rome, the Pretender was not
quite dead.  He had been speechless for many hours,
and was thought to be at the point of death ; but in

the evening he grew a little better, and took some
nourishment, so that it was possible he might hold
out a little longer, but so little that the dispositions
for his funeral were continued with all diligence.'

This was premature. On May 31st, Mann informs
Walpole that, 'The Pretender is grown much better,
but the Romans are resolved they won't lose the
amusement of his funeral, for which all the preparations are still carrying on!' The Pretender, however,
had the best of it, for the moment, and checked the
amusement which the Romans would have enjoyed in
his funeral, by declining to die. On the 12th of
July, Sir Horace states that, 'The Pretender is so
well recovered that he may live till the fall of the leaf,
and if he chooses, till the Spring. It would be indiscreet to hold out any longer, after the enormous
expence that has been made for his funeral. Twenty-
four Giants in gold, to stand round his corpse! It
was to exceed everything of the kind that has ever
been seen. Triumphal Arches, for his Entry into
Heaven, etc., etc.; and then his wife, who is continually piddling at Miracles, is to be declared a
Saint.'

Waiting these events, Mann notices the doings of
another sovereign, the King of Spain, who had ordered
that the explorations at Herculaneum should be continued, and that the building of the famous Villa at
Caserta should be 'carried on,' says Mann, 'with the
same spirit as if he was present; for which he has
promised to furnish the money. You ask if Caserta
is finished and furnished. The second story won't be
up this year, nor will the whole, in all probability, be

completed in eight or ten years more. People who
have seen it, tell me that the entrances are dark
already; what will they then be when the building is
raised to its height ? The great apartments are noble,
which are indeed the principal object; but the con-
noisseurs find fault with the upper story, which has
totally the air of a Convent. The Corridors that
receive light by holes, are neither thought handsome
or convenient. However, upon the whole, it must be
allowed that there are great beauties in the building,
and that the whole plan, with the Gardens, and the
Town *that is to be,* is noble. The aquaduct is finished,
and is a wonderful undertaking.'

In the person of Stosch, nephew and heir to the
late Baron, Mann passes to a much smaller personage
than a King. The younger Stosch was about to
leave Florence for England, to sell, if he could, his
uncle's collection, and, failing by lack of profitable
sale to procure means to support his baronial title, to
obtain employment, if possible, as a ' bear leader ' con-
ducting young gentlemen on the Grand Tour, as it
was called, and polishing them as they went. Mann
thus describes Stosch's qualifications for the post of
travelling tutor :—' Stosch has been brought up a
soldier, both in his native Prussian service, and afterwards in one of the German regiments in France ;
which has given him an air du monde. He has been
vastly well looked upon here by everybody. I have
lived in great intimacy with him, and interest myself
for him. He possesses all the qualities and languages
necessary for accompanying a young Man of Fashion
on his travels ; and he has great ambition to be well

employed in that manner.   He is well known to all
the English who have passed here, in his time, and
may hope to be well received by them in England, as
well as recommended, from their personal knowledge
of him, to any one who prefers a man of the world,
with sufficient practice in every thing that a young
man is to see,—to a Student from one of the Univer-
sities, or to any of the hackney Tutors now on the
list.   Besides that, a Prussian Baron in the suite of a
young Nobleman, will reflect as much credit on his
Pupil as a Cardinal receives from a Knight of Malta
in his Antechamber.'

In a letter of March 22nd, Mann refers to a spectacle at which some of those travelling young noblemen and their ' leaders' were present—'the terrible
execution of the officers of the Regiment de Piedmont,
at Metz; three broken upon the wheel, and thirty-
eight made to pass under the gallows,—degraded and
imprisoned.   Their crime has not been made publick.
Count Lorenzi thinks it was the murder of an officer
to whom they were all indebted.'

About this time the soul of the Pope was much
troubled by the obstinacy of princes and peoples who,
willingly accepting his rule of faith, pertinaciously
opposed his interference in the domain of morals,
which means everything else besides faith ; an interference which, if permitted, would place the
temporal, as well as the spiritual government of the
world, in the hands of a few Italians established
in Rome.   In 1760, the King of Portugal withstood
that interference.   Mann writes:—' The Pope has
had all possible mortification on account of the

Jesuits, which he has deserved from the King of
Portugal who, after having obliged his Holyness to
yield in every point, even so far as to send him the
minutes of the Brief that he had demanded, has
lately sent him word, by a Courier, that he was gone
into the country and had not leisure to consider it.
The Cardinals Corsini and Passionei are the chief
Counsellors and Directors of the Portuguese Minister
at Rome, and most of the Pamphlets against the
Jesuits have been printed in the Corsini Palace.
Voltaire, they say, has wrote something very clever
against them.'

But this trouble was insignificant compared with
that which the Pope suffered through the stiff-necked-
ness of the Genoese. He even half forgot the sick
Stuart Prince, in this greater trouble. The malcontents, or, as the Genoese called them, the rebels, in
Corsica had applied to the Pope to send a visitor to
Corsica, to put order to the affairs of the Church,
which had got extremely entangled during the late
disorderly times. The Pontiff, with extreme alacrity,
despatched for the purpose required a special commission with a bishop at the head of it. The republic of Genoa took fire at this step,—which was an
acknowledgment of the sovereignty of the Corsicans
who were in open rebellion, rightly or wrongly, against
their sovereign masters, the Genoese. On May 3rd,
Mann says:—'The Genoese opposed it with all their
might, in a long Memorial, which the Pope did not
condescend to take any notice of. . . . It was answered in a scurrilous manner by a Corsican. . . . The
Genoese, finding that respectful forms had little weight,

threatened to use force to support their right, and in order to prevent the Bishop's landing, sent two large vessels, well armed, and commanded by a Doria, to cruize on the coasts of Corsica, for that purpose. Upon this, the Pope, not choosing that his Apostle should be a Martyr too, suspended the execution of his intention, till he received news that the presumptuous Doria and his whole crew had shared the fate of Pharoah, for opposing his will.'

' The truth is that the Genoese vessels were cast away, and very few of the crew saved. The Pope declared it was a Divine Chastisement, and immediately ordered his Vicar to depart, under the protection of " St. Peter " and " St. Paul," with twenty guns each, to defend him against three Gallies which the Genoese had sent to supply the place of their Barks ; but whether the sanctity of the Commission, or the disposition in the force, of two Frigates to three Gallies, prevailed most, the Faithful may decide. The event is that the Bishop landed there on the 23rd, and was received by the Corsicans with all possible marks of respect and joy.'

' So soon as the Genoese Agent at Rome sent an Express to inform his Republick of the Bishop's departure, they issued an Edict offering a reward of six thousand crowns to any one who should seize and consign him to any of their dependants, that he might be *decently* conducted to Genoa. The notice of this occasioned a more than ordinary commotion at Rome, and offended the Pope most grievously. We shall see what he will do to resent such an indignity, and what the Genoese will do when they hear that the Bishop is actually administering the sacrament to ten thousand of their rebels in Corsica.'

*May* 17*th.*—' The Pope rejected all the violent councils that were given him in the Congregation he held on that subject, but ordered an extraordinary Brief to be drawn up and sent to the Genoese, to shew them how wrong they are to dispute his authority in whatever he pleases to call Ecclesiastical matters ; and his future conduct is to be regulated by the success of these exhortations, but it is insinuated at the same time, that the measures will be very severe if they do not shew an entire submission to his will.'

' The Genoese, on the contrary, are full of resentment, and had rather that their rebels should be damned than that the Pope, out of care of their souls, should prejudice the sovereignty of the Republick. . . . The Pope, conscious of his own weakness, and doubtful of the effect of his spiritual arms, is endeavouring to strengthen his hands by getting the assistance of all the Catholick and Christian Courts (I mean such as believe in him). A statement of the quarrell has been sent to all the Nuncios, that each may make the most of it at the Court where he resides. Unless the fundamental maxims of Government to oppose the usurpations of the Pope should prevail more than papal Bigotry, woe be to the Republick, they will make her walk barefoot to Rome to ask pardon.'

The quarrel became aggravated, and the Florentines were as excited about it as any of the Italians. The Genoese published edicts, the Pope fulminated bulls to annul them. The Republic stood on its rights, the Papacy appealed through the Nuncios to all the orthodox courts, to support the right of the Pontiff. When the Genoese were not to be moved by threats, the Holy Father overwhelmed them with exhortations, and with suggestions of their naughtiness in supposing that they knew better than he did what was fittest for them. One exhortatory brief was sent from Rome by a courier to the Archbishop of Genoa, 'who delivered it, but soon after the Republick sent it back to him by a Senator, accompanied by one of their Secretaries of State, with orders to say, they would receive no letter from Rome but through the channel of their own Agent there ; and the next day they published another Edict, in opposition to that of the Pope, of whose person they affect to speak with respect, but treat his Edicts with much contempt. . . . All this will help to kill the Pope soon ; he takes the thing very much to heart. His Bishop, however, is christening thousands in Corsica. The Malcontents received him as their Saviour, and made him a submissive appeal, but full of sedition with regard to the Republick of Genoa, whose first Edict they caused to be burnt by their Hangman.'

This quarrel, however, in which there was a little right and a little wrong on both sides, died out ;—to give place, indeed, to another. On the 12th of July, Mann informs Walpole :—'We talk no more here, or at Rome, of the quarrel between the Pope and the Genoese. It only related to the salvation of souls, and an affair of much greater importance to the welfare of Rome has succeeded to it. Rome is on the point of quarrelling with Portugal; not, however, if the Portuguese should change religion, they would turn Protestants ; they would turn Jews. Notice has arrived at Rome of an indignity offered to a Nuncio-Cardinal, by turning him out of Portugal, for not lighting up his house, as every one else did, for the marriage of Don Pedro with his niece' (daughter of Don Pedro's brother, the reigning King, Joseph). ' Notice of this arrived after the Pope had appointed the time to give an audience to the Portuguese Minister, in which (though I believe the Pope did not then know it) he was to deliver the King of Portugal's letter to notify that marriage, upon which, the Pope retracted his word and forbade him his court.

' M<sup>r</sup> Almada,' (the Portuguese Minister) 'upon this, fixed up a notification at the Portuguese Hospital, addressed to all the subjects and dependants of his nation, that, by order of his Court, both he and they must leave Rome. The rest of the Paper was little less than a defamatory libel against the *Ministero Politico*, as he calls it, of the Court of Rome, under which denomination, he, and everybody knows it, means Cardinal Torreggiani, the Secretary of State. At the same time that this strange Paper was fixed up, Almada sent a volume of two or three hundred pages to all the Ministers and Cardinals, containing the motives of the rupture between his Court and Rome.'

' There was the utmost confusion all over the town. Every Portuguese, and they are very numerous, was providing a chaise, a horse, or some *voiture*, to leave Rome. The affair, by this, growing very serious, it

was thought proper to try to accommodate it by the
mediation of Cardinal Cavalchini and Cardinal
Corsini, who is Protector of Portugal. The Pope was
induced to grant the audience to Mr. Almada, which
he had refused before, though it was afterwards
thought better that Cardinal Corsini (now become
Mediator as well as Protector) should deliver the King
of Portugal's letter to the Pope, and that the latter
should appoint Corsini to treat, for the future, with
the Portuguese Minister, instead of Torregiani.'

'Mr. Almada, having gained so much, published
a second Edict, as he calls it, to annul the former,
declaring to the Portuguese at Rome, that he took
upon himself all the danger of suspending his and
their departure, till his Court was informed of the
disposition the Pope was in to give him all the satisfaction he had a right to demand. Thus, everything
is to remain till the return of the Courier, who was
despatched with the Pope's answer to the marriage
letter, and an account of all that had been done.'

'Cardinal Corsini, who knows how to treat Popes,
talked very roundly to his present Holyness, who wept
bitterly, and owned *che era stato tradito,*—that he
had been betrayed ; a confession which does more
honour to his sincerity than to his Infallibility. The
Jesuits, who had begun to rejoice in the rupture
between Rome and Portugal, are now as much afraid
that an accommodation must turn to their great
prejudice. The Pope, who has protected them hitherto is too weak ;—and the Mediator is not their
friend.'

Their friend was Torreggiani. This Cardinal, says Mann, July 15th, 'animated by the Jesuit party, and by the fear of losing the larger pension which, it is said, he receives from the Jesuits, hastened to the Pope to complain of the affront his Holyness had put upon him by excluding him from the functions of his employment, representing the danger there was in putting his affairs in the hands of such a Jansenist as Cardinal Corsini; and that his own dignity ought not to suffer him to yield on this occasion. The Pope, intimidated by Torreggiani, as he had before been by Corsini, denied that he had given the latter any positive commission; saying, that he had only desired Corsini to try what he could do to bring about an accommodation, not having any intention totally to exclude Torreggiani. The latter Cardinal, having gained so much, had little difficulty to bring the Pope to the point he aimed at, and had prepared for; which was,—if the Pope did not trust to him, to call a Congregation of Cardinals to consult, and advise him what to do. This was immediately executed, and the majority as soon decided that it was inconsistent with the Pope's dignity, not only to yield a jot, but even to treat at all, while Almada was in Rome.'

'Corsini being informed that this opinion had been approved of, hastened in his turn to the Pope, and in very strong terms reproached him with having retracted his word. The Pope, half denying that he had, at first, given Corsini a positive commission, and not knowing what to say, burst as usual into tears,

and pointing to a Crucifix, said: " *Ci remediera lei ;
io non so piu che fare*"—*He* will find a remedy ; I
do not know what more I can do ! Corsini, seeing the
extreme weakness of the Pope, and that the Jesuits'
party had gained their point to make a rupture with
Portugal unavoidable, had nothing to do but to
inform Almada of what had passed.    Upon this,
Almada published a third notification, ordering all the
subjects and dependants of Portugal (who are very
numerous) to leave Rome by the end of September.
He then caused the Arms of Portugal to be taken
down from over his door, and left Rome, with his
whole family.'

' Almada retired to a Villa at San Casciano, belonging to Cardinal Corsini, about a post from Florence,
where I have been this afternoon to make him a
visit.    We have since heard that the Cardinals and
the Pope's Ministers are at open variance among
themselves, swearing revenge on each other, whilst
the Pope cries and prays.    They have all equal reason
to complain of his weakness, though that has at last
fixt him where his own inclinations in favour of the
Jesuits first led him, and which was the ground of all
their Imbroils.'

On the 9th of August, Mann states that the courier from Lisbon was anxiously expected ; adding :—
' Should the King of Portugal hold out, and not
revoke the order to his subjects to leave Rome in
September, their departure, it is thought, may lead to
an insurrection ; but whenever the priests get time
to treat, either by tears, or some momentary submis-

sion, they melt their antagonists into a Repentance.
Mons<sup>r</sup> Almada, with his Secretario Regio, who wears
the Cross of Malta and is a *moine defroqué*, keeps
close at the Villa Corsini. They are cautiously
employed either in writing or saying their *Rosario*.
In such a dispute with Rome, what can be expected
from such instruments ? I never could understand
how a nation, so strongly suspected of Judaism (as
Portugal) should show such an abject devotion for
the "Vicar of Jesus." So strongly is this devotion
expressed even in the writings that came from that
Court on this occasion, that one ought not to be
surprized if they were all to go barefoot to Rome to
ask for pardon.'

This, however, they did not stoop to ask. On the
13th of September, Sir Horace writes to Walpole :—
'Do not be surprized if you should hear that the
Jesuits have murdered me for being civil to the Minister of him' (the King of Portugal) 'whom they
sought to murder. Mon<sup>sr</sup> Almada, the Portuguese
Minister, the day before yesterday, left his retreat at
San Casciano, but, as he is a showy man, he contrived
it so that I should offer to fetch him into the town
and make a sort of an Entry ; for which purpose I set
forth in a Coach and Six, and ushered him in, and
afterwards carried him, in Gala, to all the Members
of the Regency, gave him a great dinner, and in the
evening, carried him out again at another Gate to his
chaise, to proceed on his journey towards Turin, where
he is to stay all the winter, as the safest place from
the revenge of the Jesuits and Cardinal Torreggiani ;

—for whom the following Epitaph has lately been made, at Rome :—

### D. M.
Aloysio Cardinali Torreggiano Florentino
Quod
Januenses (*sic*) e Catholicæ Religionis gremio expulerit
Romanam Urbem Lusitaniæ pecuniæ onere sublevaverit,
Et Jesuitorum Exulum Hospitio maximo auxerit
S. P. Q. R.
Tanti Beneficii Memor
Ad Parietem Inclinatum Extra Portam Flaminiam
Monumentum Posuit
Sepulturam Paravit.

At the 'inclined wall,' outside the Flaminian Gate, it was the custom to bury malefactors and Christians who were not of the Romish communion,— as if the evil-doer and the so-called heretic were equally infamous ! Mann says :—' The rupture between Rome and Portugal is irretrievable, for the life of the present Pope or his Secretary of State ; during which Portugal will probably find some means to do without their successors ; nor will pay a million and a half of crowns, as Spain did to the late Pope, for leave to name to its own benefices !'

Very soon the attention of the Florentines was turned from the Pope and Portugal to the singular conduct of the King of Spain. In October, Mann wrote :—' Two extraordinary Couriers passed by a few days ago to Naples, to announce the Queen's death. Marquis Viviani told me that before the King would give way to his grief, he recommended himself to the

people about him, to divert him, putting them in
mind of the example of his brother, and that he was
of the same Bourbon blood.   This pathetick, or perhaps
prophetick, truth drew tears from their eyes, and then
they set about to amuse him.   This prudent suspension
of grief puts me in mind of an instance in lower life,
but of the same nature.   Madame de la Tour, Count
Richecourt's daughter, with three other married ladies,
being on a party of pleasure with their husbands, and
having but one coach, the woemen of course were
within, and the men on and about it, as well as they
could.   Thus loaded, it overturned, and all the men
were sadly hurt.   At the sight, three of the ladies
fainted away, but Madame de la Tour, whose size
and gentleness had acquired her the *soubriquet* of
the *Grenadiere agevole*, summoned all her courage,
dressed her husband's wounds, and then (as she told
me) " Je me suis laissé tomber en faiblesse."   The best
and I believe only remedy for the disconsolate King of
Spain, will be a speedy marriage.   His constitution,
both of mind and body, requires much dissipation
with a wife.'

Mann subsequently writes :—'We are ignorant in
Florence of the fate of the two Lords (Earl Ferrers
and Lord George Sackville).   You will smile when
you hear that Lady Killmurray has wrote to all her
numerous acquaintance abroad, to announce the misfortune that was to happen to her in so near a relation
being to be hanged.   Judge how they started at the
word, when according to the Italian notions of the
Ignominy which such an action brings upon the whole
family, nobody would make any alliance with it.

Unless that good Lady had taken such pains to explain it, nobody in these parts would have known that she had any connection with an *Impiccato*.   Does not this in some measure justify Lord Ferrers's defence ? '

'I cannot help mentioning an oddity, among a thousand others, that escaped her, and which was recorded in the Italian Assemblies.   When at Rome, she was attended by the Comtessa Charofini, Cardinal Alexander's mistress, and, going into a room together, my Lady drew back, nor could be persuaded to walk in first.   The other, still pressing, received for answer, with all the gestures of Civility and Ceremony : " Non posso davero Signora Contessa, perche lei è piu *mere-trice* di me,"—meaning *meritevole*,—as a Contessa, to whom a Vice Contessa ought to give place.'   (It was as if Lady Kilmurray, declining to take precedence of the Cardinal's Countess—Mistress—had grounded the courtesy on the fact that the Countess was more *mere-tricious* than *she*,—meaning, meritorious.)

Lady Kilmurray's kinsman, Earl Ferrers, went to the gallows for the brutal murder of his steward, with such decency of bearing that even Florence regretted that his quality suffered any derogation.   On May 31st, Mann writes :—'. . . I was struck˙ with some parts of the ceremony, and with the whole of Lord Ferrers's behaviour, resolute without ostentation, cool and sensible beyond anything that one could expect, from all his former actions, insomuch that one could not help thinking that he had a species of madness in his constitution, which occasionally broke out as his passions were put in motion,—and entirely depended upon them.   The whole process, and particularly the catastrophe, is an interesting historical narrative. But few foreigners can reconcile the latter to their notions of birth. They think that no crime can level a Man of Quality with the mob. Even our Marshal, who has little else to plume himself upon, would not believe that Lord Ferrers had not been degraded from his nobility before the execution. Some few, however, there are, of a lower class, who think that this event does great honour to our nation, and they envy a people, where Justice makes no distinction of persons.'

'The same old military gentleman' (Marshal Botta) 'would not believe that after Lord George Sackville's sentence had been confirmed, Lord G. S. was permitted to hold his rank. I had all the difficulty imaginable to convince him that though the King was the Fountain of honour, it was not in his power to deprive any one of them, except in cases of Attainder or Outlawry—which distinction I could not make him understand.'

In referring to the war still waging between the King of Prussia on one side, and the French and Austrians on the other, Mann records the Florentine opinion that if the French government did not provide muffs and flannel waistcoats for their troops in winter quarters, there would probably be an insurrection in Paris, on the first report of a French nose or ear being lost by the cold in Westphalia. On September 13th, Mann writes:—'The Empress Queen fainted away when she heard of Loudon's defeat. Marshal Daun had sent to her to pray incessantly for the event of the 14th, promising her a complete victory on that

day, *if* she could engage Heaven on her side ; and she
doubted not that she might have added that to the
rejoicings on the marriage of the Arch-Duke.    Old
Marquis Ricciardi, whom you knew, used always,
before any great *merende* that he intended to give in
his garden, to cause many masses to be said for the
souls in Purgatory, to obtain a fine day.    They failed
him most unkindly once, upon which he went to the
Church and upbraided them publickly:—"Ah! anamine,
anamine ! (*sic*) non c' è d' aver una grazia da voi ne
anche col pegno in mano ! "

'I have not heard what the Queen has done on
this occasion.    You may remember that, last year,
Marshal Botta would not give leave for Masks, as
usual, for fear of spoiling a victory which they then
expected near Dresden.'    It was quite a joke in
Florence that Marshal Botta's French horns were
never to be relied upon.    They blazoned as victories
what often turned out to be "victories" on the other
side.    When the news of the capture of Montreal
reached Florence, Mann describes how he announced
*that* victory :—'I read the Extraordinary Gazette with
an audible voice to a crowd of English who were come
in upon the arrival of the post, and each testified his
joy in a manner most suitable to his character.    I own
that there was one who broke out into so boisterous
an *huzza !* that it startled the Marshal, though he lives
in the Craon palace which is at the other end of the
town.    It was equivalent to his horns which spread a
victory in an instant.    He was afraid to blow them
that day, though the same post brought him an account of the taking of Berlin, but as he is much

suspected to be a Prussian at heart, his rejoicings should be interpreted for us. He did venture to say that the sending such a man as Leichtenstein, preceded by twelve postillions, to announce the entrance of their troops into an open town, could not have been approved of by the Empress.'

At this time, a monument in honour of our young hero at Quebec was being constructed in Rome. Mann calls it a design for Wolfe's tomb:—' a bas relief done by one Berton, a Frenchman, by order of Mr. Adams ; but, pray don't mention it, lest it might do him a prejudice ; though, indeed, Berton makes little diffi- culty to show it, and most of the English now here, *and they are very numerous,* have either seen or heard of it at Rome.'

In alluding to the 'very numerous' English visitors in the Tuscan capital, Sir Horace frequently notices the unfitness of Florence as a residence for steady young Englishmen, owing to the evil example set by the reckless and dissipated fine gentlemen. He stated as grave objections to one of his nephews sojourning there :—' He would be too much his own master at a dangerous time of life ; and the example of a succes- sion of giddy young travellers might draw him into all their irregularities. We have Lord F—— losing his whole time by acting the Cicisbeo to the Marchese ——, and entertaining all her dependants. Then we have Sir B. B., nursing a dancing girl in an obscure villa, and waiting the hour of her being brought to bed. Such examples frighten me in a country where custom almost justifies them. Lord Archibald Hamil- ton lives in the woods of Tuscany. He is quite a

wild boy, has nothing human in him but the pride of
the Hamiltons, which is encouraged by a strange,
good for nothing creature he has with him, one Cargill,
who, they say, was a little schoolmaster, and indeed,
he has all the air and presumption of one. That little
Lord is very rude about his Sister in law; indeed, he
would think none but a Hamilton or a Campbell
worthy of that honour.' On the other hand we hear
that, 'Among the English, there is a Mr. Robinson,
Sir Thomas's son, *micat inter omnes*, a glorious young
fellow indeed, and most amiable. Your *recommandé*,
M^r Bunbury, is a very knowing, agreeable young man,
but too retired, out of complaisance to his companion,
Lord Torrington, but not at all out of choice, but
Mr. Robinson seeks company, and shines in it, too.
There was a Scot far more illustrious than any of the
above-named gentlemen, who arrived in Florence with
a letter of introduction from Walpole,—Strange, the
famous engraver, and the most ardent Jacobite of the
Jacobite times,—always excepting his more Jacobite
wife. Political feeling did not interfere with Mann's
readiness to honour so able an artist who came with
a recommendation from Walpole:—'Mr. Strange, the
Engraver, has delivered me your letter, and has experienced my desire to serve him, having got leave
for him to draw in all the palaces.'

The record of the year closes with a decent assurance of the grief, which Mann lightly bore, for the
death of George the Second. He immediately applied
himself not only to being continued in his representative office, but for an increase of both pay and character.
The Grand Duke of Tuscany to whom he had been

originally accredited, had enjoyed increase of dignity
by becoming Emperor of Germany, and Mann suggested that such circumstance being considered, and
his twenty years of service being remembered, he had
fair claim to be elevated to a position above that of an
Envoy, and to be furnished with additional means to
illustrate the elevation. Walpole, who had previously
warned him against sending presents to Ministers,
which had the look of bribes, now made a suggestion,
which is thus noticed in Mann's last letter in 1760 : —
'I know the King's taste for *virtu*, and should be
happy to be able to gratify it on every point; but I
fear that anything fit to be presented there will
greatly exceed my purse. I am much obliged to you
for the hint, and will never neglect any opportunity or
offer that presents itself.' Waiting such opportunity,
the English Minister in Florence found some satisfaction in hanging up Walpole's portrait, a recent gift, in
his bed-room, by the side of a sketch of his brother
Galfridus Mann's monument, set up in Linton Church,
Kent, by Walpole himself. And as the Envoy lay in
that room, reading 'Tristram Shandy,' another recent
gift from his old friend, he formed an opinion of it,
which finds this expression :—'You will laugh at me,
I suppose, when I say I don't understand it. It was
probably the intention of the author that nobody
*should*. It seems to me *humbugging*, if I have a right
notion of an art of talking or writing that has been
invented since I left England. It diverted me, however, extremely, and I beg to have as soon as possible
the two other volumes, which I see advertised in the
papers for next Christmas.' Ultimately, the Duke of

Roxburgh, who was sojourning in Florence, lent the two volumes (the possession and carrying about of which prove their popularity) to Mann, whose sententious criticism takes this form : 'Nonsense pushed too far, becomes insupportable.'

## CHAPTER IV.

### 1761.

SEVERAL letters of Mann seem to be missing. The earliest in the year 1761 is dated August 1st. Its chief record is that of the loyal joy of the English at Florence, at the news from England. 'The King's declaration of marriage has surprized every one here extremely. It has been carried on with as much secresy as if it had been really a love affair. Circular letters have been sent to all the Ministers abroad, and people talk of nothing else but the joy it will occasion. London will soon be the centre of all diversions and magnificence. This, I suppose, will exceed anything that has yet been seen. . . .'

Among the French wits, M. de Souvré was one of the most distinguished, and the most audacious. He was at Madame de Pompadour's, when she was learning German; and he remarked aloud, rudely enough, whether the equally audacious lady was present or not, 'Il me semble que depuis que Madame la Marquise apprend l'Allemand elle écorche le Français.' The King entered the room while the company were laughing at the rude jest, and as he insisted

on being told the cause of so much merriment, the
joke was repeated. The King's consequent anger was
shown in his addressing the jester: 'M. de Souvré,
est-il long tems que vous n'avez été à vos terres?'
'Oui, Sire,' replied he, 'mais je compte d'y partir ce
soir!' 'The frank *hardiesse* of the answer saved
him,' remarks Walpole, in his narrative of the story
to Mann. The Minister replied by another illustration of the witty Frenchman's ready sarcasm: 'Upon
some occasion, bread being dear in France, the King
passing down some village where he was hunting, the
people cried out: "Sire, du pain! du pain!" The
King was hurt, and on his return home, asked if it
was true that bread was so dear. His courtiers
assured him that nothing was so cheap, and that it
cost only a *sou* a pound. M. de Souvré said, with an
air of concern: "Ah! il faut que je fasse pendre mon
Maitre d'hôtel; il m'a fait payer le double!"'

Florence was full, at this time, of great English
Dukes and Lords, to whom the English Minister
publicly communicated all public news of importance.
He informed them at an assembly that the conquerors
of Pondicherry had driven the French from all their
settlements on the Coast of Malabar, and from every
place they possessed beyond the Cape, excepting 'l'isle
de France et de Bourbon,' so that the poor devils will
have nothing left to heighten their ragouts.' Mann
expressed his admiration for 'Monsieur Lally's spirited
insolence'; but Count Lorenzi, the French Ambassador,
said, 'Lally is an Irishman,' and Lorenzi, writes Mann,
'pretends, by that, to account for the easy conquest
of the place entrusted to his charge; but I have

translated his intercepted letter, to prove that he had
done everything on earth to save it.'   Sir Horace
writes, August 15th :—' I was quite ashamed yesterday only to be able to acquaint our Dukes and Lords
here with the taking of two ships of war, the Achilles
of 64, and the Buffon of 30 guns, near Calas, which
were carried into Gibraltar, and the Privateer, Prince
George, had taken a rich East India ship.   I suppose
that this and the St. Anne which Admiral Holmes's
squadron has taken, will be the last of any consequence that we shall hear of. . . .'   Our merchant
ships, however, were afraid to leave Leghorn, though,
says Sir Horace, ' there are two men of war in the
port, but they are quarrelling who shall *not* conduct
them to Gibraltar, out of zeal to the military part of
their duty, which excites them to look out for their
Enemy's ships rather than tamely to take care of our
own.'

Among the English in Italy in this autumn, Mann
notices Lord Strathmore as having ' broken the chains
that held him so long at Parma,' and returned to
Florence.   He had not yet assumed the new chains
which in 1767 bound him to the Durham heiress,
Mary Eleanor Bowes, and the breaking of which
scandalized a not too susceptible society.   His aunt,
relict of the sixth Earl of Strathmore, married George
Forbes, Master of the Horse to the Chevalier, and
a conspicuous personage in Italy.   Forbes is sometimes called a ' groom,' and he was probably that
sort of ' head groom,' who, taking the charge of
the Pretender's stables, might be called the Master of
his Horse.   Mrs. Forbes's daughter by the ' groom,'

her mother being dead, was in a convent in Rome (or
Florence) from which Forbes took her to his own home,
where ruled so cruel a stepmother that the daughter
fled, preferring her chance in the wide wide world to
the certain miseries of home.   Her fate was a singular
one.   She married a Scotch farmer's son, one Lawder,
with whom she fell into great distress.   After his
death, she lived in a poor cottage near Stirling, on
an annuity of £100 a year, granted by the Strathmore
family ; and there the daughter of the old Pretender's
Master of the Horse died in the first quarter of the
present century.   Mann calls Lord Strathmore, 'a
very amiable friend of your most amiable Mr. Pitt.'
'Lord Titchfield,' writes Mann, in October, 'leaves this
place in a few days, on his return home, without
seeing Rome, so pressing are the Duke of Portland's
entreaties to him.   The Duke of Roxburgh also left
Florence for Rome and Naples.   Lord Torrington
closed his villa and repaired to England, and at last
Lord Fordwych, who disobliged his father, and lost his
seat in Parliament by not fixing the time of his departure, seems inclined to return to England soon.'   Lady
Mary Wortley Montagu is also announced as having
'set out on her journey to England, but was herself
doubtful of being able to perform it.   She said that
when she was tired, she would winter at some place
on the road.'   Walpole said she 'would not be put in
quarantine, dirty as her condition was.'   Gouty Sir
Richard Lyttelton was turning his face homeward, ' not
at all better in health, but extremely fatigued with
seeking after remedies.'   Meanwhile, Sir Richard
rested at Naples, where, says Mann, ' there will be

more English ladies assembled this winter than probably ever met together. The Dutchess of Bridgewater, Lady Eyles with her sister and daughter, and a Mrs. Robinson were already there; Lady Orford is on her way thither, but said she would return to Florence in May.'

One of the most popular English personages in Italy at this period, undoubtedly, was Mr. Thomas Pitt. In August, Mann informed him of the death of his father. 'I traced out a plan,' says Sir Horace, 'by which, if he approves of it, he may be in England by the Coronation; as, I dare say, I could engage Count Lorenzi to get him a passport from his Court to go through France.' This was not to be effected. In October, Mann writes :—'Having been disappointed in getting a passport to go through France, he had determined to go by Loretto to Bologna, and from thence into Germany; but he has very obligingly preferred the road through Florence, to make me a visit. He will make use of your appartment for the few days he stays. . . . Mr. Pitt, not receiving his expected passport to go through France, or even a refusal, was willing to attribute the delay to the loss of letters to or from Paris; so resolved to make a second trial. I expect him in a few days. His bed is ready made in your appartment.' In November, says Mann :—'Mr. Pitt has been with me for a few days, which was the reason that I did not write to you by the last Post. The moments were so precious that I could not spare any even to you. He set out in excessive bad weather for Germany. It is a horrid time of the year for the other road, and his hurry to get into England is so great that he will despise all common obstacles and inconveniences.'

The English who remained at Florence during this autumn expected that Mann's loyalty and liberality would enable them to rejoice greatly, on the occasion of the coronation of George the Third and Queen Charlotte. On September 12th, he writes:—' Everybody imagines that I am to do something very great here for the wedding and coronation; I don't joke when I tell you that some of the Florentine tradesmen have applyed to me, to furnish me with wax, others to direct the Orchestra, and old St. John, who has dressed many a supper for you at Princess Craon's, and who has often played with you and her after, at Pharoah, has desired to preside over all the Cooks whom he hears are to be employed on this occasion. It has been asserted that I have wrote to Cardinal Corsini to lend me his house; but others, who are better informed, say that they are sure I should, at all events, make use of my own. Nobody as yet will believe that I shall not have occasion for either, on this occasion, not thinking that it would be either prudent or permitted to attempt to celebrate an affair of this sort, without order or re-imbursements. Mr. Coleman was reprimanded for acting above his character for the late King's coronation, and for expecting to be paid for it.'

1762. The most interesting event to Florence in the first quarter of 1762, was the declining power of Marshal Botta, or Botta Adorno, to call him by his proper name. The old Pavian soldier and statesman, who had taken lessons and received praise from Prince

Eugene, was now 73 years of age. He had served Austria to good purpose in Flanders, Hungary, and Italy; but the Marshal's highest distinction was in his having defeated the Franco-Spanish army, near the Tido, in 1746. He was still active. He was no longer an Ambassador, or a General in the field; but he now turned with equal zeal to the cleaning of the ceilings in the Palazzo Pitti (painted by Pietro da Cortona), in honour of the expected coming of the Archduke Peter Leopold. The rooms, the walls of which were made glorious by the same artist, were refurnished under the Marshal's superintendence. 'He has got models of chairs from France—one of the Duke of Richelieu's, the frame of which cost 700 French *livres.* Glasses and all other furniture is to be in that taste. The Marshal is very tawdry, but piques himself upon his *gout* in those things. He has made great alterations in Princess Craon's house, and much for the better, though they are very faulty.'

Botta's taste in other matters was often more faulty, and it was offensive to the English in Florence. The silly King of Spain, Charles the Third, showed an Armada-sort of arrogance, by declaring, in reference to his quarrel with England, that the 'Omnipotent had chosen him as an Instrument to chastize the pride of England.' Mann asks, in a January letter: 'Was ever such Asiatick nonsense?' He adds: 'The Marshal, however, is charmed with it. We have had very curious dialogues together on that subject; but, yesterday evening, it was near going too far. I presented to him Lord Tavistock and Lord Stanhope, upon the Circle, which was numerous. It has since

been repeated abroad, and excepting with those whom
the *bâton de Marechal* keeps in awe, it is not disapproved of.'

Mann forgot to record the speech to Botta which
was repeated in the salons of Florence.  He had other
matters to chronicle of the Marshal and of the im-
pending war between Spain and England—a war
which made the very nostrils of Botta's charger
expand with a snuffing delight, when a Spanish
courier carried the declaration through Florence.  ' It
is,' says Mann, February 6th, ' the strangest performance of that kind that was ever seen.  It has more
the air of an Ordinance of a Fishmongers' Company
than a princely Edict to be registered in the *Corps
Diplomatique*.  The Pope has contributed towards
the execution of that Ordinance and, at the same
time, he made the Spaniards fond of the war, by
allowing them to eat meat four days in the week,
during Lent.  As to Naples, Sir James Gray seems
persuaded of the sincerity of Marquis Tannucci, who
tells him that not only they desire vehemently to
remain neutral, but that the King of Spain desires
the same, and with that view will not call upon his
son' (the King of Naples) ' to sign the family con-
vention, which would oblige him to declare war.
However, they are fortifying the very Mole of Naples,
which some people take the liberty to suppose may
indicate their intention to throw off the mask, when
there is less to fear.'

In the midst of the gossip on this war question,
there came a report that the head of the Regency
in Florence was mortally ill.  Mann repeats it in

his letter of February 9th.   'Our old Marshal Botta,'
he writes, 'is dying.   He has been the most innocent Governor that any Government could desire;
but still, the Lorrainers exult indecently on his
approaching decease.   They had found means to discredit him with the Emperor, as superannuated.   So
that everything he proposed from hence was rejected
at Vienna.   This will always be the case with everybody except a Lorrainer, so long as the Emperor is
one, and has so many of that nation about him.'   In a
postscript, Mann says :—'The poor old Marshal, at his
own request, has had the extreme unction and the
Archbishop's benediction, in *articulo mortis*, but still
breathes.'   And the old warrior continued to breathe.
'The Marshal,' says Sir Horace, March 13th, 'will
disappoint the Lorrainers at last.   He is grown so
much better that *they* have no hopes.   His case is
very singular.   Given over by everybody, and even
despatched by the Priests, who seldom hazard their
benediction in *articulo mortis* when there is the
least probability of escaping it, his illness took such
a turn that he is thought to be quite out of danger,
and his nephew, who posted hither from Pavia to
receive his rich spoils, is forced to accept the compliments of everybody on his disappointment.'

The Lorraine hangers-on looked to their Lorraine
Emperor for advancement.   The Regency in Tuscany
remained closed to them, and Botta was not even
superannuated.   But all the good people of the
Florentine salons were soon cackling loudly at a new
appointment.   It was one which shows how even the
Imperial Sword of that day acknowledged it might

be served by the Pen of a ready writer.  The appointment was that of Doctor Laeni, once librarian to the famous Riccardi, as 'Teologo to the Emperor.' 'What that is nobody knows,' says Mann, March 13th, 'but the pension he has with it is supposed to be a bribe (like those which Aretin received from all the princes of his time), to speak well of him on all occasions in the "Novelle Litterarie," which he publishes every week.'

Though Botta was out of danger, he was still an invalid, and this proved to be of some discomfort to Mann, who writes on March 13th:—'I am sadly embroiled ; this is my Night, and I have got a terrible Rheumatism in my loins.  I had not time to make it known or to excuse myself.  It is Gala day, and as the Marshal is ill, nobody else receives.  The crowd will consequently be great, and I shall not be able to do the honours.'

In the last letter of this quarter, March 27th, Mann notices the mark which a noble English artist had made in Italy.  'You are rightly informed.  The Great Duke's Palace and the Church at Leghorn were designed by Inigo Jones, and the whole Square, which is spacious, was to have been the same.  You shall have drawings of them by the first opportunity.'

Occasionally, scenes occurred at the Florentine Court which, to use Charles the Second's phrase, must have been 'as good as a play.'  In the course of the war then being carried on, Count Lorenzi, when any English success had been gazetted, attended at Marshal Botta's and announced that our ships had been destroyed and our soldiers repulsed.  When we had taken Martinico, the Florentine Court was informed that we had lost 2000 men in an ineffectual attempt to land our troops. This and other falsehoods were repeated and believed at Florence. 'On the very day,' says Mann, April 10th, 'that we received an account of our success, I carried the news to the old Marshal, who really brightened up on hearing it; for though he is a very good Austrian, he is a strong Anti-Gallican. I have not met Count Lorenzi' (the French Ambassador) 'since, but I hear that he is vastly ashamed for the number of lies he had told on this occasion.'

The English Minister paid much deference to the 'old Marshal.' Referring to the retirement of the Duke of Newcastle from the administration, Mann writes, in one of his April letters:—' Marshal Botta, who is the Duke's contemporary, frequently quotes him in his system of politicks as well as of ceremonies. He has a standing story of a great dinner at Brussels, which was near being spoilt, the which he prevented by contriving that the Duke should, in fact, take place of the Nuncio, by handing some lady to the table, whilst he himself took place of them all, by leading in the Duchess of Newcastle. . . . He has cheated the Nuncio out of the *pas* twenty times by some ingenious conceit, though the Court of Venice has ordered him to yield it; and I am told that there is no circumstance for which Botta loves me so much as that of my seating myself in the lowest places, and even declining to accept of his offer sometimes to sit upon the same couch with him—an honour that he allows to so few.'

Alluding to the capture of the 'Hermione,' that gallant deed which flung such a flood of glory and of gold on England in the early days of George's reign, Mann adds the following curious details :—' Captain Sawyer, an extreme sensible, well educated man, Captain of the Active frigate, has, we hear, taken the Hermonia (*sic*), a Spanish register ship from Lima, which Mr. Dick's correspondents at Gibraltar acquaint him is worth a million. What increases my satisfaction on this occasion is, that another very worthy young man, and my particular friend, Meadows, will share with Captain Sawyer, *by a private agreement between them.* Another comes in likewise for a share, who had lately married Sawyer's sister—by being in sight when the Hermonia (*sic*) struck. I think that it is infinitely better that such wealth should be divided among several than overload one.'

But Mann's thoughts were now concentrated on one, and that an unofficial subject. Walpole had recommended to his homage, courtesy, and devotion, that beautiful Duchess of Grafton, to whom Walpole himself wrote such saucy letters. In her maiden state, she was Anne Liddell, sole daughter and heiress of Lord Ravensworth. She had now been six years a Duchess ; and she and scandal as yet had nothing to do with each other. The appearance of the English beauty in Italy excited as lively, if not the same, interest in the ladies as among the cavaliers. Mann was overcome by his enthusiasm. On April 17th, he writes :—' Your charming Dutchess is arrived. I immediately fled to her, and in a few minutes had an opportunity, amidst the kindest enquiries she made

after you, to hear that she had received the letters
you wrote to her.    You will easily imagine that I did
not omit on that occasion, to inform her of the impatience you had expressed to hear of her safe arrival
here.    The knowledge she must have had of your
goodness for me, or her own amiable character,
abridged much of the ceremony in approaching and
making acquaintance with so great a lady.'

'Madame Acciajuoli is to attend her as much but
no more than she chuses.    She has not been out yet,
having refused an invitation this evening to Madame
Acciajuoli's, where the sweet Madame Corsi and a few
other ladies had been invited to meet her, but the
Dutchess reserves her first *sortie* for me ; intending to
honour my Conversazione to-morrow evening, which
will, I am told, be very numerous.    The curiosity to
see a stranger (to which they give the name of attention to me on such occasions) will draw crowds here.
The next day she does me the honour to dine here,
with several Ladies ; and in the evening we are to
have a new Burletta by an extreme good company.
Nothing can equal my ambition to contribute to her
amusement.    If ever you should hear that I became
troublesome, attribute it to that only.'

'The Duke is very obliging.    You know that he
is the son of my great friend, Lord Augustus' (Fitzroy,
second son of the second Duke of Grafton), 'who lived
with me some time here.    I carried the Duke this
morning to the Marshal's, who was much flattered with
the visit, and rose from his chair for the first time since
his illness, on our taking leave.    This visit will, he
thinks, give example to Cardinal Rochechouart, who

is coming from Rome—the first Eminence who has
ventured to put his foot into Florence (though many
have gone round the walls) since the Marshal has
been here, on account of the ceremonial ; but, to a
sick Marshal, even a Cardinal, fresh from Rome, may
yield *sans consequence.*' Rome had not forgotten the
slight which Botta had put on the Papal Nuncio at
the dinner in Brussels, when he contrived that both
the Duke and Duchess of Newcastle should have precedence of the great official from the Vatican. On
April 24th, Mann writes :—

'Your charming Dutchess of Grafton seems to like
Florence very well. . Great attentions have been shown
to her by the Florentine Ladies—by their visits at her
house, and by crowding to mine, to see her ; and I
am proud that they should see so much dignity and
affability ; so much sweetness in her countenance and
care in her behaviour ; and, in short, so many amiable
qualities assembled in one person. She has corrected
the ideas that people had formed of our English
woemen. But still I am not satisfied. She won't let
me attend on her so much as I could wish, to see the
curiosities in the town, and has absolutely declared off
from taking any airings to the Park di San Gallo,
and further jaunts to your sweet Petraja, Castello, or
other places, as she says that going in a coach in the
afternoon hurts her, and makes her unfit for any
Assembly, or able to hold out at the theater. This,
you see, excludes the principal amusements at this
agreeable season ; but still her health is preferable to
everything. She passes her afternoons much more
profitable, it's true, in studying Italian and Musick.

She has dined here twice, and comes again to-morrow.'

' I shall have crowds again this evening ; for those who were here last week wish to see her again, and have excited the curiosity of those who were absent. I have talked to her so much of the Petraja, where you used so often to pay your court to Princess Craon, that she has promised to go there one morning early, on horseback, to walk upon that charming Terrass— where Mr. Morice was surprized yesterday to see so large a Palm tree ; larger, he said, than any he had ever seen, except in China—where he has never been!'

The Duke and Duchess were dining with Mann a few hours before their departure from Florence, when letters from Horace Walpole reached the Minister while he and his guests were at table. ' It gave me an opportunity,' he says, May 15th, ' to satisfy her constant . enquiries after your health. Pray, thank her, in my name, when you write to her, or see her, for the many marks of goodness which she con-descended to show me during her stay here,—which she seemed to wish to prolong ; and has expressed herself in such a manner as would make me flatter myself that she was convinced at least of my great ambition to contribute in any shape to make this place agreeable to her. On her part, she has done every-thing one could wish, and has quite corrected the Ideas of the Florentines of the English Ladies ; but we shall never be able to maintain the reputation which she has established. They were to stay one day only at Bologna ; two, at most, at Turin ; and then proceed to Genoa, where they intend to fix for two

months, and be in England by the end* of August.
The Duke's great exactness in keeping to his travelling
plan will admit of very little alteration in this.'

Mann asks Walpole, in a 'memorandum,' to send
him 'some late volumes of the Monthly Review, the
Court Calendar, Miller's Register, The Annual Register
for the year 1760, an account of the Revolution at
Bengall, and 12 of the best Oratorii of Handel.' He
says, in the letter containing the loose memorandum :
'The twelve Oratorii of Handel, with their scores, that
is, all the parts, are for Madam Branchi (?) a most
divine singer, who charmed the Dutchess of Grafton
twice, therefore deserves that return, or any other
acknowledgment from me.   Mr. Morice tells me that
you must ask the assistance of some musical man, to
chuse the most esteemed among those Oratorij.'

The Duchess of Grafton, according to Mann's letter
of June 12th, 'was certainly hurried out of Italy
contrary to her inclinations, and would willingly have
passed all the time here that she *must* spend out of
England.  They are, long before this time, seated near
Geneva, where she can have few amusements.  The
Duke does not seem to seek them ; or, perhaps, to
speak more properly, may find them in what others do
not.  He hates everything of a publick nature.  She
only loves to step aside from publick diversions into
retirement, which she employs in musick, writing,
and much reading, adorning by those means her mind
as much as her person is by nature.  They have no
intercourse with Voltaire, though so near a neighbour.
He is a brute, and will not deviate from his rule of
not returning visits, even in favour of a Dutchess,

for on their first going to Geneva, they both went to
see him.'

'Apropos to Voltaire. I must give you an instance in him of the unbounded vanity even of the
most cleaver people. One Mr. Craufurd, a very ingenious young man, who is now *here*, being very intimate
with Voltaire, and in his Library, took up a Homer
and desired him to read a few lines, that he might
hear whether a Frenchman pronounced Greek like an
Englishman. Voltaire was displeased, but owned that
he never knew Greek. Craufurd, much surprized,
asked him how he had been able to write so much
about Homer. "Bon!" replyed Voltaire, " est-il neces-
saire d'entendre un auteur, pour en dire son sentiment?" The learned would be able by this to
account for the many errors that they say Voltaire
has fallen into by the vanity of being an universal
author.'

When the Duke and Duchess of Grafton visited
Voltaire, the latter showed them a chapter of his
Universal History (in MS.), entitled, Les Anglais
Vainqueurs dans les Quatre Parties du Monde?
'There have been minutes in the course of our cor-
respondence,' says Walpole to Mann, 'when you and
I did not expect to see this chapter.'

Mann found some solace for being deprived of the
bright presence of Walpole's charming Duchess. On
June 26th, he writes:—'Mr. Pitt will hardly believe
you when you tell him that Lord Strathmore has
accompanied the Countess San Vitali here, and is
now in our neighbourhood. I expect them all in my
garden this evening, for I have got two foreign ladies

recommended to me, and this is the first night of its opening below stairs.'

Mr. (Thomas) Pitt then resided near Walpole, at Twickenham. 'I am very happy in my new neighbour,' says the latter. 'He calls his small house, Palazzo Pitti, which does not look as if he had forgotten you, and sounds pleasantly in my ears.' With regard to Mann's devotion to the Duchess, Walpole remarks: 'It would look like vanity in me to thank you for attentions where so much attention is done; yet, I am apt to think you did pay a little homage extraordinary on my account to the Duchess of Grafton. She tells me how charmed she is with your reception of her. I warned you to expect no great beauty; and yet the more you saw her, did not you like her the more? Her air, and manner, and majesty are quite her own.'

Walpole had not then seen his Duchess, since her return to England. He writes, however, in September:—'Well, I have seen my Duchess—you have not returned her as you received her. I was quite struck at seeing her so much altered. She wears no rouge, and being leaner, her features, which never were delicate, seem larger. Then, she is not dressed French, but Italian, which is over-French. In one point, in which she cannot be improved, she seemed so; being thinner, she looked taller. She spoke of you to my perfect content; and, as if I did not know it, told me of all your good-breeding, good-nature, and attentions.'

Mann, in his turn, told Walpole of the cost of war to Austria. No wonder that Maria Theresa and Frantz the Kaiser were inclined for peace. 'She has spent,' says Mann, in a June letter, 'three hundred thousand subjects and four hundred Millions of Florins, in this unsuccessful and unprovoked attempt to recover Silesia.'     Marshal Botta had no victories to blazon, but when the news reached him that the poor Czar Peter's enthusiasm for the King of Prussia had led the Czarina Catherine to hurl him from the throne, a preparatory step to a darker sequel, 'the Marshal,' says Mann, August 7th, 'taking the news of this usurpation as a favourable event for his Court, announced it at the *Imperiale* by his French Horns ; but, as they could not be heard in Florence, he wrote circular letters to his colleagues in the Regency, and to the French and Spanish Ministers, and he had the indelicacy to make use of the expression, " qu'il avait la satisfaction de leur faire part que le Czar avait été deposé, le 9 passé," etc.     The next day we talked indifferently about it, but he plainly discovered that if his Court had not profited by it, he should have looked upon it in its true light, as the blackest treachery.'

The Court of Vienna saw no treachery in the deposition, nor any crime in the murder of Peter the Third by his wife, Catherine.     What Mann calls ' a grand Manifest from the Court of Vienna,' was sent to Florence.     At a ' Circle ' at Marshal Botta's, that ' great personage ' gave it to the English Minister to read, saying at the same time, that ' it was a most excellent performance.'     Mann thus describes what followed (September 4th) :—' I returned it to him with a few observations that differed much from his opinions.     We canvassed the principal points of it, which warmed me so, that my sincerity quite got the better of

my prudence ; for, I concluded by saying that the case
of that unfortunate Prince was most deplorable, as he
not only had lost his crown and his life, but that he
must lose his reputation too ; that, however, one
ought not to wonder at this, as, to justify or palliate
what had been done, it was necessary to load the Czar
with everything that was odious.   The Circle seemed
to be on my side ; and *He'* (the Marshal), 'mistaking
my meaning, as if what I had said was personally
directed to him, and not to the Manifest, replyed :
" Mais, je ne pretends pas le justifier."

'Besides this famous piece in which the Czarina
imparts to Peter, as a crime, his not having wept at
his Aunt's death, she has also insinuated that his not
having declared his son to be his heir, was an omission
by which he meant to disown him !   There is not the
least shadow of proof for such a supposition ; for, at
that same time, she herself virtually deprived that son
of his crown !   In another piece she is represented as
weeping and bewailing the death she had occasioned ;
though she had exulted before in it, and looked upon
it as a sure proof that Heaven had approved of her
usurpation.   She persisted in the resolution to attend
his funeral, but yielded at last to the persuasions of the
Senate,—and out of compassion to her loving subjects,
lest *she* might sink under the weight of her grief ;
and *they,* by that means, might be deprived of so
tender a Mother ! . . . We see that all the Great
Courts are sending their Ministers to congratulate this
new Empress upon her accession ; though each, in its
own state, would have inflicted the severest punishment
on any subject that had committed such crimes.'

Austria lost much of her admiration for the
Imperial murderess, as soon as Catherine showed less
enmity to the King of Prussia than his furious and
implacable antagonist the Czarina, Elizabeth.  On the
other hand, Mann tells Walpole, September 4th, that
Cardinal Alboni covered Catherine with encomiums
and called her ' the Heroine of the North,' ' in the
circular notes that he sent about to the foreign
Ministers at Rome, to give them notice of that event
which he had received by an Express.  Count Rivera,
the King of Sardinia's Minister, flew into a violent
passion, and shewed that he did not think the term
was either judiciously chosen, by a Prince of the
Church, or prudently, as a publick Minister.  I have
been assured that the Pope was inclined to wish the
Empress-Queen joy of this event, and even to offer a
Jubilee for the future success of her arms.  He probably thought that they would be prosperous ; and, in
that case, wished to steal the merit of it.'

The Florentines, however, at this season, had been
more concerned with a calamity at home than with
battle, murder, and sudden death abroad.  At two
o'clock, in the afternoon of August 13th, their Great
Gallery, the pride of the Duchy, the shrine to which
intelligent pilgrims resorted from all parts of the
world, was discovered to be on fire.  Indeed, it seemed
suddenly to burst into flames.  The ordinary citizens,
at first, were panic stricken, and next, finding they
were not allowed to quietly contemplate the unusual
spectacle, they fled, rather than lend a hand in putting
it out.  ' All the Members of the Regency and the
Great Folks assisted, and many of the Cavaliers

carried water ; but they were forced to treat the
common people very rudely to oblige *them* to do it.
Soldiers were sent to the remote parts of the town
to get them together, but they ran into the Churches
and other secure places. The confusion was very
great, from two till sun-set, and in that neighbourhood
it lasted all night by the fire breaking out again late.'
From first to last, there was 'a want of all conve-
niences to extinguish the fire, and great difficulty in
getting up water so high.' After all, the damage was
not so extensive as was feared it might be. Mann
says :—'Had the fire that broke out yesterday at two
in the afternoon, happened towards the evening, the
whole Gallery would infallibly have been destroyed.
It began at the end where the Laocoon stands (or
stood). The space of eleven of the great windows,
which is near 200 feet, has been demolished. You
will be able to see what stood there by the exact
drawing you have of the Gallery ; but, in reality,
excepting that group of the Laocoon, and the Bacchus
of Sansovino (?) there was nothing good ; the Boar, I
believe, is not lost. They count six statues and five
busts lost. The room where the Collection of Drawings is, was on fire, but they were saved ; so that the
mischief has been much less than was apprehended
from the fury with which it began.'

Walpole's reply to the above information is :—' I
condole with you for the misfortune of the Gallery, in
the loss of the Laocoon ; yet, if a fine statue was to
be demolished, it was one that could most easily be
spared ; as there is a duplicate at Rome, and, as I
remember, not only a finer but a more authentic.

But how came the Florentines to see their Gallery burn, with so much indifference? It was collected by the Medici. If formed by the Lorrainers, I should not wonder.'

After fire,—water and hurricane. 'Besides the late disaster at our gallery,' says Mann, September 4th, 'we have had a storm that threatened destruction to the whole city. It did much mischief to the Palazzo Pitti and most of the large buildings, by tearing off the roofs and literally demolishing *all* the windows of every northern front in the whole town. The hail was of an extraordinary size and has done vast mischief in the country. My house and garden, you know, are all south, so that I have received no damage. At Leghorn too there has been a hurricane which lasted *one minute*, but which has done strange mischief.'

The year had been productive of 'strange mischief' in Italy, and superstitious people alluded to the fact that the year opened with domestic calamity at Rome, where the roof of the Opera House fell in (January 18th) during the time of performance; and though the majority of the audience had time to escape, the killed and wounded amounted to nearly seventy,—among whom were the Princess Borghese and the Prince d' Asti.

Mann now comes to the close of this disastrous year, during which England and Spain each declared war against the other; Spain also declared war against Portugal, and England continued her war with France. Austria and Prussia were also at war, but on the other hand, Prussia made peace with

Russia and also with Sweden. The great English glory of the year was the capture of Havannah by Lord Albemarle and Admiral Pococke; and the crowning event was the peace, the preliminary articles of which were signed by the French and English contracting parties at Fontainebleau, on November the 3rd. England gave up nothing she had won; and she took Canada from France and Florida from Spain.

All these events were warmly canvassed in the circle of the Florentine Regency and the representatives of foreign kings, who there assembled. Marshal Botta, now recovered, whispered scraps of intelligence which Mann received with well-founded distrust. An amiable diplomatist showed him a letter from a Spanish minister at Madrid which contained the assurance that a Spanish disaster there would only aggravate the war. Others were confident the English could never take Havannah. Mann reminded them of former confident prophecies, made in the same spirit, which were utterly falsified. On November 13th, Mann says :—'The Marquis Squillaci, writing to Viviani here, assures him that they are quite easy at Madrid on account of the Havannah. . . Would to God (said Viviani) that what he writes may be justified, but the Articles of Capitulation are coming !—And so they did come,' says Mann, 'for I had received them about the same time.' The conquest struck the King of Spain dumb, and went far to seriously disturb his very small intellects. A Frenchman compared his country's success at sea with its eagerness to follow English fashions. He said in a letter to a friend in Florence, who allowed Mann to see it : 'Nous nous anglifions beaucoup, mais il est vray que ce n'est pas sur mer ! ' Leghorn took a practical view of the peace.  'Leghorn,' writes Mann, 'rejoyces much in the recovery of Newfoundland, in hopes that the fish ships may still arrive in time to furnish all Italy with fish, and save the Pope from an uncatholick stretch of his authority, by declaring Beef and Mutton to be *maigre* for the next Lent, which might be a bad example for the future.'

Of the English in Italy, there are significant records.  Lord Strathmore, says Mann, 'would go to England as fast as French post horses could carry him, *but* he had not consulted the Countess Sanvitali, who still detains him at Parma . . . Mr. Bouverie, Lord Folkestone's brother, will be more expeditious, as he could not strike up the bargain with a great Lady here, whom he intended to allow as great an ascendant over him.  In which case, we should probably have kept him as long as we have had Lord Fordwych.'  Mann alludes to a far more remarkable man than either,—that wayward, ill-fated, accomplished, and misrepresented son of Lady Mary Wortley Montague,—namely, Edward Montague :— 'Mr. Montague has been for some time in these parts, making dispositions for his journey to Ethiopia. They say he has put a daughter into a Convent at Rome.  He wears his whiskers, I am told, and, at home, sometimes the dress of that country, to accustom himself to it.'

But there was a British subject in Florence who has left a brighter mark in the world, and the history

of Art, than Mr. Montague.   Strange, the ardent
Jacobite, whose services in collecting pictures neither
English Whigs nor the English King declined, had
returned to the Tuscan capital.   'Mr. Strange has
returned hither from Rome and Naples, with such a
numerous and well-chosen treasure of his own drawings from the most capital pictures there, as will
abundantly repay him for the time he has spent
abroad.   He has been very much distinguished
wherever he has been, and particularly admired, for
a new method he has invented, of *drawing in colours*,
which, by great application, he has reduced to certain
and fixt principles ; so that at the same time that
this elegant invention will, as he says, be of great
use to him in engraving those drawings, it has a
more extraordinary and beautiful effect in them than
can be either described or conceived, without seeing
them.   They give the clearest idea of the originals
and of their colourings, and by that means they themselves have the merit of becoming pictures of a much
more delicate nature than miniatures.   Mr. Strange
is impatient that you should see them, and begs his
very respectful compliments to you.   Many people
*I know* will vye with each other for the purchase of
those drawings, though the cost will be very high ;
but nothing will tempt him to part with them, till
he has engraved them ; and by one or two at a
time, the whole will at least employ ten years to
engrave.'

George the Third was a great purchaser in the
Italian markets of art and *virtu*.   'Have you heard,'
asks Mann, 'what a quantity of things have been

bought and are buying for the Queen ? Cardinal Alboni's collection of drawings and prints were paid 14,000 crowns. Mr. Smith's whole collection and library has been purchased at the price of 20,000*l*. sterlin'; and Mr. Dalton is now at Venice, packing it up. Many expensive things of that sort were lost in a ship that took fire at sea some months ago ; the crews of which saved their lives by becoming prisoners to the Spaniards, at Carthagena. In short, I believe that there is no ship departs from any port in Italy, that has not something for the King.'

While 'King There,' as some Italians called George the Third, was thus profitably laying out his money, 'King Here,' as the same persons styled the old Chevalier, was gradually fading out of life. On the 12th August, 1762, Walpole wrote to Mann :—' A Prince of Wales was born this morning. The prospect of your old neighbour at Rome does not improve. The House of Hanover will have members in its own family sufficient to defend their crown.' In October, Mann replied:—'The Pretender seems to be at the last period of his life. He has lately had two apoplecktic fits ; by which his mouth is much drawn aside, and his speech is hardly intelligible. His devout son contents himself with praying for him. The other will probably get drunk to drown his sorrow.' On December the 4th, alluding to the extinction of 'a certain party which distressed former Ministries in England,'—that of the Jacobites,—Mann says :—' The object of it is languishing in a sick bed at Rome, forgotten by everybody except the few about him. His eldest son, more the object of contempt, or

perhaps of compassion than of alarm, is hidden in
a corner of France ; and the other, by putting on
the Cowle, has done more to extinguish his party
than could have been effected by putting to death
many thousands of their deluded followers.'

# CHAPTER V.

## 1763.

THE most conspicuous English travellers of rank whom Mann received during the first half of the year 1763, were, incontestably, the Earl and Countess of Northampton. The Earl was on his way to Venice as English Ambassador. The Countess, formerly Lady Anne Somerset, was the daughter of the Duke of Beaufort. Walpole described them as ' young, handsome, and happy '; and he spoke of life as being ' very valuable to them.' But the shadow of the Inevitable Angel covered them both. Mann writes, April 30th :—

' We have a melancholy scene here which must end in a catastrophe. Lord and Lady Northampton are here ; she with an intention to proceed towards Naples'—(the young, handsome, and happy Countess had been suddenly attacked by rapid consumption)— ' but I fear much too late. He ought to go there, and probably might recover, for he has all the symptoms of the beginning of the same disorder. The separation, I fear, will be a distress to both. I had proposed an appartment for her but she would not accept it. I carry her out twice a day, and by deceiving her,

with regard to her own situation, and persuading
her that my Lord will follow her to Naples as soon
as he had made his Entry into Venice, have brought
her to a certain tranquility on that subject.   This is
my own opinion :—their separation will be for ever.
I don't see how he can go through the ceremony of
his Entry.   He is obliged to be carried up stairs, and
even without the least motion, has frequently a
thickness of breath that indicates the danger of his
disorder.'

In those days Ambassadors entered the cities to
which they were accredited with much public show
and pomp.   No Envoy entered London with more
magnificent circumstance than the Ambassador from
the Venetian States.   From the Tower, where he
landed, it was one triumphal procession, escorted by
troops and enlivened by music, till his Excellency
arrived at his official residence in Soho.   The Earl
of Northampton resolved to enter Venice, indeed he
was bound to do so, by courtesy and custom, with
equal show of dignity.   Mann, however, says, May
21st:—'I fear that the distress in Lord Northampton's
family will spread further and sooner than I expected.
Mr. Dick ' (the English Consul at Leghorn) ' who
went to Venice to see my Lord's Entry, has informed
me by a letter which I received two days ago, that
my Lord's Physician had told him plainly, that the
Earl hastened, every hour, to his end, and that he
doubted much if he could hold out to make his Entry,
—which was then fixed for the 29th of this month.
One cannot figure to one's self a scene more afflicting.

' Mr. Bagot and the Physician who accompanies

my Lady, have acquainted me from Paris that they
had little hopes of her reaching Naples.  They were
then unacquainted with the dangerous position of my
Lord, who did not seem to know it himself, as, the
post before, he wrote that he should soon see me again
here.  Such scenes are very distressing.'

The dying Ambassador braced himself for the
entry into Venice in state.  A Venetian physician
said that he seemed as one going to the gallows in
*Gala!*  On June 18th, Mann says:—' Lord Northampton performed the ceremony of his Entry with
evident risk of dying in the attempt, according to
the opinion of his Physician, and by all accounts he
was as near it as possible.  This was before he knew
my Lady's death, which they concealed from him two
days; but the notice of that added so much to his
oppression, that the Republick had compassion of
him and dispensed with his returning to their Colledge in the same State he went before '—(This refers
to the second Entry in State, when the Ambassador
went to receive the reply to the notification made by
him, of his appointment, the previous day)—' but sent
their answers to the King's Letters by a Secretary;
and everything after passed by the same means.  My
Lord was to leave Venice on the 9th, with a view of
consulting M. Tronchin at Geneva, in whose reputation he has confidence, and if he survives the hot
months, they intend to carry him to Lisbon, the place
of his nativity.  Never was so much Pomp joyned
with so much distress.'

' Lord Northampton,' said Walpole, ' will, I fear,
be little better for Tronchin, who, I am assured, from

very good judges at Paris, is little better than a char-
latan.' And Mann replied : 'Tronchin is certainly a
quack ; but perhaps none other would give him hopes.'
The Earl was beyond the reach of human aid. His
agony ended in October. There was one more awful,
which Walpole communicated to Mann, namely, the
death, by fire, of Lady Molesworth, her brother, two
of her daughters, and four servants, by the burning of
her house in Upper Brook Street. This led to Mann's
remarks on building in England and what was thought
of it in Italy. 'There is no instance,' he writes, May
30th, 'of so complicated a scene of horror, all owing to
the sad method in England of making all the stair-
cases of wood, and of having only one in a house.
Surely, this melancholy accident will terrify people
into such precautions as may on most occasions secure
them from perishing so miserably. It is an object
worthy the care of the Government. I hope to hear
that an act is passed to oblige every body to make their
stairs of stone, and in poorer houses at least of brick.
The same power has obliged people to make partition
walls. Basta ! the houses in London are the ridicule
of all strangers, both for their size and the weakness of
the building ; but the safety of them against such
terrible accidents ought absolutely to be provided for.'

If the Italian method of building was superior
to the English, our climate, at least in spring, was
equal to that of northern Italy. Mann not only
complains of several weeks of damp weather, but of
the abominable fogs. 'Fogs so thick that at any
eminence at a mile distance the whole of Florence is
frequently invisible for a considerable part of the day.

This I lately' (end of February) 'experienced from Fiesole, where I stayed a fortnight. It was exactly what I have seen from Linton, looking towards the Wilds ( *sic !* ) of Kent.'

Mann refers with some melancholy to failing strength and increasing years ; but he was not quite devoid of ambition or of desire for promotion if he could only propitiate the King. 'But,' he says, 'it is absolutely impossible to make any merit here by culti-vating the King's love for *virtu*. There is nothing of any kind to be got worthy his notice after the vast collections that have been purchased for him. . . . . I assure you that neither in medals, pictures, or drawings, anything is to be got here. I had, purely in complyance with your opinion, given commission to Mr. Strange to look out both at Rome and Naples for anything capital and worth presenting there, but all in vain.'

There was a subject, however, much more impor-tant to the Florentines than the question of Mann's abiding with, or departing from them. That new order of things appeared to be about to be established, viz. those sovereign Grand Duchies, which were so recently finally swept away in the revolution which has made one united Italy. 'The prospect,' says Mann, 'of this State becoming again independent under Great Dukes of their own, rejoyces the Florentines, who are persuaded that they shall owe that benefit to England.' England had nothing to do with the arrangement. 'But,' said Walpole, ' *I* am glad you are going to have a Great Duke ; and a new Court will make Florence lively, the only beauty it wants.' Mann

narrates at somewhat tedious length how the Emperor's
second son, the Archduke Leopold, was to reside in
Florence 'as his father's Lieutenant in Tuscany during
his life, and to succeed as Great Duke at the Emperor's
death. This archduke, by marrying the grand-
daughter of Modena, is to succeed to that duchy if, as
there is very little probability, there shall be no male
heir. The Duke's people, to prevent the extinction of
his family, wanted him to marry a proper person to
get heirs ; but he (like Louis XIV.), it is agreed, has
married, *par conscience*, the Countess of Simonetti,
whom he is ashamed to own.' ' You divert me,' writes
Walpole, ' with my friend the Duke of Modena's con-
scientious match. . . . But, for Hymen's sake ! who
is that Madame Simonetti ? I trust, not that old
painted, gaming, debauched Countess from Milan,
whom I saw at the fair of Reggio ! ' To which out-
burst Mann makes answer, May 28th :—' Why should
you doubt of Madame Simonetti being the same whom
you knew so long ago, when you know that the Duke
is the same senseless personage whom you knew at
Modena ? And, in England, if great examples can
justify folly, did not Louis XIV. do the same thing ?
Victor Amadeo the same ? though the latter was in
different circumstances.'

This Duke had one son by his former wife, a
daughter of the Regent, Duke of Orleans. ' He is so
indifferent to that son,' writes Mann, ' that he is dis-
sipating everything he should leave to him. He has
lately sold the Allodials of the House of Guastalla
(which he was heir to) for 73,000 zecchins to Don
Phillip ; and they say has secured the money in the

Bank of Vienna. . . . . This step and some others of a like nature, have made an open quarrell with his son.   The whole family was dividing—the son and his wife to Massa, and the Antient Maidens, your old friends, to Bologna ; but some people have interfered, and say they will prevent an *eclat.*'

In making preparations for the new-comers who were to be the future Grand Duke and Duchess, Prince Lichtenstein came from Vienna, to assist Marshal Botta ; ' but,' says Mann, ' they seem to forget the example of the Medici, the ceremony of whose Court put it in their power to make a figure in things of more importance.   Prince Lichtenstein is now at the Baths at Pisa.   Cardinal Stuart is also there, in so confirmed a scorbutick habit of body as make his dependants and the Jesuits fear that he cannot live many years.'

Mann despised the ill taste of Botta, who spoiled rather than improved the Palazzo Pitti.   ' He is of the stile of the old Cosimo Riccardi, whom you knew, whose Government in the Medici family is only remembered by the Luster of thick Cristal of an enormous size which he added to the Gallery that his father had painted by Giordano, and which the smoak of those candles spoilt.'   Botta went to Vienna, to receive the additional dignity of ' Grand Maistre to the Archduke and Duchess,' as soon as they took up their residence in the Palazzo Pitti.   ' He has made sad work in the Palazzo,' says Mann, ' and in the Garden.   His arrangement of the Pictures is to make it depend, first upon the freshness of the gilding upon the frames ; and then, upon the position of the figures in each picture, which figures must not turn their back to the throne! Calvin and Luther, by Giordano, were turned out with a most pious contempt, as not worthy to stand in the presence of so orthodox a Prince as is coming here! His mother' (Maria Theresa) 'will not permit any picture to hang in her department that shews either a naked leg or arm. This ill agrees with the Medici taste or the collection they have left. Imagine only that grave Matron' (Maria Theresa) 'running the gauntlet, through the Gallery! Ah! Quelle horreur!'

Later, returning to the same subject, Mann writes: 'A famous picture, by Titian, was turned out of the room where the Canopy is, because the figure almost turned its back to it, and none are to be admitted there but such as respectfully present their faces to it. The picture of Luther and Calvin was dismissed with a Catholick fury, and, I fear, will find no better place than in that horrid ill-painted room of Hell, at the end of the appartment, that the young Prince may see how the enemies of the Church ought to be treated. You will think I exaggerate, but what I have said is literally and ludicrously true. Botta tells the Florentines who criticize his operations, that he knows more of architecture and Painting than Andrea del Sarto, or their ancestors who invented their Tuscan Order! Such are his occupations, for as to Government, *cela va son train!* Nobody interferes and nothing can be taxed' higher than it is. . . The Farmers of the Revenue, though Tuscans, are more rigorous than the Receivers or Collectors used to be under the Medici, who were indulgent to their subjects, and spent their revenues amongst them.   This will not be the case for some time, though a young Prince is coming, for the Emperor will still have the principal share.   The Infanta is certainly to debark at Geneva, in the Spring, and to go to Inspruck, where *La Famille Imperiale* is to meet her, but the young couple will probably not be here till September, 1765, and great diligence must be used to get everything ready even for that time.'

There was another couple, the Duke and Duchess of Grafton, who now considerably surprised the Italians (who had admired and envied both) by taking a course, after their return to England, which is explained in the following paragraph :—' I *was* more concerned than surprized to hear of the separation of the Duke and Duchess of Grafton.   I saw such seeds of disagreement when they were here, as too plainly shewed that they neither of them meant to contribute to the other's happiness.   This point, I am persuaded, is better understood abroad.   Less is expected in a conjugal state, consequently, the Duties of it, which naturally produce aversion, are more easily fulfilled ; and when there is a real, reciprocal indifference, they don't exact the profession or the appearances of the contrary.   However this may clash with our ideas of Matrimony, it is more agreeable to general Society and attended with less inconvenience, for few can afford here to purchase their quiet by a separate maintenance.'

In some respects, indeed, the Italian system might be more agreeable to general society than that pursued by the Duke, the Duchess, and immediate friends mixed up in their social arrangements.   For example :

The young Duke lived publicly with ' Nancy Parsons,' (Anne Horton) when the young Duchess lived on the most intimate and familiar terms with Lord Ossory, who (after her divorce) married her, and accepted an accompanying paternityship, with the utmost alacrity. The Duke then turned off 'Nancy,' and married a baronet's daughter, Miss Wrothsley. Lord Maynard, a man who was not rigidly particular, wedded with Nancy Parsons; and, finally, the Duke, who lived to a 'good' old age, took to the study of Theology, and died an Unitarian! The social arrangements here recorded, were matters of surprise and amusement to the Florentines. They ordered these things better in Tuscany.

There was another English visitor to Florence, who gave much opportunity to censure, and whose ghost has pertinaciously kept its place in the most blundering and baseless of ghost-stories ever built out of nothing, namely, Thomas, Lord Lyttelton; but he was as yet only plain 'Mr.,' the good George, Lord Lyttelton's son:—' A very odd young man, a near relation of our friend, Mr. Pitt, and the son of Lord Lyttleton (*sic*), one who has already taken a resolution to make himself considerable by opposition, and whose ambition will bear no controul. If he does succeed, it must be by the force of that and the harshest means only, for his contradictory temper makes it impossible for him to agree with anybody; and his behaviour in general disobliges and offends so that he is shunned both by the English and Italians, whom he in return' despises. Don't mention this to his amiable cousin, on his return to England. He must soon make himself be talked of, as he has given occasion in every place he has passed through, much to his disadvantage.'

Meanwhile eccentric visitors were not wanting at this time in Florence. 'We have a young Spaniard here, who, to outdo the English Cicisbei, gave a *Cocchiata* to his *bella*, first at her house, and then on the river, this evening (August 20th), which will cost him 500 zecchins. The windows and scaffolds are let at great prices.' Another visitor was simply a passer-by,—the Hereditary Princess of Modena, 'who returned to Massa, her own dominion, when her husband was just under arrest, for want of respect, I suppose, to his Mother-in-law, or at least for not complying with everything which she had long ago settled at Vienna in regard to his Daughter. That Princess, who travelled with most of her Court, Ladies of Honour, Gentlemen Ushers, Groom of Her Bed-chamber, etc., to the number of near 40 people (almost as many as the Chancellor of Russia has) had instructions from the Duke *not to set her foot* in Florence, on account of the Etiquette and the Marshal, who is a greater Lady here than she is. She was therefore led about the principal streets in her Post Chaise, to see as much of it as she could *en passant* to a Villa of Marquis Costi, about a mile off. She was most sumptuously entertained that night, and at a Meat breakfast the next morning; I assisted at this. The generosity of the Marquis Corsi (for he is at Naples, whence, they say, he is to return a Duke) was so great, that her Serene Highness's Chaises, and the pockets of all her servants, were stuffed with good

things more than any Stage coach in England, though
the next stop was but 16 miles distance.'

Among English visitors to Florence were young
ladies accompanying their families, and attracting the
eyes of Romish priests. Mann kept the circle at
Marshal Botta's excited and attentive, by his altercations with the representative of the Emperor,
respecting 'some Protestant Girls who have been
seduced by the priests to escape from their Parents
and to change their religion. It would divert you
extremely to see how zeal on such occasions triumphs
over reason, and how meritorious they think it is
to set aside all promises and obligations for such
a cause. The affair is now in the hands of Lord
Stormont, and though in itself it is extremely trifling,
yet by the *hauteur* with which it is treated at Vienna,
it may be attended by very serious consequences.
Lord Stormont has had orders to protest against the
Emperor's decision, and not to treat any more ; this
has alarmed them, and will probably bring the affair
back to Florence, with the old Marshal (now absent),
with whom I shall have some warm altercations
about it.'

Next appears on the scene the William Hamilton
who subsequently became so familiar to us in history
as *Sir* William, the husband of Nelson's Emma.
'Your friend, Mr. Hamilton, and his wife, were cast
into Leghorn some days ago by a storm, and very
kindly came to make me a visit whilst the wind
changed. The poor, good, sickly lady was seized with
a fit of the asthma, as she got out of the coach, at
my door, and could with difficulty get to her appart-

ment, but it was rather a slight fit and did not last so long as usual, so that she could dine at table the next day. Did not your ears tingle ? for we talked of nothing else but of you and your Château at Strawberry. You will easily believe that I wanted to keep them, but his hurry to get to Naples would not permit it ; but we are to be very good neighbours. They sat out (*sic*) the day before yesterday, and hope not to be detained at Leghorn.'

Mann now sent some of his letters to Walpole, by Earl Cowper's courier. The courier's master was one of the most eccentric of the English residents in Florence. Sent, when young, by his father on the Grand Tour, he visited the Tuscan capital and never again left it. He fell in love with a Florentine lady, and kept household with her. In this year, 1764, his dying father entreated him to return to England, but the dutiful son paid no attention to the entreaty. When the passion for the Florentine lady died out, the used-up lover married a Miss Gore. Their children were, in due time, sent to England to be educated, but the Earl and Countess lived and died in Florence.

One English visitor considerably embarrassed Sir Horace Mann. Garrick, this year, devoted part of his professional holiday to travelling and sojourning in Italy. 'I shall be expecting Mr. Garrick and his wife,' Mann writes, 'but shall be much embarrassed to know what to do with them in regard to the Italians. Senesino, after having been courted for twenty years by the first nobility in England, was not permitted to sit down in the presence of a Siena Countess.'

Subsequently Mann says:—'I expect Mr. Garrick daily, who with Lord Palmerston and others were to leave Genoa last week, to come hither. I won't say a word to him of Powel'—(This was the young actor, ex-clerk in the city banking house, who had been brought forward by Garrick, after receiving good instruction from the Great Master of his Art, and when fairly successful was absurdly supposed to be a source of jealousy to Garrick himself)—'I won't say a word to him of Powel, but he will probably repent of having defeated his own scheme for fresh applause on his return to England, by having given occasion to that young actor to supplant him. I shall be as civil to him as possible, and am persuaded that all the English will show him attention. I will get another box for Mrs. Garrick in the Theater. A *Dama* goes always into mine, to whom I am Cicisbeo only in the evening, for that and a coach home; and Mrs. Garrick, who will be called *The Violetta*, must too well remember the customs of her own country, however Lady Burlington and others may have spoilt her, to expect that these stately Dames will associate with her.'

Of Garrick's visit there is no further mention, the letters referring to it having apparently been lost; but Davies tells in Garrick's Life how he was honourably entertained in Parma, and the actor's correspondence supplies what is otherwise wanting.

Walpole now announced to Mann the approach of a more illustrious visitor than any that had gone to Italy, of late, from England—Edward, Duke of York, brother of George the Third. Walpole, 'knowing the

young Duke's gallantry,' foretold that he would be a
great favourite with the Florentine ladies. Mann, at
once, placed his house at the Duke's disposal, and
proceeded to set it in order. 'I flatter myself,' he says,
'that I can make my house convenient for him, and
for those that are immediately necessary about his
person, though upon examination into the detail of
linen and of everything that falls under the inspection
of woemen, I find that much is to be done. . . . My
only concern is how to do things properly, not the
expense . . . I wish he may not defer the visit till
everybody is in the country, and the approach of
Christmas, when no publick nor even private amusements are permitted. Nothing had been provided in
the theatrical way for this Autumn, but the Marshal
sent for some of the leading people, yesterday, and
told them that it was a shame that a *Corpo di No-
bilità* like this should not on such an occasion make
an Opera in the Great Theater. The hopes of this
first pleasant effect of the Duke's arrival please the
female Nobiltà much.'

Marshal Botta's notion of the etiquette to be observed somewhat startled Mann :—' He says, I ought
to quit my house, leaving, however, my servants to
serve the Duke, and never appear there myself but to
pay my visit as other people. I have wrote to Captain
Hervey, to know if this can be esteemed an act of
respect, in which case I will instantly do it. So soon
as the Duke arrives at Leghorn, His R. Highness will
receive great attentions wherever he passes, and in
spite even of the Incognito, under which he travels.
Even Rome, in defiance of their own King, and of his

namesake, *their* Duke of York, is disposed to show our
Prince all the honours due to his rank.    Cardinal
Albani had orders from the Pope to tell me so, and
the Nuncio here has had instructions to wait on him
to repeat the same, and to invite him to go there,
promising him all safety, honour, and amusements.
The latter, I should think, would be his chief inducement.    I wish we may succeed in amusing him here ;
but he comes at a bad season, when most of our Dames
are at their Villas.    However, the Marshal has at last
consented to a Burletta, provided it begins next Tuesday, the Emperor's day, to exclude all idea of its being
made for the Duke of York, thinking it an entertainment unworthy of him. . . . Niccolini has declared
his intention of making a ball for him.    The Republick
of Lucca has ordered its ministers to make one at their
expense, which I am persuaded will outdo us all.'

On the 12th of November, Mann narrates how the
Duke was making his progress to Lisbon, Gibraltar,
Port Mahon, and Genoa, and adds:—'We are now
forced to hope that he will defer his arrival in Florence till the melancholy Advent is over, during which
it would be impossible to amuse him.    The Burletta,
which was made on purpose, draws near to an end,
and the Ladies, tired of waiting for His R. Highness,
are going into the Country ; judge of my additional
distress, if he should come before they return and the
theaters are open again.    Should this be so, he will
reflect that all Italy is in the same case during this
season, and I hope will not have the worse opinion of
Florence for it.    I am not sure that he will go to
Rome.    No plan, I am told, was fixed before he set

out, either with regard to the places or the manner of
his visiting them.   I opened my house (which is very
clean, to receive him) some days ago, by an Assembly
for Lady Spencer, who said it was like a Northumberland Rout.   I must do many of these things for the
Woronzow family, if they come before the Duke,
having had the King's orders to show him every mark
of respect, and to contribute by all that may be in my
power, to their amusement here.   The commission
will be expensive, but one only considers the honour
on such occasions.'

Mann looked upon his entertainment of the Russian Chancellor and his wife as rehearsals of the ceremony which he was to observe towards the Duke of
York.   It was a strange rehearsal; for he says :—' I
have regaled the Count and Countess Woronzow with
a large quantity of English beer, more acceptable to the
Countess (who by the artificial ruddiness on her face,
and her Star and Garter, which she wears like a man,
you would take for the General of an Army) than all
the other wines I offered them, or than Nectar.   I
have given them a large provision of Tea, and, last
Tuesday, had a numerous *Rout* for them ; and, to-
morrow, am to give them another; the Ladies, I mean,
for the Great Chancellor is out of order, and probably
will not come.'

The Russians had left, travelled, and returned,
long before the Duke of York made his much-desired
appearance.   Mann continued his expensive dress rehearsals, ' practising,' as he calls it, the part of host
which he was to play to a more august guest.   As late
as February 18th, 1764, the Duke was slowly wending

his way to Florence. Meanwhile, Mann thus treated his Russians. 'I gave them a Ball on Saturday, but the crowd was so great that it was quite unpleasant and inconvenient to the Dancers. The number of Ladies can at any time be limited by invitation, but not easily by me, who cannot well exclude any. They were about 80, but as all men of their rank have a right to come without invitation, they were at least three times that number. In the midst of these constant dissipations, the Russian Chancellor gives evident signs of the agitation of his mind; and, I am persuaded, would not be surprized, and probably not sorry, to hear of a revolution in his country; and, as his situation there would necessarily expose him to a dangerous share in it, the most prudent method is to pass some time at a distance, during which, as the Italians say, *starà a vedere.* . . . By what I have gathered from his people, my friend, Lord Buckingham, has not had the good fortune to succeed at St. Petersburg. They quote strange instances of his inexperience and want of prudence, which make me sorry that he went there. I am told that complaints were sent home of his behaviour.'

But Mann, as he affirms, can think of nothing but the coming of the Duke of York. Early in October, 1763, every one in Florence, interested in the matter, was ready for him. English residents renewed their leases, and crowds of new-comers poured in—'Lord Fordwich, who now stays to pay his court to the Duke of York, will do all he can to entertain his *half-brother.*' In November, his Royal Highness was 'diverting himself at Genoa, exceedingly. . . . He has graciously accepted of my invitation, but upon condition that I do not leave the house. The Marshal prides himself now that his advice was the means of procuring me so obliging a command.' The Florentines, weary of waiting, began to speculate in January, 1764, as to the reasons which led the young Prince to see the world. 'I have seen a letter from a Personage, whose rank gives credit to his absurdities, which says he has very good grounds for believing that the principal motive of the Duke of York's journey into Italy is to get himself out of harm's way; and a great Politician here, who is an Oracle for English affairs, has pronounced, *che questo povero figliuolo s' era lasciato sedurre dalla minorita; m' intende?* The audience did not understand, the speaker could not explain himself, and everybody was satisfied that some other object than pleasure was the motive of the journey.' Gallantry detained the amorous Prince on his road. 'H. R. H. is still at Genoa (January 24th), where Madame Durazzo amuses him, and he has declared his intention of staying there till the Squadron returns from Malta.'

In February, Mann hears that the erratic Prince is enjoying the Carnival at Turin, and is to enjoy the close of it at Milan. What route he was to pursue was not known, except that he was to be in Rome for the Holy Week, 'after which he is to come here till "the Ascension" at Venice.' The letters in which Mann described the Prince's sojourn in Florence are missing, but he gives some curious details of H. R. H.'s progress afterwards. On April 10th, the Minister writes:—'He set out from Florence on Tuesday.

Colonel St. John and I had the honour to go in his coach. Sir William Boothby and others in that which followed. Our first stop was at a place to which I had sent my servants the day before, to prepare a little dinner. This was soon despatched, and we proceeded towards Leghorn, at two miles distance from which the Consul and the Factory were waiting to pay their first respects. The Governor, Bourbon del Monte, with a train of officers, was waiting a mile from thence. Here I got out, to embrace him as an old friend, and to yield him my place by the side of the Duke, in the coach. A large detachment of Dragoons escorted H. R. H. into the town, and three rounds of 24 cannon saluted him. A Captain's Guard was placed at the door of the Consul's house, where the Duke lodged, which however he dismissed immediately. So soon as the Factory could be assembled, they were presented, and had the honour to kiss his hand. Then, the Governor with his officers were presented distinctly; the Consuls of the different Nations, and anybody who had any right to come there. This ceremony lasted till the evening, when more company of both sexes made a numerous Assembly for Cards.'

'The next morning, early, the Duke visited the Mole and the fortifications, dined at the Consul's, and passed the evening at the Governor's. The next day, the Governor gave H. R. H. a very fine entertainment in the Park near Pisa, twelve miles from Leghorn. It was to have been a hunt of Deer and Wild Boars, but that part of it did not succeed. The Dinner, however, and everything else succeeded *over* Expectation. We

returned in the evening to Leghorn, where there was
a very handsome Ball at Mr. Dick's.  The next day,
after dinner, the Duke went to Pisa, where he was
received with all the military honours, as at Leghorn.
He passed the evening at the Casino.  The next day,
after dinner, we set out for Lucca; H. R. H. having,
before he left Florence, accepted of an invitation to
pass through that civil Republick, and though he had
prescribed many conditions, nevertheless at a mile
distant from the town, a deputation of six of their
Nobili in abito di Ceremonia waited to compliment
him, to which he ordered me to make an answer.  He
then advanced towards the Town, from the walls of
which a great many cannon were fired.  The Duke
had refused a house, so went to an Inn, where however, the Republick, without taking any notice of it,
had made some preparations soon after his arrival.'

'The same Deputation came with a vast present of
Oyl, wines, hams, wax candles, coffee, etc., etc., conducted by a Maitre d'Hotel of the Republick, and
brought by fifty Servants in their Livery; for which,
besides thanks, a generous return was made to the
Servants.  On all these occasions I acted as Master
of the Ceremonies (excepting as to Presentations) on
account of the Language.  They then invited H. R. H.
to an amusement which they had prepared for him at
the House which they had hoped he would lodge at—
the same where they entertained a King of Denmark
at the beginning of this century; a very spacious and
fine palace most splendidly furnished and illuminated.
The musick struck up on the Duke's entrance into
the Hall, where all the Ladies were assembled, and,

H. R. H. danced with the Mistress of the House, and
in the course of the evening, with those who were
offered to him.   At Eleven, he was desired to pass
into another appartment, where there was a concert of
vocal and instrumental musick, for which they had
sent for people from Genoa.   This lasted till past
twelve, when another invitation carried him back to
the Hall, where a most sumptuous Supper was spread.
They told me there were sixty covers, and though the
crowd was very great behind those who were seated,
everybody was served with great order as well as
profusion and delicacy.   The Duke returned home at
about three ; in the same manner as he came.'

 ' The next morning the Deputation came to attend
him to his coach, and to receive the most gracious
expressions of thanks for their civilities. The Republick
which, you know, is all civility, would not omit
on this occasion extending it even to one of His
Majesty's Ministers, though so totally eclypsed by
H. R. H.'s presence.   They sent two senators apart to
make me a compliment !   We proceeded to Pistoja,
but without going into the Town, as the post-house is
without the walls, and there is nothing to be seen
within.   The Governor was there to compliment the
Duke while they were changing horses ; and the
cannon saluted them. From thence we went to Poggio
and Cajano, a house of the Emperor's, where my
servants from Florence met us with a dinner, after
which we reached Florence late, and found a numerous Assembly for the rest of the evening.   This
was Sunday.   Yesterday, the Duke dined with Ladies
at home ; and passed the evening to hear Manzuoli,

at Lord Fordwich's. To-day other Ladies dine with him.'

'H. R. H. waited only the arrival of letters from Rome to determine his departure thither, for the Holy Week, and though the accounts are very bad indeed for want of corn, and that,—to discourage Pilgrims and other strangers going there,—most of the Ceremonies of the Holy Week will be omitted, nevertheless, as things must grow still worse in a month or two, the Duke has fixed the day after to-morrow, to set out, and has permitted me to attend him as far as Siena. I send people to prepare a dinner on the road, and shall return the next day to Florence in expectation of seeing Him back again very soon, as it cannot be proper for him either to stay there long, or to go on to Naples, in such dreadful scenes of misery as we hear of, for want of bread. His great condescention and affability make me flatter myself that he will prefer this place to any other, till the Ascension of Venice. He is most gracious and good himself, and has good people about him,—Sir Wm. Boothly and Col. St. John; nothing can be more obliging than the behaviour of them all.'

Half Italy was raging, in famine, or in fear of it, for lack of corn. Sixteen thousand troops kept the starved Neapolitans quiet. Spain was as badly off as Naples, and her ships intercepted the corn-laden vessels from England for Italy. Rome murmured and menaced, but the holiday Prince made the hungry there forget their appetite for a time.

'He set out on Thursday morning. My people went the evening before to a proper place on the road to prepare a dinner for him. He arrived at Siena early and found the Ladies in their Coaches, and the troops drawn up to salute him. The Inn where he lodged was, by Marshal Botta's order, cleaned up, and a little furnished from the Wardrobe there. The Commissary and crowds of their Nobility came to pay their Respects, and attended him to the Duomo and the few other places worth seeing. From thence He returned to dress for the Assembly which, by the Marshal's order, was prepared for his amusement, and which consisted of Cards, a Ball, and a Supper at Madame Sansidoni's, a very polite lady, who has not given over her pretentions to please ; but, unluckily, she has two beautiful neices (the daughters of the Marchese Ghigi) who employed the Duke's whole attention.'

' On my kissing H. R. H.'s hand the next morning, and thanking him for the great honour he had done me, He said the most obliging things, and promised to return to Florence soon. He will arrive at Rome tomorrow, and unless he should alter his mind with regard to his stay there, which he said should not be above a fortnight, and, unless he should accept of the solemn invitation which the Constable Colonna was to make him, by order of the King of Naples, to go there, it is highly probable that He may stay here till it is time to go to Naples, for the Ascension, which falls on the 31st. We shall then have a theater open and many more amusements than the Lent would admit of. The weather too will be more proper for excursions to the Emperor's Villa, of which I gave him a specimen, by carrying him to Castello and your favourite Petraja, where Princess Craon passed the summer.    We are to have rejoicings too for the King of the Romans' (the election or nomination of the Emperor's eldest son, Joseph, to that dignity), 'and they will endeavour to continue them so that the Duke may partake of them and put them, if He please, to his own account.    The Duke left one of his Pages here so ill, that the physicians despaired of his life ; but I have now good hopes of his recovery.'

*April* 24*th.*—' The Duke arrived in Rome the Sunday after he left Siena, without any *éclat,* just as he had prescribed.    Instead of going out to meet him with all the Cortége of Casa Corsini and Casa Borghese, the Grand Prior and Don Paulo presented themselves to him at his lodgings with the most respectful offers of being his Ciceroni,—in return for the great civilities which they themselves had received in England. By this easy and genteel method, the Pope conveys his attentions to the Duke.    The present of ceremony was sent to him, in their name, the day of his arrival.    It consisted of wine of different sorts, Chocolate, Coffee, *Cedrati,* etc., etc., and a live calf dressed out with flowers, Peacocks, and Guinea hens.    The latter he ordered to be sent to England, and the former to Lady Spencer, with whom he had supped that evening.'

' Some days after, he took the opportunity of the Pope's being at the Vatican, to see his Palace at Monte Cavallo, and the Gardens . . . where a magnificent refreshment was prepared.    Two great basons of Cedrati and a prodigious Sturgeon were sent to him, in the name of the Pope's Major Domo as the

fruit of the Garden and of the Tyber. Greater
presents, they say, are designed for him ;—a Picture in
Mosaick, when he goes to see them work in it, another
in Tapestry, and a collection of all the Prints of everything valuable at Rome, finely bound, when he goes to
the Capitol. The day after the Duke's arrival, the
Constable Colonna in full dress, went to invite him
in the King of Naples' name, to go there, but he
declined accepting of the invitation, on account of the
unhappy situation which the whole Kingdom is in for
want of corn. The same motive will oblige him to
escape from Rome soon, as the want there is still
greater, though the Government has hitherto endeavoured to conceal it, but is now apprehensive of the
consequences, and has disarmed all the lower classes of
people, but the Trasteverini have stones, with which
they have frequently threatened to demolish the
Pope's Nephews, and it is feared that some strange
disorder will happen.'

'Great preparations are making by the Corsini and
the Borghesi to give the Duke great Balls, with the
permission of the Pope, who has forbid dancing the
whole year round. Cardinal Albani is to give him a
Concert of Musick at his famous Villa near the town,
which surpasses every other fabrick and collection
there. But in the midst of all these attentions, what
will you say to the Vicomte Aubeterre, the French
Ambassador, who has refused to make the Duke a
visit, because he had not announced his arrival to the
Ambassadors ! I will lay any wager that this will be
a precedent of unpoliteness to all French Ambassadors
wherever the Duke goes for the future, as the French

think they gain a great point by starting absurd pretensions.'

'. . . Some attempts were made to bring the Pope and Duke together ; but when it was found they could make nothing of H. R. H., or fix any precedent to the advantage of the Court of Rome, by any concession on his part, they declined it, well seeing that any concession on their own part would fix a precedent to their disadvantage ; so, the Dignity of each has not suffered the least diminution.    It cost the Pope some tears, however, for you must know that he has so tender a heart, that all the overflowings of it, either of joy or grief, nay, the least embarrassment, is expressed by them.    However, every personal attention was shown to the Duke.'

' *But,* who do you think prostrated himself to our Protestant Prince ?    You would never guess that the General of the Jesuits waited upon him publickly and desired his mediation with the King, his Brother, for his protection in favour of the Jesuits, now his subjects, in America, and all others wherever dispersed or concealed !    The Duke's answer was very proper, as His whole Behaviour has been.    He and Cardinal Albani were very fond of each other.    His Eminence waved all Etiquette with him, feasted him, and made him fine presents ; nay ! gave him a Ball, though all dancing is forbid by the Pope.'

The Chevalier de St. George, or ' the old Pretender,' ill as he was at this time, was not so prostrated but that he felt keenly the honours paid to the son of the ' Elector of Hanover.'    ' In effect,' says Mann, ' he is dead, for he is very seldom in his senses.

Nobody, except his Physicians and a few servants, goes to him; his Son, never! When the latter was in Florence' (on his way to the Baths at Pisa, to which the Cardinal of York resorted, to relieve his distressing scorbutic malady), 'he complained to Niccolini of the manner in which the Duke of York was received at Rome, but said that his only concern had been to hide it from his father, who would have been much hurt; and that he had succeeded. I was forced to make a little complaint of the military people here, for showing certain honours to the Cardinal that could only concern the Duke of York, and they were reprimanded; though I never thought it of consequence enough to mention to my superiors at home.'

Roman fever kept some of the gentlemen of the Duke's suite in Rome, where they struggled between life and death, till health was, at least, temporarily restored. The Duke of York was received with hearty though ceremonious welcome in every part of Italy visited by him. Sir Horace Mann was as liberal as any of the native potentates, in entertaining the English prince in Florence. Walpole gently rebuked him for his reckless outlay, but Mann protested that he would not regret the cost, though it left him as bankrupt as the Spanish Ambassador, and his body unburied till the bankruptcy was superseded. There is something noble and (if the word be permitted) thoroughly English, in his own remarks on the subject to Walpole:—'I do not say that on such an extraordinary occasion as the present, a larger income would not have been agreeable, but there are certain situa-

tions in which it is impossible not to exceed the
common bounds. The world expects a great deal on
such occasions, and one's own vanity prompts one to
satisfy it. The Duke's affability is so enchanting that
it commands everything in return, and it will never
permit me to reflect on anything but the great honour
he has done me, and of my being so happy to be in a
situation to receive it.'

It is due to the Pope to say that under the circumstances he acted with a certain sort of decency. If it
was impossible for the Prince and the Pontiff to meet
personally, Clement XIII. extended to the former a
vicarious hospitality, and used his influence to encourage other States to give the Duke a right royal
welcome. Bologna especially distinguished itself by
the magnificence of its reception. Venice outdid
Bologna. Two thousand workmen laboured in the
Arsenal to prepare a regatta for the illustrious traveller,
and the Government presented as its tribute a gift of
wax and crystal. The details of the royal progress,
in other respects, are only repetitions of the same
incidents, and they would weary the most courteous
of readers. Suffice it to say that, when the Duke
took final leave of the English Minister, his grateful,
graceful, and gracious acknowledgments quite over-
came Sir Horace. The Minister's eyes were full of
tears, and his purse was empty of zecchins. His
indignation was subsequently raised at hearing that
France had refused to grant the Duke passports to
cross that kingdom, on his way home ; and H. R. H.
had to return by sea. He had certain tender memories
of his progress abroad. There was a Madame Durazzo

to whom he wrote an assurance that he would revisit
her, at the head of a fleet.    Mann rather anxiously
asked Walpole if such an exhibition of love and
triumph was likely to come off.    Walpole thought
the Duke was as 'likely to carry a fleet on a visit to
Diana, and cast anchor off one of the horns of the
moon !'

## CHAPTER VI.

### 1765.

AMONG the Englishmen of note who visited Florence
this year, John Wilkes was perhaps the most remarkable. 'He is going to Naples,' says Mann, February
9th, ' to write the History of the present times *up*
to the Revolution. By the death of his Bully-back
Churchill, he will probably be deprived of the materials
for the first part ; and, I should think, will not be able
to instruct further up. I speak of him in a publick
light, for I have no reason to complain of him in a
private one. On his arrival, he desired Lord Beauchamp, your amiable cousin, to deliver me a civil
message in his name, which was returned, and I
advised Count Lorenzi,' (the French Ambassador)
' who came to consult me whether he should attend to
the strong letters of recommendation, which Wilkes
brought to him from Paris, to show Wilkes all the
attention he thought proper ; and I answered for
Wilkes's rank, to remove the Count's scruples about
presenting him to the Nobles. Marshal Botta criti-
cizes my Brother of France much, on this occasion,
though wrongfully, and he has desired me to return

the compliment when Deon ' (the Chevalier D'Eon)
' comes here.'

' Lord Beauchamp, I *must* say, is the most amiable
youth I have seen among all our young Noblemen.
His figure, as the French say, " est noble comme le
Roy," it announces all that affability, sense, and goodness, which is hereditary in his family, and which he,
most early, has improved by the politest education.
In short, he is most amiable, and I really do not
exaggerate, when I tell you that whenever he appears
in publick, he attracts the attention and admiration
of everybody—though he is the only one who does
not perceive it.'

There were other young Englishmen in Italy
who attracted as much attention, but less admiration.
On March 22rd, Mann says :—' Pray make my
respects acceptable to Lord and Lady Milton, for
their acceptance of my endeavours to be civil to
their sons. I am sorry for the uneasiness they will
have, when they hear the melancholly Event of a
drunken riot of the younger at Rome, who, with Sir
Thomas Gascogne, exacting such offices from their
Coachman as the Valets de place only are used to
render, and meeting an opposition which Wine could
not bear, a violent skirmish ensued, in which the
young Gentlemen wounded four men, one of whom so
dangerously, that it was thought prudent that they
should immediately retire from Rome, whilst the
Governor, from a motive of the greatest civility and
partiality in their favour, suspended the Justice of his
Office ; and even assisted their escape at midnight ;
affecting twice the next day to make strict per-

quisitions for them. They first came to Siena, but
were afterwards permitted to return to Ronciliogni, to
be nearer Rome, to wait the event, and to regulate
themselves by it. This soon became desperate, so
that it was again necessary that they should hasten
out of the State, whilst their friends made all the
attonement for them that the nature of this affair
could admit of, by giving money to those that had
been hurt, and a small provision to the wife of the
man whose life was despaired of.'

'The Governor of Rome (Piccolomini) has been
indefatigably partial to us on this occasion, by which
he has drawn upon himself the reproach of the
Publick; but he has still promised to persist, and to
obtain an act of oblivion of what has past, that the
Gentlemen may return to Rome, next year, if they
please. The Damers have gone towards Venice. Sir
Thomas Gascogne arrived here yesterday. I think it
will be best not to say anything of the affair to Lord
and Lady Milton, but to let their sons represent it
to them in whatever manner they please. In the
account which I was obliged to send to Lord Halifax'
(Secretary of Foreign Affairs, in the Granville Administration), 'I have avoided all detail, saying only
that the insolence of the behaviour of the Coachman
drew upon them the resentment of the two gentlemen
who, in the heat of their fury, and in their own
defence, unfortunately wounded them.'

'Sir Thomas says that he was not present when
the fatal blow was given by George Damer, but was
gone home for his pistols, which he discharged among
the people; not perceiving that they were without

balls, otherwise the mischief must have been very
great. The scene happened in a country, where by
the frequency of such accidents it has made less
impression. It was lucky too that the offended came
of a rank to be quieted by money, but above all, it
was lucky for our countrymen that the Governor so
zealously assisted them. I this instant receive advice
that the poor man died last Sunday morning.'

On May 14th, Mann refers to Wilkes's progress
in Italy :—' Wilkes is at Naples, making an addition
(*sic*) of his friend Churchill's works. He stayed a
very few days in Rome, where he was not courted
(as our Gazetteers have said), neither is he at Naples,
where Tanucci, for whom he left a letter of recommendation, takes no notice of him, for political
reasons. His chief intimacy is with Sir William
Stanhope.'

*June* 15*th.*— ' As people are inclined to think that
everything relating to Wilkes must be produced by
some extraordinary cause, the Italians have, first,
greatly exaggerated the circumstances of his Mistress's
separation from him, by asserting that she has robbed
him ; and then they have supposed that his enemies
have made use of her to get at his papers. . . . I
believe there is no more in the affair than that they
could not agree, or that he was tired of the expence ;
and so they separated.'

Of one of the Italian potentates, Mann speaks in
terms of praise rarely, if ever, awarded to others of
the same rank and little power. ' You will have
pitied,' he writes, July 27th, ' the Duke of Parma, to
be carried off in the midst of much (domestick) joy

They could not conceal it from his daughter, because he used to write to her from Alexandria twice a day. All amusements which the Genoese had prepared on this occasion, and which were immense, were immediately suspended, excepting the Theater, to the great disappointment of crowds of strangers who were assembled there. The loss of this Prince will make no alteration in the political world, but in private, it will be greatly regretted, as he did as much good as his little income would permit ; and his little court was a compendium of all Civility, Politeness, and Ease. He was unhappy only in having the means of exerting it so limited, and in reflecting on the injustice which he was forced to submit to in being deprived of a kingdom.'

The Pope does not stand forth so creditably in this record as ' benevolent Parma.' On August 17th, Mann says :—' There has been, or I should say *is*, at present, a terrible fracas at Rome on a subject that hurts the Infallibility of the Santa Sedia more than anything that has happened a great while. The Holy Vicar sheds floods of tears and finds no consolation but in a good dish of Sturgeon. Some weeks ago, one Abbé Fiore was condemned to death by the unanimous votes of the Sacred Colledge, for falsifying the Pope's Briefs,—though the sentence has been changed to imprisonment for life. Soon after, a little narrative came out which has alarmed and offended the Court of Rome extremely, as well it might. This soon produced an Edict by the Governor of Rome, condemning it as a false scandalous libel to be burnt by the Hangman (which was performed on the 9th of this month),

and with orders, under the severest punishment in
this and the next world, to everybody to carry in the
copies of this scandalous paper. This, as usual, has
multiplied the copies of it both in print and writing,
and even the most orthodox are at a loss how to
reconcile the confession and punishment of the Abbé
Fiore with this Edict, and pity the Infallibility of His
Holiness, which is so easily imposed on.'

The 'Personality' of the Pontiff was as much to
be pitied in August.   On the 24th, says Mann:—' We
have just received advice of the danger of losing
the other head of the Catholick world.'      (Francis I.,
Emperor of Germany or of the Holy Roman Empire,
died at the above date.) 'The Pope has eaten so much
Sturgeon and enjoyed so plentifully those advantages
of the Thiara (*sic*) that he has brought upon him the
natural effects of repletion.   On Monday, he was struck
with a fit too, which deprived him of his senses for
some time, but three copious bleedings so far recovered
him, that they could administer all the Sacraments to
him ; and, as if there could have been any doubt of his
Orthodoxy, he made a publick profession of his Faith.
At the departure of the letters, he had a strong fever
which in his circumstance was rather thought favourable, but his shortness of breath made him suppose
that he would not last long.   The Jesuits and his
Nephews alone will lament him.   The Church itself
will exult on this Event as the only possible means
of her preserving France and Portugal.   It is thought
by many, that these have already taken the resolution
to make their Patriarch and Bishops do their business
for them, for the future, without applying to any
other Holyness.'

His Holiness, however, had other troubles. On the 12th of May, Walpole, writing to the British Minister at Florence, said:—'We believe, past all doubt, that the Pretender's eldest son is turned Protestant; in earnest so; and in truth I think he could have no other reason now. What is more wonderful and more believed is, that he came over and abjured in St. Martin's Church, in London. There he risked so much. What Clergyman could expect it was he? I asked if Johnson, Bishop of Worcester' (the ex-Jacobite, translated from Gloucester, A.D. 1759), 'had given him absolution. He declares he will never marry, and his reason does him honour;—that he may not leave England embroiled. What a strange conclusion in the House of Stuart, to end in a Protestant and a Cardinal! I pity the old phantom, if they have told him of his son's apostacy.'

To this information as to a circumstance which some have dated as happening in 1753, Mann replies, Sept. 7th:—'I cannot think you are in earnest about the Young Pretender. Nobody suspects it at Rome; but, at all events, his father is incapable of understanding it, if they should tell it to him; and his Brother would assist at a Congregation to damn him to all Eternity.' By November 14th, however, Mann had more to say, not so much, indeed, on this matter as on what followed it. 'I have the greatest piece of news. It is so extraordinary and destroys so compleatly a late supposed conversion in St. Martin's Church that, unless I quote the respectable names of two Cardinals, I should not expect you would believe it. Cardinal Alexander Albani has informed me that,

by Commission of the Pretender's eldest son, his
nephew, Cardinal John Francis Albani, has communicated to the Pope, the disposition which that Person
is in to return to Rome, upon condition that he should
be treated with the same distinction as before his
Exploits ; and that on his father's deccase (which may
be daily expected) he may be acknowledged under his
new titles, and enjoy the Pension which the Camera
Apostolica has always given to his father (which
consists of twelve thousand crowns a year, and a
house in town and country), though that pension, in
the time of the late Pope, Lambertini, was settled on
Cardinal Stuart.'

The Pope's answer is very sensible :—' That he
will receive him with pleasure ; that he shall be
treated with distinction ; and that he may depend
on the continuance of the pension which his father
enjoys.   But that, as to any marks of Royalty, he
neither can nor will take upon himself to grant anything ; resolving to regulate himself on that point by
the Example of *some other Sovereigns.*   Whether this
answer will satisfy him or not, time only can show ;
but as it is highly probable it will engage him to use
his utmost endeavours to induce the Courts of France
and Spain, to connive as usual at their Ministers at
Rome giving him the same titles as they have, publickly, always given there to his father, I have wrote
by this post to the Duke of Richmond (who, I judge
by the Gazette, may by this time be at Paris), and
to Lord Rochford, that they may be attentive to what
may be proposed on this subject, and be prepared for
any Instructions that may be sent from England

about it, if the King should, as I imagine he will,
think it worthy his attention.    The opportunity
seems very favourable totally to suppress for the
future, even at Rome, the titles that that Wanderer
may attempt to assume on his father's death.    That
Court, I know, think it their interest to oblige
England, in return for the lenity with which the
Catholicks are treated in all the King's Dominions.
Besides *that*, they are tired of the Phantom which
is both troublesome and expensive ; and they would
be glad of an opportunity to get rid of it.'

   *December* 14*th*.—' Cardinal York, they say, very
willingly relinquishes his pretentions to the twelve
thousand crowns that were settled on him after his
father's death.    The latter knows nothing of all this.
The faculties of his mind being too weak to compre-
hend anything.    He was thought to be dead a few
days ago ; but cannot live many days longer.'

   Meanwhile, there was a matter in hand which
concerned the Florentines more than the Stuarts, the
Pope, or the English eccentrics in the city, put together.    The English Minister too had an absorbing
interest in the matter.    The Archduke Leopold and
his intended wife, the Infanta of Spain, by taking up
their residence in Florence would found a gayer Court
and establish a more important form of government,
than that of the Regency which existed, with Marshal
Botta at the head of it.    With such a Court and Administration, there would be increase of expense, and
Mann's salary did not suffice to maintain the hospitality which both English and Italians expected
from him ; and for which—especially for his profuse

hospitality to the Duke of York and his suite—he could never obtain such poor acknowledgment as might have been made by awarding him the red ribband of the Bath. Accordingly, Sir Horace wrote to Lord Halifax, laying before him at length the above circumstances; and adding:—'By the nature of my situation here, I have every year been obliged to exceed the narrow bounds of the appointments annexed to my present character.' He modestly alludes to the 'zealous assiduity and attention to duty' which he had practised during five and twenty years that he had represented England in Tuscany. Those were his only pretensions; 'but,' he says, 'if from the pure effect of His Majesty's goodness, that circumstance alone could have sufficient weight to stand in lieu of all personal merit, it might excuse my presumption in flattering myself that, if your Lordship would condescend to honour me with your protection on this occasion, by making a favourable representation to the King of my situation, His Majesty might be graciously pleased, either to grant me an encrease of character, equal to that of His Ministers at the two other Courts of Italy, or such an addition to my present appointments as may enable me to support the great expense which the arrival of a Court must necessarily occasion.'

The answer of the Earl of Halifax, written at St. James's, June 25th, is marked 'Private,' but there will not be much indiscretion now in copying this part of it. 'His Majesty is graciously pleased to allow you the sum of £400, on that occasion' (the marriage of the Archduke and the Infanta) 'when it shall take place. You will therefore, in the proper time, transmit a separate Bill for that sum under the Article of Extra Extraordinaries, by His Majesty's special command, specifying likewise in such Bill the purpose for which that Sum was granted.'

The sum was small enough for so great an occasion, but Mann was content therewith, and he addressed himself to criticize Marshal Botta's buildings-up and pullings-down, by which he was defacing the exterior of the Palazzo Pitti. One addition to it, erected for the accommodation of the Archduchess's women, he rather rudely styles ' the *Harem !'* But the greatest measure of his contempt was for Botta's new arrangements in the interior. ' Everything,' he says, ' is calculated for the meridian of Germany, nay of Muscovy. Stoves and chimneys in every room. For the furniture, the *gout* is not less Gothick. All the freshest gilt frames are to be put together. The famous picture of Luther and Calvin, by Pordinoni, has been discarded from among the Madonnas.' Then, respecting what he had previously said of the Empress's nasty niceness, he adds : ' not only will she not permit a naked leg or arm to defile the walls of her appartment, but she never will set her foot into any house, where the Emperor keeps his *Virtu,* though there is nothing there that is *indecent.'*

The preparations went on through the summer. ' Nothing,' writes Mann, in August, ' is attended to here, but the preparations for the arrival of our new Court, which is expected the 10th of next month. I have not yet been able to go to the Marshal to ask his Instructions as to how, when, and where I may pay my first homage, nor have I learnt to make a curtsey as yet, which is necessary on approaching an Arch-Duke; this, I am afraid, will be a difficult task for stiff or weak knees.'

Suddenly there came a change, and instead of an Archduke, presiding at Florence for the Emperor his father, who was Grand Duke of Tuscany, Florence was destined to receive an independent ducal sovereign. Francis (as before said) died in August,—with this consequence, as regarded Tuscany. ' His successor' (his son, Joseph II.) ' has ordered the Regency to cause the Arch-Duke Leopold to be proclaimed Great Duke of Tuscany ; who, in that quality, has confirmed all the ministers here in their employments, till further orders. The Courier who brought the news of this great event, arrived here a few hours ago.

'. . . The Emperor's death occasioned some consternation for a few hours, not from any affection in the people for their Sovereign, but from a doubt whether the Prince they expect was to be acknowledged Great Duke. The doubt arose from a known repugnance in Leopold's older brother, Joseph, to give up the only State he would possess *en propre* in the case which has now happened, and though there were all the reasons to suppose that everything of that kind had been settled, yet not only no publick act had appeared, but Marshal Botta absolutely forbid the title of Great Prince or Hereditary Prince, to be inserted in any paper or notification that has been published on this occasion, and, what was still more extraordinary, caused that title to be erased from the collars of some dogs which the Arch-Duchess brought with her from Spain and had sent hither from Genoa!'

'Spain and Naples were outrageous at the refusal
here of that title, and as soon as the time would admit
caused the strongest complaints to be made at Innspruck' (where Francis suddenly died, — after the
marriage there celebrated of the Archduke and the
Infanta) 'but there had not been sufficient time for
orders to be sent from thence as to the puerile cavilla-
tion (*sic*) in the Marshal. . . . So soon as the people's
apprehensions had been removed, their joy broke out
and the meanest sort now look upon this Event as
most advantageous to Tuscany.   The poor Marshal is
afflicted extremely, forseeing probably that his reign
will not be long, though he has already been appointed
Plenipotentiary of the new Emperor, and he may still
appear with the four Pages and two High Dukes . . .
with a numerous and rich set of Liveries that he has
prepared to figure with on this occasion.   I attempted
to see him yesterday, but though he had held a
Council and had dispatched many affairs, the dignity
of his Grief did not permit him to receive compliments
of condolence.'

In September :—' We are at the Eve of the Great
Duke's arrival, and nobody knows what he is to do.
People flock to the Marshal for instruction but,—for
the first time he ever made use of the expression,—he
says *mi non so niente!*   He used to say, when
altering the Palazzo Pitti : *mi so tutto!* and when
people persisted to show him the absurdity of any
order, he added, with a strong expletive : *Lo vo
cosi!*   But affliction humbleth the mind, and the
Boys in the street have been taught ridiculous songs
to mortify him.   One says that *mi* is no longer a note

in musick.   Another, that two pair of his *Attelage*
with which he used to go about the town are to
be let.   He is gone to meet his new master, whom he
is to entertain at *Pietra Mala*, the first stage in his
own dominions.   From thence he comes to Pratolino
to sleep.   How long he will stay there, or whether
anybody will be furnished to pay their court there,
*mi non so!*   The only orders he has sent are,—to
discontinue all the preparations in the Duomo, for the
*Te Deum*, which was to have been performed with
great *éclat;* and, not to illuminate the town on his
entry.      But, the Marshal intends to remonstrate
against the first, thinking the Great Duke ought to
perform the Act of Devotion before he goes to his
Palace. . . . . It is said that the Great Dutchess will
decide all these difficulties.'

'Apropos to the Great Dutchess, I must tell you
that Madame Antinori' (who, with the Marchese
Riccardi, was sent to attend their mistress, from
Bolsano), 'describing in her first letter from thence
the great affability and *graziosità* with which they
were received, says, that the Great Dutchess asked
them, *se tutte le Dame di Firenze erano spiritose
quanto lori Signori.*   Madame Antinori's Brother in
law, an Archdeacon, to whom her letter was written,
shows it about as a proof of the condescension and,
at the same time, of the penetration of that Princess
in distinguishing so early the merit of his *cognata,*
in asking her if the Ladies of Florence were as witty
or mettlesome as their Lords.'

*September 14th.* — 'The Florentines seem very
sensible of their good fortune in having a Prince

again to live among them, after thirty years' bondage
under unexperienced Lorrain ministers and óthers so
little fit and desirous to contribute to their welfare.
They have nothing more to wish for at present, than
that this young Prince's health may become more
robust than it is at present, and that he may have
a numerous issue to exclude the danger of Tuscany's
becoming again a Province for a certain number of
years.'

'The Great Duke and Dutchess arrived at Pratolino late on Wednesday night, and came to Florence
yesterday morning.   He wanted to avoid all *éclat*,
and many arts were employed to deceive the people
as to the time of his coming; but it was impossible to
elude their vigilance.   They expected him the evening
before, and waited all night in the streets.   The crowd
was so great that his Court with difficulty moved on;
and when they were in their appartments, they had
the complaisance to comply with the boisterous desire
of the Mob, that they should shew themselves in the
Balcony.'

'It had been settled by the Corps Diplomatique
that we should go to Court to visit the *Grand Chambellan*, only to put ourselves in a way to be admitted
to the G. Duke when he should direct us.   I was more
lucky than my colleagues in being conducted into the
room destined for the Chamberlains.   I was very
politely received by Count Thurm, but was told that
the G. Duke's health requiring some repose, he would
be *en retraite* for some days, and that I should be
informed when I might be admitted to the Prince;
but the reason is they have got no regular mourning

yet, and wait for notice from Vienna on that subject; till when, the G. Duke will only admit his own servants. Everything that he has said or done yet is sensible and good, but no business of consequence has been entered upon. It is said he has given some visible marks of his dislike of some of the Marshal's dispositions in the Palace, and that his personal reception of him does not denote any impression in his favour.'

' The people, amidst their acclamations, mixed some injurious expressions of the Marshal, attributing to him the dearness of bread and every inconvenience they labour under. . . . He possibly may have presumed too much upon the favour he was in with the late Emperor, but those who make his process add a thousand despotic acts and expressions to aggravate matters. The truth is that Botta is no longer in favour, and will ill brook the necessary restraint of that illimitated (*sic*) authority with which he has acted hitherto.'

On September 20th (misdated 1762):—'The Court is still *en retraite* which is to last six weeks compleat, from the death of the Emperor. The G. Duke has given audience to the Heads of the Tribunals and to his own Servants. Strangers are excluded and he does not show himself in public about the town. The G. Dutchess is extremely tired of this rigour. She wished to hear Manzuoli, but was told that any deviation from what had been prescribed from Vienna would ill please them. What hurts her still more is that the Theaters are not to be opened for a whole year, for such is the Etiquette at Vienna. In this

the publick are concerned and will probably remonstrate against it.   The only amusements the G. Duke
and Dutchess allow themselves is dining with a large
company, walking in Boboli, and playing at cards
with their own people.   But the Arch-Dutchess is
of too gay a temper to be satisfied with this.   The
expense of the Court is immoderate.   The table and
other daily expenses, they say, amount to 700 Crowns,
which would be £175 sterling, which is hardly credible;
but there is all the appearance that Luxury will run
very high.   All one Gala provided for this occasion
must lay by for a year.'

   The usual presentations, however, were not deferred.   On October 12th, Mann tells Walpole:—'I
have been admitted with all the English to the
presence of our new Sovereigns—not as a Minister,
for the Marshal, who is omnipotent again, says we
cannot be received as such, without new Credentials;
and those, I replyed, would never come till the G.
Duke announced his accession and arrival here.   The
delay in complying with so common and necessary
a formality proceeded from the G. Duke's delicacy
towards his Brother, upon whom he thought it
depended to announce to foreign Courts the cession
he had made of this part of his inheritance, to him.
However, whether they, here, have received an order
from Vienna, or reflecting (as the Marshal told me)
that the delay might give offence to those Courts, I
have just received private notice that the Letters of
Notification to England, France, and Spain, have been
wrote, and that our's are to be sent by this post. . . .
I have been assured, in confidence, that the G. Duke

waits to see what Character the King may give me by
the new Credentials, with an intention, if any addition
should be made to that which I have hitherto had,
to appoint a Florentine Gentleman to go to England,
instead of a Mon^{sr} Lottinger, a Lorrainer, now Consul
at Genoa, who was nominated, long ago, by the late
Emperor, to succeed Mr. Pucci. . .'

'. . . The Duc de Choiseul has notified to Count
Lorenzi that the Court of France had determined to
send a Frenchman here in his place. This was softened
to the poor Count, with all the flattering assurances
of satisfaction of his abilities and zeal for the King's
service which, nevertheless, the Duc says, requires
that a French subject should attend to, for the future.
He then gave the Count hopes of a Pension, with
which Count Lorenzi will content himself, if it be a
considerable one. . . .'

Count Lorenzi's successor, according to Mann,—who
was dying to be raised from the office of Minister to
the dignity of Envoy, with proportionate increase of
pay,—would probably have a higher rank than the
Count had, 'and *that* could never get him admittance
into the Chambellan's Antechamber at Court; so that
hitherto both he and Viviani (Naples) have been
excluded from it.' Mann adds: 'Thursday next is
fixed for the Ladies, *en habit de Cour*, to kiss the
Great Duchess's hand. Both she and the Duke were
so tired of the constraint which the rigorous Etiquette
of Vienna imposed upon them on this occasion, that
they could hold out no longer. It was therefore
thought sufficient that the late Emperor's name-day'
(St. Francis' day, Oct. 4th) 'should in some measure

put an end to it, instead of the ceremony of the obsequies, which was fixed as a proper Epoque, but that cannot be ready for some time yet.'

'In the meantime,' says Mann, Oct. 11th, 'I have been received at Court with the most flattering marks of distinction. I had les Entrées the first day, though the others were not admitted. The Great Officers and those about the Court take all opportunities of the Assemblies to come to my house, and the most gracious expressions of their Superiors are reported to me ; and, last night, having accompanied Captain Murray, the Duke of Athol's brother, to the Grand Chambellan's Appartment, in order to obtain his admittance to-day to the G. Duke and Dutchess—the G. Duke came on a sudden into the room and stayed nearly an hour, talking in the most affable and indeed the most sensible manner. It was very plain that it was concerted on their part. There was nobody but the Grand Chamberlain and his Brother in the room. Two days before, I had procured admission for General Walmoden, who dined at Court the same day.'

'On Tuesday evening, there was the first Drawing Room, and the Ladies of the First Class attended, by order, to kiss the Great Dutchess's hand. Many were excluded by that distinction, which has mortified them beyond expression, and it will be a lasting prejudice to them and their children. All those who have bought their nobility, or had it by favour, and by the Patent of the late Emperor, and who, from the first words of it, "Nous voulons," have acquired the ridiculous appellation of *Nuvulloni*, being excluded, regret the

money they gave for it; whilst the Patrizii exult in
this distinction.'

'Poor Count Lorenzi, who kept up his spirits for
some time by hopes of a good pension, has received
notice that it will be only 3000 livres (120*l.* a year),
yet, miserable as that is, his circumstances won't
permit him to refuse it with disdain.   It is terrible in
one's old days to be obliged to such a favour for one's
maintenance.'

'The Great Duke applies himself very assiduously
to the affairs of his Government; his only amusement
is riding.   In every other respect, he and the Great
Dutchess seem to lead a very dull life.   Very few,
except at Audiences and Dinners, are admitted at
Court.   Their evenings are lonesome.   They sup at
nine and are in bed by ten.   It is decided that no
Theater is to be opened for a year, excepting at
Leghorn, where there will be an Opera, in the Carnival.   Their Capital will be the dullest part of the
State, but the influence of Vienna will, for some time,
be very great.   *There*, the rigour of mourning is such
that the Empress has forbid the Ladies wearing *rouge*,
for the whole year.   Your French Dames would never
submit to that species of tyrany.'

From Court circumstances, Mann turns to consider
his own official position.   Hitherto, he has only been
Resident, or Resident-Minister.   The next step is
Envoy or Minister Plenipotentiary.   The trumpery
Republic of Lucca now raised its representative at
Florence to the dignity of Envoy; and it was a
positive 'disattention' on the part of the English
Government to the Grand Ducal Court not to raise

their Resident to an equal position; Spain too had done the same for Viviani, who, for a score of years, had been a mere Chargé d'Affaires for Spain and Naples at Florence, with nothing more to do than to open the post-bags brought by Spanish or Neapolitan couriers, and to forward the letters. The English Resident, as Mann describes over and over again, was of more importance than all his diplomatic colleagues in Italy together, inasmuch, as he had to look after the rights and wrongs of the English mercantile colony at Leghorn, and there was nothing like that duty to be performed by any other diplomatist. On the first of November he thus narrates the aggravating progress of his grievances :—

'Marquis Viviani, our new Envoy of Spain, is beginning to set the example' (of increasing his expenses) 'by a ministerial dinner, next Tuesday, St. Carlo (November 4th) to all the great Officers of the Court, Foreign Ministers, etc. The Envoy of Lucca, to instal himself in the privilege of imitating a Great Court, is to do the same the week after; and, though I have constantly dinners for our own, and other, strangers, I must follow their example, by making that sort of repast too, for the same company. The *Galas*, when they are to take place, are very numerous ; twenty seven, at least, obligatory ; among which, several are lumped together by the births and names happening on the same day' (that is, when the august personage in whose honour the gala was given, happened to be born on the saint's day after whom his Highmightiness was named, the birthday and the name-day were lumped together, in one gala).

'Surely,' says Mann—when he hears that Captain
Murray was sent to Constantinople in place of Mr.
Grenville, as 'Ambassador,'—'this may make the
English Cabinet think that the character of Minister
Plenipotentiary may not be too much for another
"Resident" in this Christian part of Europe.' And then
the £400 which he had been promised wherewith to
defray the 'Extra-extraordinary expenses' for mani-
festing in Florence the joy of the English nation on the
marriage of the Archduke Leopold and the Infanta at
Innspruck, had not come to hand at this last date.
But the prolix writer forgets this solid grievance for a
while to tell what he knows of the *Nuvulloni.*

'On the day appointed last week for the *Nous
Voulons* to be admitted at Court, the morning was
fixed for the men, and the afternoon for the Dames of
that class. The number of those who received the
order was about a hundred; but, to the astonishment
and great mortification too, of the G. Dutchess, only
thirteen presented themselves to kiss her hand. This
occasioned so much displeasure, that it was instantly
determined to exclude that class for ever after from
the Court. Since that, orders have been given to
inquire into the real cause of what is called so great
an Insult, on a suspicion that it may have proceeded
from pique for their not having been admitted with
the other Ladies the first day. Probably, some may
have acted on that principle, but the greatest part
could not go, for want of time to provide the proper
dress, which was a Sack with a Hoop, and the Linnen
prescribed. All their preparations for the time when
they expected to be received with the greater Ladies,

like their's, were for the Court Dress. You will easily
judge of their mortification, first in being so distinguished as *Nous Voulons*, and then chastized for not
humbling themselves.'

The greatest gala day in Florence, after the Great
Duke was installed, was that of the saint from
whom he was named, Leopold, November 15th. A St.
Leopold's day in the Tuscan capital was celebrated
with the completeness of a St. Joseph's day in
Vienna; and this was how the stage was prepared and
the drama was acted. 'Invitations or, as I should
rather say here, Intimations, are sent by the Fouriers
of the Court, to be there at such hours; every Class
has its turn; between ten and eleven has been announced to us, as that in which we may see the Great
Officers, Chamberlains, etc., kiss hands. After which
the Great Duke and Dutchess go to Church in State.
At their return from thence the First Class of the
Female Nobility are to be in the Appartments, *en
habit de Cour*, and jewels, to kiss the G. Dutchess's
hand, which ceremony is repeated by every Class of
Nobility every Gala day; and those same Ladies, with
every one who can get a place, are to attend at the
Dinner, which is to be served in the Great Hall of the
Palace, under a Canopy of State, decorated most
sumptuously for this occasion. Other tables are to be
served afterwards; and in the evening there is to be a
great Drawing Room. Marshal Botta would willingly
have saved this last expence, by substituting the
Entertainment which the Accademy dei Nobili are
to give to their Princes this afternoon in the Great
Theater, where the Nobili are to perform all their

exercises, dancing, fencing, vaulting, etc., etc., which is to begin by a Cantata performed by mercenaries. The summons is for five, and it will last till nine. . . . All this can now be done, as the late Emperor's obsequies (on the 5th) are over. In the Cathedral Church, where the funeral ceremony took place, on the 5th *inst.*, the drapery of one of the Statues that wept on the *Catafalco,* took fire and occasioned some disturbance. The G. Dutchess was alarmed; and some attribute to that the disappearance of the first and very dubious appearances of her being with child.'

The day of St. Leopold passed according to the above description, but it was not the last gala day of the year. 'The *Baccia Mani,*' says Mann, on the 22nd of November, 'began again yesterday, for the *Nous Voulons'* (whose feud with the Court seems to have been made up) 'to prepare for Sunday, the Great Dutchess's Birth-day, which is to pass as that of St. Leopold.'

In this joyous way was established in the House of Hapsburgh-Lorraine that Grand Duchy of Tuscany, which is now absorbed in the Kingdom of Italy,— which may God preserve! The Emperor Francis was only a nominal and ever-absent Grand Duke. His second son, Leopold, resided in Tuscany from 1765 till his accession to the Empire, on the death of his elder brother, Joseph, in 1790. Leopold's son, Ferdinand, succeeded in the Grand Duchy, from which he was expelled by the French in 1800. He was restored in 1814, when the kingship of Etruria and the grand-duchessship of Eliza Bonaparte (Princess Bacciochi) became things of the past, and Ferdinand kept his seat till his demise in 1824. The second Leopold, his successor, abdicated in July, 1859, when Ferdinand, the last of this line of Grand Dukes, inherited the little greatness, and kept it for a short time. In March, 1860, he was an uncoroneted Grand Duke, going about Austria, loudly protesting against the annexation of his Duchy to the Kingdom of Sardinia. It went, by the vote of the Tuscans, as by similar process went Parma, Modena, and the Romagna. In 1861, Victor Emmanuel changed his old title of King of Sardinia for that of King of Italy ; and in 1871, after the Pope had made himself equal in one respect with God, by assuming Infallibility, the temporal power fell from the Pontiff's hands. Mann did not exactly see all this succession of events, but he was constantly referring to the inevitable overthrow of such a condition of civil and ecclesiastical government as prevailed about him in Italy.

## CHAPTER VII.

### 1766.

WHILE at the New Grand Ducal Court all was out-
wardly brilliant, a disinherited heir of royalty was
unceremoniously dying in Rome. On January 3rd,
1766, Sir Horace Mann makes this communication
to Walpole :—'At the departure of the last letters
from Rome, the Pretender was expiring ; he had had
the Extreme Unction, and the Cardinal, his son, was
employing the Jews to fit up an Appartment for his
brother, who was daily expected ; an odd disposition
for one who was to go thither to take possession of
Royalty. We are told that the elder son's Catholickism,
notwithstanding that he has no religion at all, is uncon-
taminated, and that what gave rise to that injurious
supposition was, that the Heir of a Sir Nathaniel
Thorold (a Romanist) who died at Naples, performed
the abjuration in St. Martin's Church, as a condition
of the inheritance.' On January 10th, Mann says of
the luckless son of James the Second :—' He died on
the night of the first of the month, and was exposed
on a Bed of State in his own house ; from thence, he
was removed to the Church contiguous to it ; and on
Tuesday was to be carried to St. Peter's to be buryed.

The Romans were vastly impatient to bury him, that
their Theaters might be opened. It is said that he
has left in the Publick funds at Rome—in money,
jewels, and plate—to the amount of a Million of
Crowns. I should think that the sum is exaggerated,
as I am perswaded that for many years he received
little from his friends. The Baili de Breteuil, now
Ambassadour of Malta at Rome, whose mother was a
Fitz-James, and who attended the Young Pretender all
the while he was in France preparing for his expedition to England, assured me that he had a revenue in
France, of near 15,000l. sterling, arising from money
which King James, in the Regent's time, deposited in
the Hotel de Ville, at Paris. I never could perswade
myself of the truth of this; and yet the Baili had
such connections with him, and such opportunities of
being informed, and asserted it so positively, that I
did not dare contradict him.'

'A Roman Courier has passed by, in search of the
Heir of the Palazzo di Santi Apostoli, for as yet his
appellation is not decided ; but, not to keep the world
in suspense, the Pope, with a few of his Cardinals,
intends soon to pronounce whether George or Edward
shall be King of Great Britain. As Advocate in
these parts for the former, I had a warm debate yesterday, with the Nuncio, on this subject, and I really
think that I made him quite sensible (because he was
quite confused) of the ridicule which his Holyness
has already drawn upon himself, by calling a Congregation to debate on the subject, and of the inconveniences which might attend a decision, though
dictated by their consciences. Monsieur D'Aubeterre,

the French Ambassadour who behaved so uncivilly to
the Duke of York, when he was at Rome, and who
was chosen by the Duc de Choiseul, to treat the Court
of Rome *de haut en bas*, on all occasions, is, they say,
warmly engaged to procure a favourable sentence for
this new candidate.   I can't say he does it by order of
his Court, but he has had time enough to consult it
and to receive instructions, since the Pope gave his
first answer to Cardinal Stuart on that subject.    I
have wrote a letter to Cardinal Albani (who is as
staunch as a Heretick in our favour), in answer to
the notice which he gave me of it, which I dare say
he will be glad to make use of; for it is a rule with
all Cardinals, who either have been or wish to be
" Nephews," to criticize the proceedings of those who
govern the Pope or the reigning Nephew. . . Cardinal
Stuart has desired his Brother to stop where the
Courier meets him, and to wait for fresh instructions,
in consequence of the afore-mentioned consultation ;
hoping, no doubt, to introduce him with all the
Ensigns of Royalty.'

*January 17th.*—' I am eager in the pursuit of my
cause now depending at Rome.  By writing, reasoning, and brawling so much, as I have done of late,
about it, I think I see so many good consequences of
suppressing a title that cannot fit two, that I figure
to myself, that in case the Pope should bestow it on
another, a Squadron will be sent to Civita Vecchia
to chastize him for such an Insult, and to make him
eat his words.  The present situation of the affair is
this.'

' The Pope is vastly fearful of offending England,

to whom, he says, he is so much obliged for the great lenity with which the Catholicks are treated ; but then, he is persecuted by the French Ambassadour, by that of Malta, by the Minister of Spain, and by Cardinal Stuart with all his numerous Parasites and Zealots, who are really perswaded that their Religion is concerned in England's having a nominal Roman Catholick King. You see with what powerful antagonists I have to combat, and yet I do not despair. My weapon would receive great force, indeed, if I could, as in the year '45, send for Admiral Matthews with a few ships and a Bomb vessel, to sound the Harbour of Civita Vecchia, which, however, I afterwards saved from the resentment of that furious Admiral.'

'. . . The Pretender died, they say, even richer than I mentioned in my last, which is accounted for by the money he drew from Poland, for some lands that belonged to his wife ;—by large sums which he formerly drew from England ;—by what he had in France ;—and, latterly, by a strickt economy. He has left all he had in France, to his eldest son ; and what he had in Rome, to the Cardinal—who is charged with the Legacies and Pensions to his family. Two Couriers were despatched by different routes, to meet the traveller ' (Charles Edward) ' and to advise him to stay somewhere till he should receive notice how he was to proceed. I am afraid the perplexity in which the Pope is, may affect his decision,—that he will dye, and so the affair be reserved to another. Many of the Cardinals, I dare say, will advise this, that they may not expose themselves to an exclusion at the next Election, on the part of France or Spain, for not acting in this affair according to their dictates. Every menace and every insinuation is put forth on this occasion ; and this is the stile of Rome.'

Pope Clement's health was indeed in an unsatisfactory state.     Early in January, Mann writes :— ' The Pope has had another attack of his fits ; and they are not occasioned now by too much Sturgeon, as formerly ; for they set no more before him than it is proper for him to eat.  He complains horribly of this ; but, his Nephews starve him, that they may continue the longer to get their Bellysfull ! '

How our Minister worked at this Papal Court, and with what result, is joyously told in a long letter dated January 24th, from which this extract is made :—

' You will have seen by my late letters how deeply I have been engaged to bully the Pope and all his Cardinals and to suppress the titles of a Popish Pretender even at Rome ; did you believe that I should succeed ?  Knowing that I should have to fight with all the foreign Ministers there, who to be sure were ordered to whisper in the Pope's ear that their masters wished to have two kings of England, and that in conscience he could not deprive the Catholicks in our three kingdoms of such a means upon any favourable occasion of restoring them to the obedience of his Thiara.   These and every other argument have been made use of in a long but extremely weak memorial that Cardinal Stuart presented to His Holyness, to convince him of the obligation he was under to acknowledge his Brother's titles.   But in spite of all,

I have been a more successful advocate for the King. I have acted by my Emissaries of all sorts ; my first letter was read in the very congregation that was to decide this great part, for which all Rome stood in suspense. The 'secret of the inquisition' (as it is called there) was imposed on all those who assisted at that meeting, which denounces Damnation to anyone who should reveal it, but nevertheless the result was known before they separated, and in order to save the tender consciences of the Cardinals who could not keep a secret long, the next day Cardinal Torregiani, the Secretary of State, wrote the enclosed billet to Cardinal Stuart. 1 have sent all the papers relating to this affair to General Conway ; do you think they will approve of my zeal ? I cannot help applauding myself most prodigiously ! Among those papers there is one very curious which I must explain to you. In the month of October, the Hero at Bouillon (Charles Edward) wrote to his brother to acquaint him with the disposition he was in to return to Rome, provided he could obtain such promises from the Pope as might encourage him to do it. This letter was shown to the Pope, who, after taking some time to consider of it, sent for young Cardinal (Francesco) Albani, the protector of Scotland and the most intimate friend of Cardinal Stuart, to talk with him about it and to convey his sentiments to him; this Albani did by a letter to Frascati, but the contents of that letter appearing too loose and weak, Cardinal Stuart engaged his friend to compose another more capable of inducing his Brother to return to Rome, but in return for so great a mark of his little honesty yet of his great complaisance, he gave copies

of that second letter, with all those that had passed
between his Brother and him, with his own composi-
tion, to the Cardinals who were to compose that congregation;—you will easily judge of the surprise of the
Pope and his Ministers, and of the indignation of
Cardinal Francis Albani, to see himself thus exposed;
in short, it has occasioned a total rupture there, and
what will probably appear more ridiculous, is the
astonishment of the Pretender himself to hear on his
arrival at Rome that a sentence has been pronounced
so different from what he had reason to hope for from
the letter of Albani, upon the strength of which he
set out from Bouillon. He passed by here on Monday,
entered into no house but stayed in the street whilst
they changed the horses; his own coach had eight, two
others, six; he travelled under the name of Douglas,
with a french passport, but his people called him
publickly the Prince of Wales, so he is to be called
at Rome where they saw him come into the world
under that denomination;—as to the absurdity of
the continuance of it now his father is in his grave,
it matters not at Rome, they are forced to reconcile
greater absurdities every day, and it is sufficient for us
that the greater titles are suppressed, and after all, if it
produces nothing more than the most glaring proof
of the submission to George the 3rd of the Court
which excommunicated Elizabeth and indeed all her
Descendants, it is no small triumph, but if it is not
sufficient, I will send the Pope to St. James's with
his triple crown, that the King may tip it off with
his foot !'

The reply given to the request made by Cardinal

York—or Stuart—further exemplifies what Mann calls 'the stile of Rome.' Its chief point is that the Pope cannot, for the present, accede to Cardinal York's request, for the recognition of his brother,—and meanwhile, the Secretary, 'full of respect,' most humbly kisses his hands! This, however, did not settle the matter. On February 7th, Sir Horace writes :—

'I thought that I had quite exhausted the subject of the Pretender, but the rage and disappointment of his brother has suggested to him the means of showing his contempt for the Pope's decision, that has drawn upon them both an additional mortification from the Pope and the disapprobation of all the *Sacra purpurea Romana.* You know that it has long been agreed among themselves that they are too great to give the right hand to any but a crowned head, therefore to convince the world that he was such, Cardinal Stuart carried him in triumph about Rome in his coach, in that distinguished place of honour. This and a visit which Cardinal Orsini, Minister of Naples, and Cardinal Guglialmi, formerly an humble dependant on the family, made to the new comer, in which it was supposed they had given him the title of "Master," gave such offence, that the same congregation was immediately assembled, in which it was resolved that Cardinal Torreggiani, the Secretary of State, should go in person to the Cardinal Dean of the College to desire or to bid him in the Pope's name to send a gentleman to all their Eminences and to the Heads of the distinguished orders, to acquaint them that the Pope having refused to acknowledge that personage

as King, they must regulate their behaviour to him
accordingly. Circular letters have been wrote to all
the Nuncios, and the notice of it was conveyed to me
by an order (in disguise) that I might not suspect
that the Pope's decision was illusory. This rigour,
however, regards themselves chiefly, in order to command the respect due to a Pope's order ; for my part
I would not desire to deprive him of the comforts of
Society, nor trouble myself how his friends treat him
in private, it is thought that he will not stay in Rome,
but that if he is not permitted to return into france,
(at Bouillon they say they were quite tired of him),
he will fix in some town of the Ecclesiastical State.
Does he succeed to the obligation which his father
was under, to live on this side the Alps ? I have
nothing this post worth troubling the Duke of Richmond with, just mention to him, however, this last
step of the Pope, as it shows how fearful he is of
offending the real King of England, and as it may
produce the departure again from Rome of his
antagonists. It is whispered that he is to marry,
whom I don't know, nor should I think after this
decision at Rome that it would be easy to find any
principessina to accept of him. Twenty years ago,
when his Royalty at Rome was not disputed, the
Dutchess of Massa rejected the offer for her daughter
with great disdain, come ingiuriosa al suo decoro.'

On the 28th February, Mann announced his complete triumph. ' The disapprobation which the Courts
of France and Spain have shown of their Ministers
conduct at Rome, in regard to the Pretender, has
accomplished my Prophecy and made my triumph

compleat. For, the last week, they both declared to
the Pope, to his Nephew, and to the Secretary of
State—by order of their Courts—that for the future,
they were not to concern themselves, in any manner
whatever, for the person in whose favour they would
have induced the Pope to take so false a step. The
Pope and his Ministers, and the Congregation of
Cardinals now applaud their decision, and the whole
Town, nay all Italy, laughs at Mons. D'Aubeterre and
the other Advocates of the Pretender, for their indiscretion. The Court of Naples, too, has publickly
disavowed its Minister, Cardinal Orsini, and has given
Mr. Hamilton a copy of the letter that was wrote to
the Cardinal on this subject. So that, ' Monsieur Le
Baron Douglas' sticks to his Incognito, and it is as
much treason to call him King, at Rome, as at
London.'

Walpole thought it was a matter of perfect indifference to England, whether the Pope recognized
Charles Edward as king, or not. Mann thought
otherwise, but he adds of the Prince himself :—' I
have as much compassion for the young man as anybody, nor would I disturb him in anything, but his
vanity is the sole point that relates to us. He is rich,
and if he is capable of being in any degree happy, the
being deprived at Rome of a title which was denied
to his father in every other part of the Globe, ought
not to make him otherwise.'

There was another deprivation of dignity which
must have wounded the Chevalier's feelings. On
March 14th, Mann says :—' To suppress all signs, in
Rome, of the royalty of the Stuarts, the arms of

England, with those of the Pope and Senate of Rome, were, last week, in the night, taken down from over the Pretender's door. The last letter which I wrote to a zealous correspondent there, was carried immediately to the Pope, who was glad to see that he had averted the effects of the King's resentment, which General Conway's letter to me on that subject announced to any who should countenance and favour the Pretensions *dont il s'agissoit.'*

One of the Chevalier's warmest friends visited him in September. 'Miss Jenny Cameron, with a female companion only, has been lately at Rome, to make a visit and to solicit (they say) the continuance of her pension, from her Hero; but, it is said, she did not meet with so kind a reception as at Holyrood House. She returned again to Leghorn, and embarked on board a Merchant-ship (Captain Mangle) for England.'

If the Romans treated the Chevalier with scant respect, that also was the measure which they paid to the Pope himself. The famine, which distressed so many nations this year, was felt most painfully in Italy, and most of all in Rome. The scarcity even of such bad bread as could be made from bad grain, mixed with worse materials, exasperated the people, and that exasperation took an offensive form of demonstration in August. 'The calamity, more severe at Rome, by the constant confusion and disorder in the Government, has broke out there, and the populace have riotously surrounded the Pope's coach, to show him the wretched bread they are forced to eat; they threw it into him; so that, the poor old man is forced

to abstain from going abroad, as he has no better
bread to give them, nor money to purchase corn from
abroad.' In Tuscany the famine was nearly as severe
as in the Papal States. As there was little money in the
Duchy wherewith to import corn from Hungary, which
had it to sell, the Grand Duke proposed to appropriate
portions of the Church plate to purchasing food.
This was at the close of the year; and Mann writes
in reference to it. 'The Great Duke is going to
quarrel with the Pope . . . but the former is not
aware that the Spiritual Arms of his Adversary will
be too strong for him. He has already had the
mortification to see a Superior of a Convent here
suspended, for having complyed with his Exhortation
to send their useless Church plate to the Mint, without
the Pope's leave.'

The year was an important one to the Tuscan
Duchy, whose Grand Duke, not so sovereign as he
assumed to be, was the slave of much ceremony, and
got 'snubbed' when he disregarded the ceremony
which other Courts expected from him. His addressing George the Third, on announcing his accession to
the Grand Ducal dignity, as, 'Sir, my brother and
cousin,' so irritated that ordinarily good-natured king,
that he was on the point of ordering the letter to be
returned. However, the matter was looked over,
as it was by half a dozen other potentialities who had
been similarly offended. The Grand Duke made some
amends by attentions to English guests. All ' of condition' were invited to the Grand Ducal dinners.
Mann says of one of them :—'The Comptroller of the
Table has pleased the Great Duke much by his giving

Lord Cowper and Lord Tylney, Beer and Punch, which he thinks is the constant beverage of the English.'

'Everything in our little Court,' Mann subsequently writes, 'is regulated on the footing of Vienna, without making the least difference between the size of an Imperial and a Great Ducal crown. I speak of their Etiquette only; for the personal affability of the Great Duke and Dutchess is quite Medicean. . . . Their invitations to dinner, which it is not respectful to refuse, come so late, it frequently happens that one has engaged company at home, whom one leaves to dine alone; but, as the hours are very different, one can get back to them at the first course.' On points of ceremony, Marshal Botta ruled their Grand Ducal Highnesses, and the Imperial Court at Vienna ruled Botta. The Duke and Duchess could not even go to a burletta and ball without approval from that Court; and the Duke, who was much addicted to the profuse swallowing of physic, received trunks full of medicine, sent to him from the Empress. 'If it depended on the Dutchess,' says Mann, 'she wouldn't miss a single Harlequin Comedy.' They were popular, and the Florentines loved even their great ceremonies, happy in having Ducal sovereigns of their own. But when, at the ceremony of taking possession of the Grand Duchy, a document was read which limited the succession to the male heirs only of the young reigning couple, the Florentines were alarmed, 'as it shows,' says Mann, 'a prospect of the danger of their country reverting to the head branch of the House of Austria;—a situation even worse than that they were in before.'

The Tuscans, nevertheless, enjoyed the present
time, at all events before the famine set in.   The
Grand Duke Leopold paid his first visit, in state, to
Leghorn, and the various bodies of foreign merchants
established there, entertained him after their respective fashions.   'The English merchants and their
dependants gave him a *Calcio*,—a fine football in
Gala, performed in the Great Square; fifty on a side,
with their officers very richly dressed,—at the cost of
above a thousand pounds.   One uniform was rose-
colour satin; the other, blue.   The first appearance
and their march made the prettiest show imaginable;
but the sequel did not answer,—both from the inexperience of the players, and an absolute prohibition to give serious blows with their fists, without
which the game must be languid.   The repetition of
it, two days after, was animated by a greater liberty
in that respect, and gave more satisfaction.'

'The Dutch spent as much as the English, in a
race of boats at sea, in the Mole; at the head of
which a Palazzo, as it was called, was erected for
the Court.   This succeeded the best of any.   The
French gave a Chariot race.   The Jews another horse-
race, of small expense; but they had been ordered,
besides that, to build a solid front to the barracks,
which will cost a large sum, for which they have been
taxed by the Marshal.   The Pisans made their illumi-
nation richer than usual; it is always a very fine
sight.   But Leghorn outdid anything that was ever
done before.   The *Place*, which is very large, and
regular, was surrounded by a uniform Scaffolding,
under which were above 150 shops, many of them

furnished with the richest stuffs from Lions, and toys
from Paris, and which as well as the whole Square,
were illuminated the whole night; and the Fair
lasted the whole time the Court stayed there. Every
afternoon some *Spectacle* was exhibited. The first
was a procession of all the different shows that were
to be performed, and a horse race which the Magis-
trates of the town gave. The football, etc., followed
on succeeding days. . . . Neutral Cockades, of the
richest French ribbands embroidered, were given to
the Great Duke and Dutchess, and, with a proper
degradation, to the whole Court, which both men and
women wore at their breasts. This article alone cost
above three hundred pounds. The whole, it is said,
will be upwards of 2000*l.*'

'There was a table at Court everyday, of about
20 covers, to which the Foreign Ministers and others
were invited by turns. The Great Duke was much
pleased with the sea; he took all opportunities to go
upon it, and said he would frequently go to Leghorn,
where he was so well received. But as the Great
Dutchess is supposed to be with child '—(Mann says in
a June letter, that as yet people were only allowed to
suppose, and only to whisper the supposition. There
was to be no assertion of the interesting fact till after
official proclamation—so the etiquette of Vienna and
Madrid required—of the Great Lady's condition)—
'this will confine them to the neighbourhood, at
least of Florence, for several months. They are now
at Poggio Imperiale, from whence they are to make a
publick Entry, the Day of St. John, when he receives
the homage,' and on occasion of one of the fêtes, the

announcement as to the Duchess was published, and
people might talk of it aloud.

'The Entry was duly made on Midsummer-Day.
The Great Duke and Dutchess went in procession
from the Poggio to the city gate, where he mounted
on horse-back, and, attended by all his Great Officers
and his whole Court a-foot, went to the Ducal palace,
where,' says Mann, 'you have seen Prince Craon perform the same ceremony of receiving the homage
for the present Great Duke's father—Francis. The
Dutchess and her whole Court followed in coaches.'

Ceremonial etiquette so ruled everything at the
Florentine Court, that when Mann took to that Court,
in some state, Queen Charlotte's brother, 'the youngest
Prince Mecklenbourg,' the punctilious Botta complimented the Minister on having introduced the Prince
'avec décence.' 'We dined at the Poggio, on Wednesday,' says Mann, July 19th, 'which they say, is
more than dining with them in town; and, afterwards, we were admitted to drink Coffee with them,
*debout*, which it seems is infinitely a greater honour
than sitting with them at dinner.' Queen Charlotte's
brother is described by Mann as, 'a very good little
Prince, who pretends to nothing; but whose very
civil behaviour attracts respect.' Mann adds: 'The
Great Dutchess, first from a joke, and now in earnest,
is engaged to learn English. She bid me find her a
master, and I have recommended an English Carme-
lite Friar, whom chance threw in my way, by his
applying to me from Rome, for leave to dedicate an
English-Italian Grammar to me. She has almost
asked me for an English Dog and Bitch of King

Charles's breed; could you get them of the very smallest size and of particular beauty among the Royal Descendants? If it were (*sic*) I should make my court much by presenting them to her.'

The Court, with all its new polish upon it, was but a dull place; and it was made duller by the death of the Queen of Spain, for whom the Imperial family was bound to wear mourning for fourteen months! This dullness had its effect on English travellers who, after arriving, declined to tarry. 'This little Court,' says Mann, in November, 'is jealous, seeing fewer English of late than usual, and that they give the preference to other places. But the case literally is, though they themselves, perhaps, do not suspect it, that this place has lost a little, on account of the agrémens of Society, since the arrival of the Court, where there is too much Etiquette for undignified strangers who cannot brook distinctions. Saturday was a great Gala: the Duke's name-day (St. Leopold). It began with the Bacia Mano of the *Nouvoullone* (*sic*), but here the G. Dutchess, for the second time, received a slight,—only three went! If she is wise, she will, on her own account, strike off this ceremony. Duke Salviati was declared Grand Chambellan, much against his will, and more so against that of his Roman Dutchess who hitherto refuses to reside here.'

Poor Count Lorenzi died in the winter of grief, at losing his post at Court, of representative of France. Marshal Botta left it in joy, real or affected, at losing his office of Major-Domo to a Grand Duke, and being appointed Imperial Commissary at Pavia—

where he promised to let them know who he was and
what his office meant. The last English flitting
through Florence this year, were 'Lord Bristol's
youngest brother and his wife, both very amiable
people, with the particular gentility of the Herveys.'

## CHAPTER VIII.

### 1767.

THE year 1767 began and ended with a Siberian winter, which swept away many gay Italians, very reluctant to go; and the summer of the same year was accompanied by an influenza, which proved a heavy and often fatal affliction. It was in the better period of this year that a scene took place in the Vatican—one to excite sympathy even now, and which Mann thus relates, and on which he also makes comment :—

*May* 17*th.*—' The Eldest Son of the late Pretender has at last been induced by his Brother to make a visit to the Pope, with an intention, it is supposed, to live in society for the future. But for that visit he was forced to desist from all his pretensions whatever from the Pope, who treated him without any distinction. His Brother carried him there, but he was made to wait, though the Cardinal, by right of his Hat, was immediately introduced and seated. He was then called for, by the name of—the Brother of the Cardinal of York. He knelt to kiss the Pope's foot, and remained on his knees, till the

Pope said *Alzatevi!* (Get up !) and he then stood for a quarter of an hour, the whole time of his audience.'

'All this was settled before and made the condition of his being admitted ; but, for fear any misrepresentation of it might make this step appear contradictory to the declaration of the Court of Rome in regard to him, after his father's death, commission was given to a Cardinal, to inform me of it, to exclude all danger of offending the King.   Nothing, surely, can be a stronger proof of their respect for our nation than the caution with which the Pope has acted on this occasion.   I am this instant going to answer the letter that I have received on this subject, from Rome, and to express *my approbation of their conduct.'*

Nothing more is heard of the degraded Chevalier this year, but much of the Pope.   The Jesuits, accused of actual sedition and of contemplated regicide in Spain, were summarily expelled.   The first intimation comes to us in a letter of May 19th.   'The event of the Jesuits surprised everybody and much afflicted the Pope, who is their great Protector, and is weak enough to suppose that though they are persecuted by the principal Courts of Europe, he can still support them for the few years he has to reign ; but he cannot be so weak as not to foresee the great probability that his successor will dissolve the order.   The first Convoy, consisting of 570, arrived at Civita Vecchia a few days ago.   The Pope still declared his reluctance to receive them, but that he submitted to force, under which pretext they were to be received a-shore.   He is embarrassed where to place them, not having

Colledges or building sufficient for such a number in
or near Rome, so that many of them are to be sent to
Ferrara, which wants inhabitants.  It would be lucky
indeed for that spot, if the people were of a more
propagating or industrious species, for as long as the
King of Spain maintains the Jesuits' *pension*, the
circulation of the money in so poor a town may be
advantageous to it.'

*May 23rd.*—' When first the Pope received the
news from Spain of their expulsion, and that they
were to be sent to him, he was thunderstruck ; but he
expressed it by tears and humiliation, and as soon as
he could take any resolution at all, it was to expos-
tulate with the King of Spain upon the inconveniences
which his sending them to Rome would occasion,
begging him at least he would let them remain at
home as Priests, under whatever absolute restrictions
he should think proper, or as had been practised in
France.  But the Plan was notified to him only at
the time of its execution, so that the Courier that he
sent with these exhortations to Madrid, returned with
a negative to all his proposals, and with notice that
the ships were actually departed from several ports
for Civita Vecchia, where the number I mentioned in
my last soon after arrived.  Before this, he was
dubious, and then yielded to the advice of his prudent
counsellors to admit the Jesuits, and the plan was
formed to send a considerable part of them to Ferrara.

' But, at first, when he received notice of their
being actually before Civita Vecchia, he suddenly sent
orders to the Governor there to oppose their landing,
by force, in case the Spaniards should attempt it.

Immediately, the Garrison was put under arms, and the cannon of the works towards the sea so disposed as to sink his beloved sons rather than receive them ashore. . . . I have been assured by my brother-minister here, that the King of Spain has authentic proofs in his hands, that the Jesuits were the sole promoters of the late Sedition at Madrid, and that their Plan was to kill the King and seize the whole family, on Holy Thursday, as they were visiting the churches on foot; which plan was defeated by that sedition breaking out too soon, and by the popular fury being carried to greater lengths there, than the Jesuits designed or foresaw, which obliged the King and his family to escape into the Country, and by that means, saved themselves. Another Minister told me that he had not heard that the Jesuits intended to kill the King, but *only* to seize him and shut him up as an Imbecile, and put the Prince of Asturias on his throne. *Bravi davero!'*

*June 6th.*—After lengthily stating that a freight of expelled Jesuits had been allowed to land in a part of Corsica occupied by the French, Mann says:—'The Pope is vastly criticized for his unnatural behaviour to his favourite sons, and the General of the order who encouraged him to reject them deserves to be hanged. (!) The Pope ought to have obliged him to maintain them; for, the vast wealth they possess in Rome belongs to the whole Society, and not to any one body settled in any spot.'

*June 24th.*—' Some hundred Jesuits more arrived lately at Civita Vecchia, but did not meet with more favour than their brethren who preceded them. This,

as well as a third Convoy, was driven by the wind to
Porto St. Stefano, before which Port they remain, as
the others do at the Bastia. The only favour they
have obtained from the French Commander there, is
leave for a certain number at a time to go a-shore to
stretch their legs, but with an obligation to return on
board at night.'

*July* 11*th.*—'I am persuaded that your compassion and humanity can extend to the members of
the Society of St. Ignatius, and that you do not
approve that two or three thousand of them should
be crowded into a few ships and, after a long navigation, not be permitted, for near a month, to land at
the Port they were carried to. The implacability of
the Pope and their General, though they assert their
innocence, has made this scene of too great a length
for many of them to support; many have died of
fatigue and want of fresh air.'

*August* 8*th.*—In this letter, the Pope is said to be
severely censured by all parties for his inhumanity
towards these Jesuits, who were now exposed to the
greatest hardships. 'They have been permitted (by
the French) to land in Corsica, but the places allotted
to them are void of every convenience of life. Two
parties of twelve Jesuits each, disguised like sailors,
escaped from Calvi, and arrived last week at Genoa
and Savona, but being discovered, were not allowed
to land, and the Padrons of the boats had orders to
return from whence they came, or to proceed to any
other port out of the Genoese state; but every other
State has given the same orders to exclude them.'

At the end of the year, the little King of Naples

drove out these 'Sons of St. Ignatius,' who found
their way into the States of the Church, and, says
Mann, December 27th, 'The Pope cries aloud at the
violation of his sovereignty and at that of the Duties
of his Vassal, the King of Naples, in forcing upon
him so many useless mouths, with six Ducats a head
only, for their maintenance. . . . The Neapolitan
Ambassador made no other answer to the Papal
remonstrance than that his master, being dissatisfied
with his Jesuitical subjects, had no other road to
dismiss them by, from his dominions ;—like our
Beadles in the country driving vagabonds into the
next parish !'

The whole of Italy suffered excessively from sickness, the source of which was at Siena, throughout the
year. During March there were a thousand fever
patients in the great hospital at Florence, 'and 586
died there, besides a great number in private houses ;'
so that, as Monsignor Perelli wrote on a like occasion,
' Il Santissimo' (meaning the Sacrament) 'corre per
la Città come il Diavolo !'

Notwithstanding, it was a year of immense gaiety
as well as of deep mourning in Florence. Early in the
year the Grand Duke, who scrupulously fulfilled every
law of etiquette to please Vienna, indulged in a free
and easy way of life to please himself. ' He is fond
of masking,' says Mann in the Carnival season, ' and
profited of the first opportunity to go in disguise to
one of the Theaters. The company there was small ;
but he sent to the Casino to let the nobility know that
it would be agreeable to him that they should go there
this evening. It is supposed from this, that the Great

Dutchess will be there too, and that she will not be
permitted to go out any more.' Then Mann goes into
details of significant dates, calculations of the Duchess's
'woemen,' and counter-reckonings of physicians, all of
which ends with the remark: 'An Heir to the House
of Austria, expected so soon, ought to be waited for
with care.'

After a few days a little princess was born, 'to
the great disappointment of this place and Vienna'
(January 27th). 'The Empress' (dowager) 'wanted a
grandson to console her under the despair she is in of
the Emperor' (Joseph) 'having children by the wife
she has given him, with which she reproaches herself
continually.' This wife, Joseph's second consort, was
Marie Josepha of Bavaria, daughter of the Emperor
Charles VII. He married her in 1765 out of filial
obedience, and coldly neglected her out of positive aversion. Joseph had a daughter by his first wife, Elizabeth Marie, daughter of Philip, Duke of Parma, but
she died in 1770. This was the wife whom he loved,
living, and he never ceased to mourn for her, dead.
'Only a Princess!' was the expression of disappointment at the birth of the daughter of Leopold and his
young Spanish wife, the Infanta Maria Louisa; but
there was consolation. 'The early proof of fertility,'
says Mann to Walpole, 'which our Great Dutchess has
given, will endear her to the whole family, much.
The Empress' (dowager) 'has found out the only
ornament the Great Dutchess wanted among the load
of jewels she brought from Spain, and has sent it to
her on this occasion,—a set of diamond buttons for
a *Corsette;* six, which are said to be worth about a

thousand zecchins each.   Your friend, the Marquise
Albizzi, has been made *Grande Maitresse* of this little
Arch-Dutchess—an honour which totally deprives her
of her liberty, and subjects her to a confinement little
less than that of a Nun.'

In February we find that, ' The Great Duke par-
takes of all the diversions of the Carnival, with the
eagerness of a young man when he first gets his liberty.
He leaves his Dutchess and goes masked every night
to the Theater, where he is as well known as in his
Palace, and walks about for six hours together.   She
is to come out in a few days, for which great preparations are making.   Everything is being done with
Austrian Pomp.   A Ceremonial has been sent from
Vienna for her being Churched that will employ the
whole Court for a whole day.   It is astonishing what
slaves they make themselves to the Etiquette of that
Court in the most trivial circumstances.'

On March 27th, referring to the past joyous
Carnival, Mann writes:—' It was the first of the sort
the Great Duke had seen, and the first time he had
been permitted to enjoy his liberty.   He not only
permitted Masks at the Theaters sooner than usual,
but was always the first there, and at every place
where Masks resorted, and though in a Venetian Mask,
took no pains to conceal himself, but spoke to everybody he knew ; consequently, he had frequently crowds
about him who were ambitious of that honour.'

' The Great Dutchess could only enjoy the last ten
days, which she employed with such assiduity as not
to loose a moment of them.   The *Chambellans* gave a
great festival for her being brought to bed, which was

reserved for her to partake of. It consisted in the marriage of a hundred poor girls to whom a small, though a sufficient portion, to induce them to couple, was given. Both they and their Sposi were dressed in a uniform, and all were married on the same day at the Cathedral Church, from whence they marched in procession through the streets to the Great Hall of the Old Palace (preceded by Madame Cardoni (Cecco Suares' sister), who represented the Great Dutchess, and was attended by Guards, Coaches and Six following) ; where a cold dinner was prepared for them in the presence of the whole Court—to whom a Ball was given in the evening, with the admission of all tolerably well masked people. The size of the Hall requires crowds to fill it, and it was filled ; besides which, there were other Halls and Appartments contiguous to it where refreshments were served, and consequently were crouded. The Great Dutchess danced there and at every other Theater, afterwards, incessantly. All which added a very extraordinary vivacity to these amusements.'

In the course of the spring, the anniversary festivals at Siena and Pisa enjoyed the presence of the Grand Ducal couple. 'The famous Battle of the Bridge at Pisa, was fought with more animosity than usual, and much mischief was done, which offended the Great Duke, who will either suppress the show for the future, or so model it that it may at least become an innocent diversion and not a slaughter.'

But death was in other places besides the bridge at Pisa. Smallpox had slain the Emperor Joseph's first young wife, Elizabeth of Parma, in 1765. In

June, 1767, when Florence was looking for a probable
Imperial visit, with galas, operas, and tournaments,
to celebrate the arrival in Florence of Maria Theresa's
daughter Josepha, as the affianced bride of Ferdinand
King of Naples, the whole city was thunderstruck
by the arrival of an express with the news that both
the Empresses had the smallpox! (Maria Theresa,
and Joseph's wife, Maria Josepha of Bavaria.)  'An
Estafette arrives every night with fresh accounts of
its progress.  That of yesterday brought news of the
young Empress's death; but the anxiety for the
Empress Dowager makes this Court indifferent to that
Event.  Not but that our Great Duke must reflect
that the accident will make room for a more fertile
Sister in Law; and that he may spare himself the
trouble of furnishing Heirs for the house of Austria,
as his flatterers had told him he must do.  The loss
of His Mother would indeed be great to him at this
juncture.  His Brother (Joseph) gave him early
proofs, after their father's death, that he was not to
expect great assistance from him, and it was that
reflection that afflicted our young Prince much more
than the loss of the money he gave up to Joseph, and
which he was forced a few months after to supply by
a loan, at 4 *per cent.*, from the Genoese.'

'All public amusements were suspended on the
arrival of the first Estafette.  The Great Duke and
Dutchess remain within the walls of their Villa at
Poggio Imperiale, invisible to all but their immediate
attendants; and tho' all the accounts of the Empress
Queen are till now favourable, they have still many
days of anxiety to undergo, as the nature alone of the

disorder is too much to be feared in a body so replete and at her age.' Maria Theresa was as adverse against inoculation as some persons are, at the present day, against vaccination.

The Court, however, found leisure to be unceremoniously amiable to Lord Holland, who was there in Florence with his wife,—she was the daughter of the Duke of Richmond, and Charles James Fox was one of Lord and Lady Holland's children. 'The Court meant to be very civil to them. I omitted nothing which her high birth and their situation could suggest to tickle Austrian ears ; and they gave leave that my Lord should be carried in a Sedan chair, into the most sacred parts of the Palace, where none but the *Dame dell' Accesso* can approach. Of this, you will laugh at the following instance—When the Great Dutchess was up after her Child-bed, but had not leave to go out of her room, the Great Duke, out of good nature, said he would dine with her there ; which, being with joy accepted, he said he would go and give orders to Julian, the head *maître d'hôtel*, about it. To the Great Duke, the Grande Maitresse said, "I hope your Imperial Highness does not intend to let any man approach this room ; this, my instructions will not allow ; and, if you *will* dine here, you must be served by woemen." This he would not comply with ; he was out of humour and his Dutchess cried ; but they dined separate.— She is now supposed' (June) ' to be again with child.' Only whispered suppositions were as yet permissible. Maria Theresa had confidence in her Spanish daughter-in-law, who fulfilled it by becoming the mother of nearly the same number of children.

The Great Empress had sixteen; six sons and ten
daughters. The Great Duchess; nine sons—among
whom was the great Captain, the Archduke Charles,
—and four daughters, who survived her; but there
were one or two brief lives that are left unchronicled.

The year closed in gloom. Florence had expected
to be brilliant on occasion of the coming of the Arch-
duchess Josepha, daughter of Maria Theresa, the wife
that was to be of Ferdinand King of Naples. Her
elder sister, Joanna, had been betrothed at the age of
twelve, to Ferdinand, but smallpox carried her off
before the betrothal had further consequences. Josepha, not gladly, succeeded to her sister's expectations,
and was to be married by proxy, in August, 1767.
She had great reluctance to separate from her family;
and she took sorrowful leave even of her dead father,
Francis, by descending to the vault of the Capuchin
Church, and passing some hours, weeping and praying,
by the side of his body. The poor young creature
was ill at the time; emotion increased her illness;
smallpox declared itself, and Josepha died on the day
she was to have set out for Florence, on her way to
Naples. Maria Theresa, however, had no mercy on
her daughters, when there was a chance of establishing them on thrones. Florence, which mourned for
Josepha, had to rejoice for her sister Caroline, who
took her place, and is remembered as Nelson's Queen
of Naples. The Empress sent her youngest daughter,
Marie Antoinette, to France, where she was maligned
so ignobly, persecuted so cowardly, and murdered so
unnecessarily.

But long before Florence was tossing fireworks to

the stars in joy for the fatal marriage of Marie Antoinette, the travelling English were sulky at the lack
of courtesy they expected to find at the Grand Ducal
Court.  'The English here are quite out of humour,'
says Mann, ' and I see no possibility of pleasing them.
There is no exact rule at Court, and the very means
by which the Great Duke thinks to please them produces a quite contrary effect.  Several had been
presented, but had not been invited to dinner ; some
days after, I presented five more, when one of them,
Mr. Gore, Lord Arran's son, and Mr. Fortescue of the
first company, were invited to dinner ; upon which
the others have pouted ever since, and would not
return to Court, on two Gala days, by which they
meant to show their resentment, not doubting, from
a perswation of their own importance, it would be
observed that they were not there.  Seriously, I see
it will be quite impossible to reconcile the notions of
a Germanick-Spanish Court with those of our countrymen, who of whatever rank indistinctly, think themselves entitled to the greatest distinctions.  Some have
founded their pretensions on being Members of Parliament,—the Great Council of England,—consequently
equal to a *Conseiller Intime,* or any other distinguished
post whatever, abroad ; and superior to a mere titular
Lord who is nothing but by courtesy ; and here they
frequently fall foul of each other's family.'

' A German, or an Italian, who has no idea of the
importance of that rank, asks if they are all Gentlemen ; and is surprised to hear that that circumstance
is not requisite ; while he and all his countrymen are
perswaded that nothing but a long series of Family

Quarters ought to give admittance into the ante-chamber of an Arch or Great-Duke. In short, how-ever unjustifiable the prejudices on both sides may be, they are so widely different that I despair of giving satisfaction to those who are obstinately attached to them.'

Walpole laughed at Mann's distresses between ' your plaything Court and our travelling boys ; ' but he is disposed to side with the 'boys.' 'What is so insignificant,' he asks, 'as a Duke of Tuscany, and does his being a slip of Austrian pride make him a jot more important ? . . . An English member of Parlia-ment is part of the Legislature, and what is a Tuscan nobleman part of ? Has not that haughty Empress Queen been our pensioner ? In short I approve of bearding all other Courts, and particularly an Austrian one, for their ingratitude.'—Mann had expected to have the Duke of York again for his guest this year, but the Duke's 'silly, good-humoured, troublesome career,' as Walpole calls it, was brought to an end, by fever, at Monaco, in the month of September.

## 1768.

A fierce and deadly winter desolated Florence in the opening months of this year, and the peculiarly severe visitation was attributed to the German Grand Duke and his countrymen, who were accused of intro-ducing it with their German stoves. The Florentines recovered their spirits with the coming of May, but they had a short yet sharp alarm during that month of a near visitation of plague. 'We have been

alarmed,' Mann says, ' by the notice that the Plague
was on board a French ship at Leghorn, that had
brought thither from Tripoli a Minister from that
Bey designed for Holland. He, with his son and
five servants, were landed at the Lazzaretto, where
two of the latter died with the most manifest signs of
the Plague, and four others died on board the ships.
This induced our Regents to oblige those who were on
shore, to return on board, in order to send the Vessell
back to Tripoli, escorted by two Tartans, well armed.
They were to depart as yesterday. Few of them it is
believed will get thither, as the whole crew had the
most manifest signs of having that dreadful disorder.
Self-preservation only can justify the obliging those
who were in health on shore to return back to the
infected ship.'

For those who were ill from fright, or any other
cause, the Baths of Pisa were supposed to offer sovereign cure. This year they were crowded, first from
fright; but, in the autumn, from fashion. The Florentine Court led the way and loyal people with ' wanton
purses,' as Evelyn phrases it, followed suit. ' It will
be a most expensive jaunt,' remarks Mann, who felt
bound to be where the Court was, ' two or three
months at Pisa. They ask me a hundred zecchins for
an Appartment during the stay of the Court there ;
besides the transport of one's family and all household
necessaries !'

The Grand Ducal family was increased this year
by the birth of that little Duke Francis who lived to
be the last Emperor of the Holy Roman Empire, or of
Germany, and the first Emperor of Austria. ' The

Great Dutchess and Great Prince,' Mann tells his
friend, ' are perfectly well. The former has begun the
amusement of giving her hand from bed to be kissed
by the Ladies of the different Classes. Dame di Corte
the first day ; Dame del Zutritt the second day; and
then those of the Camera Zutritt. We don't yet know
what the words mean, but, in the high Court dress, we
saw them preceed the others.'

' On the Emperor's Birth-day and Name-day,'
(St. Joseph) ' the Great Duchess is to be *relevée de
ses couches.* The young Prince is to be invested on
that day with the Toison d'Or, with which the Secretary of that Order is on his way hither, from Vienna.
By this mark of distinction, they acknowledge him
to be the Heir of the House of Austria, to whom it is
given at their births. The other Arch-Dukes have it
only at twelve years old, but the Empress (dowager)
will be impatient for the Emperor's disinheriting him
again by a son of his own.'

All Italy was in pleasurable excitement at the
coming progress of the young Queen of Naples to her
new home. The Grand Duke and Duchess were to
accompany her on part of her way. ' The Pope and
Cardinal Albani (the younger) are much mortified
that they will not stop at Rome, nor at the Cardinal's
villa, as both had made expences for their reception.'
The cause was, the feud touching the Jesuits, and a
quarrel between the Pope and the Duke of Parma,
which exasperated the most Catholic sovereigns. The
Pontiff, in his right to rule morals as well as faith,
had claimed, or spoken of, the duchy of Parma, as his
own. The Parliament of Paris vigorously supported

the Duke against Rome. 'We don't know yet how
the Pope has received the news of it ; but we are
very sure, let his grief be what it will, he will console
himself with a good dish of Sturgeon, and leave the
rest to his Master, to whose hands he will remit the
Chastizement of the rebellious Princes of the Earth.
Too many, indeed, are joyned together for him to deal
with.'

Mann calls the affair ' a sad scrape for the Pope.
All the Bourbons have taken up the quarrel of the
Duke of Parma with incredible warmth. An Edict
which that Duke has lately published is equally strong
with the *Arrêt* of the Parliament of Paris.' This
edict, like the *Arrêt*, denounced an arrogant Brief
issued by Pope Clement XIII. The Ministers of
France, Spain, and Naples (the last a Cardinal), respectfully remonstrated with him with regard to the
Brief, 'but he declared that they might take Benevento, Castro, Ronciliogne, and Avignon from him,
nay, even Rome itself, but that he will never revoke
his Brief. The contempt that such a step would draw
on his Infallibility is probably the chief reason for
their insisting upon it, as well as of his refusal.' The
harshest counter-blow came from Spain, the Government of which Kingdom 'forbade the introduction
into Spain of any Brief, etc., etc., etc., from Rome,
on pain of death ; as such papers tend only to disturb the tranquility of Kingdoms and States, and to
dispute the Authority of the legal Sovereigns of
them.'

Mann states that the Duke of Parma was accused
by the Pope of committing acts that were prejudicial

to the rights of the Church, and publishing an Edict, 'by which the Duke forbids all his subjects, and even the Bishops, to apply to Rome, in any case whatever, without his leave ! This was touching to the quick. The Pope in wrath assembled his Cardinals and, with their advice, published the Brief, which he refused to revoke. In this Brief, he recapitulates all the injuries which that Infant of Spain had dared to commit *in Ducato nostro Parmansi;* and concludes by annuling the Duke's Edict, which he commands his Bishops and Clergy not to obey on pain, for all Laïcs, of whatsoever Dignity, of incurring all the censures contained in the Grand Bull of Excommunication, *In Cœnâ Domini.*' Such was the reply on the part of Rome to the act by which the Duke of Parma expelled the Jesuits,—to whom Rome granted shelter with a reluctance which almost amounted to denial.

While the dispute was raging, Florence was unusually gay with greeting and entertaining the Queen of Naples, the Grand Duke's sister. ' She is a most amiable little Queen, but it is feared that her extreme delicacy and good sense will only make her feel the more the want of both in her Royal Consort, whose deficiency in both has made many people interpret it as an organical defect approaching madness, on some occasions. But Lord Stormont assures me it proceeds totally from the want of Education ; and that he is now what many school boys are in England at ten years old. If so, the scandalous neglect may be repaired by his most excellently well-bred Queen, whose great propriety of behaviour and most sensible questions and replies raised admiration in every body.'

'The Duke of Parma went to make her a visit at Mantua, and among others of his Suite, presented to her his late Preceptor, "who had the care," said the Duke, " of my education." "And everybody says," was her reply, "that he may well be proud of it." It was really astonishing to see how well she held the Circle here in Florence. They will all set out on Tuesday towards Rome; which, however, they are not to enter. The Disturbances of the times and the Etiquette with the Cardinals would not permit them to gratify their curiosity in that respect. They are to stay at Ronciglione, on this side of Rome, and to pass on to Marino on the other.

' The King of Naples had ordered those Cardinals who were his subjects, to go to pay their Court to her; but a difficulty had been started about their dress. The Pope has ordered them to appear there in travelling costume (Abito Viatorio), but the Court of Naples has ordered them to go in their full dress. People are curious to see how this important point will be settled ; or, if not settled, how they will avert the personal resentment with which the Master of their Temporals has threatened them in case of disobedience. This little interlude employs people's attention in expectation of the great catastrophe, which is supposed to be suspended only till the young Queen is got safe home.'

The young Queen, with the Grand Duke and Duchess, went on her way rejoicing. It was a pathway of flowers, and the Italian enthusiasm and

hospitality.    One incident of the royal progress has
a comic aspect.   'They could not resist the temptation
to see Rome ; and therefore suddenly took the resolution to drive through it, taking all the principal
streets to St. Peter's where, only, they alighted.   They
were complimented on the part of the Pope by his
two secular Nephews, and were saluted three times
by the Castle of St. Angelo.   They afterwards dined
at Villa Borghese, and lay that night at Marino, from
whence they sent Prince Schwartzenberg, a *Chambellan*, to thank the Pope for his civilities.   The next
day, the Great Duke and Duchess went to see several
of the Villas at Frascati, and dined at another belonging to Prince Borghese.   The Queen was forced to
stay at Marino, to receive the homage of her new
subjects settled at Rome ; not the purpled ones, for
the Cardinals were all prohibited going there, on
account of the Etiquette in regard to their dress.'

'One does not know how to reconcile the above
civilities with the hostilities that were only to be
suspended till the Queen gets home.   The Bourbon
family are then to put their menaces against the Pope,
as a Temporal Prince, into execution.   Benevento will
be occupied by the Neapolitans, Castro and Ronciliogne for the Duke of Parma, and the French will
take Avignon.'

The royal progress through Italy had an unpleasant side to it.   'The Germans say the expense
of it will amount to a million and a half of Florins.
Then, the young Queen's going through Rome was
absolutely forbid by the three Courts ; but it will be
forgiven.   Not so with the Neapolitan Cardinals who,

not being permitted to go to Marino in *Abito Viatorio*,
alias, a frock, would not go there at all. This has
offended the King of Naples, who ordered his Minister,
Cardinal Orsini, who did go there, to assemble them
at his house, and read from a Royal despatch,—" that
the King might justly punish their disobedience, but
as he did not regard either their fidelity or their obsequiousness, his Majesty passed it over in silence." '

The Pope was pressed by France, Spain, and
Naples, to dismiss his secretary, Cardinal Torregiani,
but though the Cardinal would have resigned, Clement
bade him stick to the cause of the Church. The
Pontiff, however, was disgusted with the family
compact of the Bourbons. 'He seems so terrified
by it,' says Mann, in July, ' that he now begins to
relent. He has actually appointed four profound
Theologists to examine the case, and whether in conscience, he can revoke the Brief against Parma. It
is supposed that they will advise him to do it, and
that though there is little probability of his recovering
Avignon, or Benevento, in conscience he ought to
avoid other Evils that may befall the Church if he
persists in his obstinacy.'

Clement did persist, and found the Duke of
Modena added to his enemies, and the state of
Ferrara likely to pass from under Papal dominion to
that of the Duchy. His spirits, too, gave way—
' Literally, when the Pope is tired of shedding tears,
he tells his Crucifix : " It's your affair, now, to look
after your own Church." ' The Pope's affairs went out
of public notice in Italy, which was now exclusively
directed to the actions of the patriotic Paoli, who was

struggling to rescue the island of Corsica from the
French. The King of France declared in an edict,
'We have adopted this people among our subjects,
*avec complaisance,*' and he threatened fire and sword
against all Corsicans, who did not acknowledge the
adoption with equal amiability. 'The Great Duke is
too young to conceal his sentiments about this usurpation, and foresees all the bad consequences that may
ensue from it to his town of Leghorn; but he can do
no more than lament it. The Court of Vienna, while
Kaunitz reigns, will be Bourbon, and they are afraid
of disconcerting the match between an Arch-Duchess'
(Marie Antoinette) 'and the Dauphin, in the year
17—.'

Crowds of English wanderers of quality passed
through Mann's hospitable house and pretty gardens
during this year. There is little more recorded of
them than their names. A remark is added to that
of the invalid Lord Holland, to this effect:—' Lord
Holland has put Nice into great reputation by the
benefit he has received there.' This reputation has
continued to the present time. Some of the English
in Florence had character or oddity enough about
them to give opportunity to a caricaturist, Captain
Stewart, to take them off. 'He has made most
excellent Caricatures of most of our countrymen who
have passed by here, by their own desire, and in
societies.' Mann says of a friend and indweller with
him:—' Lord Stormont's health seems much impaired
by the deep melancholy that continually hangs upon
him, and even the pains which he takes to conceal it
seem to make it the greater afterwards. I have used

my utmost endeavours to keep him here for some
time ; as, independently of the infinite satisfaction
which I have in his company, I am persuaded that
the air and manner of living here would contribute to
the recovery of his health ; but he is determined to
set out next week, and intends to make a considerable
tour before he returns to Vienna.   This, perhaps, may
divert his melancholy for a time; but I fear it has
made too great an impression upon him, and that it
has essentially hurt his constitution.   We have crowds
of strangers here who are confined, for want of horses
to go away ' (this refers to the time when the young
Queen of Naples was on her way to the south), ' but
many of the English left this place before the Court
set out, in order to get to Naples before them.   Lord
Exeter has wrote to inform me that he intends to
return to Italy.   Lady Orford is preparing to go to
England, and for that purpose is expecting a ship
which Commodore Spry promised to send to Naples
to carry her to Marseilles, from whence, through
France, she will proceed to England, where she proposes to stay two months only and then return to
Nice or to Naples, where she has a most elegant house
both in town and country ; she has two here, likewise,
but there seems no probability of her ever returning
to reside in Tuscany.'

But, in or out of Tuscany, there was no happier
Englishman this year, than Sir Horace Mann.   He
now enjoyed the dignity of Envoy from his Britannic
Majesty to the Grand Duke of Tuscany ; and there
was at last forwarded to him, through Sir John Dick,
British Consul at Genoa, that red ribband, with the

other insignia of the Bath, for which he had sighed
long, striven hard, and, till this time, canvassed
vainly. His exulting letters to Walpole, written in
October, give full account of the ceremonial of investiture.

*Florence, October* 18*th.*—' I have but barely time
to acknowledge the receipt of your letter, dated the
22d past, and to acquaint you that Sir John Dick
with my cap and feathers are all arrived safe, of
which the Great Duke having been informed has
appointed fryday to put it on with the same ceremony
as was observed by the King of Sardinia when he
invested Lord Carlisle, which is the same as that
when the Great Duke invested his newborn babe
with the *Toison* in the name of the Emperor. You see
what great names I quote on this occasion. I am
going to dine with Count Rosenberg' (the successor of
Marshal Botta), 'with Sir John and Lady Dick, to
settle with them some other points relating to it, of
all which you shall be immediately informed when
the ceremony is over. The Italians expect a great
deal on this occasion, and it has so happened that the
extraordinary number and great rank of the English
here at present, many of whom have stayed on
purpose, will make my cortege or procession to Court
that morning most brilliant. I should not be surprised to hear that the windows were paid as dear
as for a house, and all through the streets I am to be
*en attelage*, which with my Gala liveries that were
new for the Queen of Naples' passing here, make a
very decent figure, especially when the sun shines upon
them. The Duke of Devonshire will condescend to

accompany me thither; Earl Cowper, Earl Tylney, Lord Algernon Percy, Lord Fortrose, Sir William Watkin W. Wynne, Sir Gregory Turner, and at least thirty more English Gentlemen all as fine as the richest Peers. There will be a ball here on Saturday, and Lord Tylney has for this fortnight past been preparing a Dinner bigger than his house will hold, and a greater expense in new laced Cloaths for a crowd of upper servants than anybody but himself could afford; but if I go on I shall leave nothing for the description of this Lord Mayor's Show afterwards.'

*Florence, October 25th.*—'The Ceremony was performed by the Great Duke on fryday last with all the marks of respect on his part for the King, whom he then represented, and with all the decency, nay, show, that we (I mean myself and a numerous body of English, many of whom of the highest rank) could exhibit on this occasion. The Gazette will inform you of the particular circumstances, which would be needless even if I had time to repeat, but you must still excuse my Vanity, which has guided me in all this, and which indeed I have not attempted to conceal, if I add that the whole town has expressed a satisfaction on this occasion that has flattered that Vanity extremely, and that the English have done everything they could to show their respect to the King, by honouring his Minister on this occasion. The Sun, as I told you in my last was necessary, shone on our equipages the day of the procession, and crowds of spectators were assembled to see it pass. I gave a great dinner at two tables, one of thirty covers, the other ten or twelve, to all the English and the great officers of the Court who had acted any part in the ceremony ; and the next evening I gave a publick Ball to everybody who would come. Next day, Sunday, Lord Tylney gave a dinner still bigger, the best and most magnificent I ever saw, and so said those of the Court who were there ; he dressed all his upper servants in new laced cloaks. The Desert was very fine built on the occasion, and charged with the Ensigns of the Order, with Trophies and Emblems which Lord Tylney's good nature induced him to place there. Yesterday many of us dined at Court, and in the evening Lord Cowper had Alexander's Feast, by Handel, performed at his villa, about a mile from the town, and it was followed by a Ball. To-day, Sir W. W$^{m.}$ Wynne gives a great dinner at a country house belonging to the master of the Inn where he lodges (as ladies could not go to this latter), which is to be followed by a great concert of Musick and a Ball in the evening. This great compliment is the more extraordinary, as I had not the honour to know Sir Watkin till a few days ago ; and I must add too my obligations to the Duke of Devonshire on this occasion, for having stayed many days longer here than he intended, to assist at this Ceremony, and to honour me by his presence at it. To-morrow, there is to be likewise a national dinner at Count Rosenberg's on this occasion, and our Colony is increased by the arrival yesterday and the day before of Lord (*illegible*) with a family, Mr. Neville, and Mr. F. (*illegible*). I shall be glad when all the bustle is over as I must then prepare for Pisa, which is no small embarassment, and will be horridly expensive.'

# CHAPTER IX.

## 1769.

MANN'S first extant letter of this year is dated from
Pisa, where the Grand Duke and his Court resided
during several months of the year.   Leopold preferred Pisa to Florence.   ' I never saw your residence,
Pisa,' says Walpole, ' but have a notion that it is
a charming place ; but how German, to take an
aversion to Florence, the loveliest town upon earth !
Has your little Prince no eyes for pictures, statues,
buildings, prospects ?   Where could one like to reign
if not there ? '   The Grand Duke detested Florence ;
he affected to think the Florentines insincere, and
despised the nobles for their poverty.   The Florentines in their turn detested Pisa.   Mann writes
dolorous pages of the ruinous expense to which he
was subjected by his having to follow the Court in
its migrations.   ' Were the Pisans,' says the Envoy,
' either more lively, learned, or meritorious in any
respect than the Florentines, there would be some
excuse for the Great Duke's preference ; but, a more
clumsy, insignificant race of people is in no other
part of Tuscany.'

The great event in Italy, in the early part of the

year, was the death of Pope Clement XIII. 'It was
'à propos,' says Mann, in February. 'The Jesuits,
however, thunderstruck by the event, suddenly took a
resolution by every means in their power to prevent
the consequences of it, and so managed matters that
they were well nigh making a Pope devoted to their
interests, on the second day of the balloting. The
cabal was discovered a very little time before it was
to have been executed, and the choice was to have
been either Ghigi or Tentuzzi. Cardinal Corsini
spoke high in the Conclave, and showed his brethren
the dangers of such a complot. The French Ambassador said publickly, that if they alone made a
Pope of their own, they alone would engage him.
By which he gave them to understand that such a
step would infallibly produce a schism ; and Cardinal
Orsini, the Neapolitan Minister, came to the door of
the Conclave, and said aloud (to those outside) that
he had great news to give Rome—which was, that
the Pope was *not* made. This mine having failed the
Jesuits, there seems to be no danger of any other, but
that the Inspiration of the Holy Ghost will wait for
the arrival of the foreign Cardinals, and will be
guided by the dictates of their Courts. I greatly pity
the poor old Cardinals, who will be confined so long,
and who must twice a day play at chusing a Pope,
though their only care must be not to chuse one by
inadvertency.'

While the issue was pending a curious incident
occurred. The Emperor Joseph and his brother, the
Grand Duke, were in Rome in the month of March;
'and though,' says our Envoy, 'he observes the strictest

incognito, the Romans are quite mad to see their
King' (Leopold was Rex Romanorum), 'whom they
greet under that name.     The Cardinals sent him
Guards and Deputations, which he refused; but they
received him in the conclave and shewed him their
method of Balloting, and made a Mock Election for
his amusement.' This elicited Walpole's justifiable
sarcasm : 'I delight in the mock election of a Pope,
made to amuse Cæsar! How the Capitol must blush at
such a Cæsar and such an entertainment!'

The Romans were, at all events, not ashamed of
their 'Rex Romanorum.'     Nothing, according to
Mann, could exceed or even equal 'the magnificence
of the entertainments given by the Nobility of Rome
to the Great Duke, of which the Emperor partook.
That of Prince Doria surpassed them all.   He converted the great court of his Palace (formerly *Pamfili*)
into a spacious Hall, by raising a floor level with the
Appartments round it.   Many of the windows were
cut down and became doors into it.   They say it cost
ten thousand Zecchins' (about five thousand pounds).

On May 23rd, Mann begins his letter with a shout:
'Habemus Pontificum Maximum! This son of a
Tinker (*Caldorajo*) at a village called St. Angelo, in
Vado, in the Duchy of Urbino, and a Monk of a
branch of the Franciscan Order called *Minor Conven-
tuale*, I don't know what that is in English; his name
was Ganganelli, but he has assumed that of Clement
XIV., in honour of his immediate predecessor, by
whom he was made Cardinal in 1759.   He has many
Nephews by both Brothers and Sisters, who exert the
meanest Imployments; one is a fiddler at Rome; one

a monk here in Florence, who fell into fits upon receiving the news, and remained out of his senses the whole day. A very near relation to His Holyness is a Coachman to the Great Duke.'

Cardinal Ganganelli ' always lived in the Cell of his Convent at Rome in the most private manner, having no more to keep his Court with than the *Piatto*, as Cardinal, of 3000 crowns from the Apostolick Chamber. He was always much embarrassed with his Attendants, and used to say that he wished Quegli Signori would not give themselves the trouble to wait on him ; but that he would send for them when he went out. He never would be of any Congregation, not to be of any party ; by which it is thought that he had long had an eye to the *Triregno*. His brethren of the Convent of Santa Croce say that he was a most troublesome *Frataccio* when he lived among them, and has never done them any good while he was Cardinal.'

' It is said the choice is most acceptable to the Bourbon Ministers as, in common with all other Monks and Friars, he is a natural Enemy to the Jesuits, and that the secret conditions of his Election are—the destruction of that Order, and a total compliance with all that the Bourbon Courts have been contending for. Much indeed is expected from him. Many, they say, had not courage to accept of it on such conditions. He has made choice of a very prudent man for his Secretary of State, Cardinal Palavicini, who has been Nuncio in Spain and Naples ; a very polite man, and who will not personally offend the Courts by a rough inflexibility as Torregiani did. Upon the whole, people seem rather inclined to believe that by the *Fourberie* of Fra Ganganelli, with the knowledge of his Minister, means may be found out to accommodate matters with less *strepito* than could be done in the last reign, as both master and man were biassed by their own personal inclinations and engagements.'

On June 14th, Walpole thanked Mann for the history of the Pope and his genealogy, or rather for what is to be his genealogy ; 'for,' says Walpole, ' I suppose all those tailors and coachmen, his relations, may now found noble families.' Mann, pursuing this subject, says : ' Since the Pope's exaltation, they have found out a better origin for his family ; for, though they declare that the decision of the Holy Ghost makes all objects equal, they are nevertheless inwardly persuaded that Nobility adds to the dignity of His choice. However, most people agree that in point of personal qualifications, there were none better. He has already discovered a particular desire to be well with the foreign Courts, and has received their Ministers most affably. He has made few changes in his own, but those are very judicious. He has not clearly explained himself about the Jesuits, but he has removed the late Secretary of Briefs to Foreign Princes, who was notoriously devoted to them ; and he has spontaneously declared to the Spanish Minister, that he will re-assume, tho' Pope, the canonisation of Palifox, which cause was formerly entrusted to him by Spain, though, by the credit of the Jesuits (Palafox's persecutors), it was laid aside in the last reign. Do but imagine the suspension of a Saint at the door of Paradise by the Cabals at Rome ! Oh ! they will continue to make Popes as long as the Princes of the Earth allow that they can make Saints.'

*June 27th.*—'The Pope goes on very prudently. All parties seem convinced of his prudence and moderation ; and such confidence will enable him to bring things to a better conclusion than more hasty measures.'

*July 22nd.*—'He does not attempt to deceive the Jesuits themselves. The distinguished coldness with which he has received their General, and the tranquility of their Enemies, seem to denote a concerted plan for the suppression of the Order which, as a Mendicant Friar, he never loved, and, as Pope, he will not venture to support in opposition to so many potent Sons of the Church.' France, Spain, and Portugal had declared that the existence of the Society was incompatible with the safety of any Government, and they put such pressure on the Pontiff that little doubt existed as to the course he would take. Ganganelli took precautions also :—'He has shown some indications of apprehension of their' (the Jesuits') 'attempt to prevent his design, and is extremely cautious of what he eats ; and trusts nobody to prepare it but his faithful *Laïco* who served him in his Convent. He has altered all the locks of the private Accesses to his Appartments ; and from the tranquil security of a Mendicant Friar Cardinal in his Cloister, is reduced under a triple crown to the anxiety of warding against the secret attempts of religious vengeance.'

Ganganelli took his own time and kept his own council. In November, Sir Horace writes :—'The Pope has neither dissolved the Society of Jesuits nor

relieved them from the fear of his doing it.    He gives
fair words to the Bourbon Courts, but they begin to
be displeased with the delay and to doubt of his
sincerity.    He begins, too, to lose ground in the
opinion of his Cardinals, but for a reason which
most others applaud,—his want of confidence in
them.    They have, by a deputation, even upbraided
him with it ; pretending to have a right to be consulted.    He answered, that he had been a Cardinal
many years, without being called upon ; and that,
though those who composed any Congregation were
tied by the strictest oath of secrecy, the most jealous
affairs that had been treated in it were always known
a quarter of an hour after.'

Interested as the orthodox Florentines were in these
ecclesiastical questions, there was a personal matter
which concerned them more nearly,—the coming of
the Emperor Joseph among them, in April.    They
expected to see him crowned, mantled, armed, and
all the old imperial grandeur about him.    This is
the fashion in which Joseph challenged the admiration of Firenze :—

*April* 15*th.*—' The Emperor arrived here *incognito*,
at noon day ; for though he passed through crowds of
people of all ranks, who went out to meet him, nobody
would believe that so great a Prince would make so
shabby an appearance.    His Coach, or rather an open
German Waggon, was so loaden with Matrasses (*sic*)
that the spectators took them for the *Fourriers* of the
Court who preceeded with the Baggage.    His dress is
as plain.    He always wears a military Uniform, without the Ensigns of any of his Orders.    The Great

Duke and Dutchess received him in Boboli' (part of the gardens of the Grand Ducal Palace), 'they soon after set down to dinner with the people of the Court who are always admitted. Had he come the day before, as was expected, I should have had that honour, having dined there with the other Foreign Ministers. The Emperor went to the Theater in the evening, in the coach with the Great Duke and Dutchess. He sat backwards, and in the Box took the lowest place. They went to Pisa yesterday ; and were to go to Leghorn this morning; where, for the first time, he will see a ship of war, though very small. We happen to have two Frigates there. The Great Duke has, likewise, a very pretty one, on board of all which he probably will go. They will hasten back to Florence, lest the Great Dutchess should be brought to bed, (her constant yearly custom) during their absence.'

*April* 29*th.*—'The Emperor seems quite happy in the enjoyment of his liberty, and has reformed all kinds of state both for himself and his brother. There are no Guards at the Imperiale ; and he often walks into town alone, or with only one servant, at a great distance behind him ; and has a key of the back door, near the Gate, into Boboli. He and his brother came last night to the Theater in a chaise and pair, without any attendants, and went back in the same manner, after the first dance. The old Germans at Vienna would faint away to see the Imperial Dignity so totally suspended !'

One of the reasons for the coming of the Emperor Joseph to Florence, was that he might be present at the inoculation of the Great Duke for smallpox. The

Empress-Queen had a horror of the disease which she herself had not escaped, and which had been fatal to several members of her family. She had almost an equal horror of inoculation. To this process, however, the Grand Duke submitted himself. ' The Emperor nurses him, which he does in the most assiduous and affectionate manner ; and will stay here till there is no room to doubt of the success of the Operation.'

Early in June, the kind-hearted Imperial nurse left Florence, ' highly pleased with the success of his Brother's Inoculation, which has been the mildest that Ingenhause has ever performed. The Italians were surprized to meet their Prince in all the lanes and highways near the Imperiale, and in all weathers, with the smallpox upon him, distributing zecchins to the Contadini who, for his want of a servant, helped him over a ditch or a hedge. This example, the Emperor was, however, the first to show him ; for he always rambled about the country alone ; and the people affected not to know him ;—their least instruction to him to turn to the right or the left, was rewarded with a zecchin.'

' The Emperor seemed to enjoy his liberty much, and to like Florence better than his Brother ; the *Exterior*, I mean, for neither has shown any great esteem for the fine things they possess. This friendly visit has increased the affection between the Brothers, and the birth of the last Prince has rivetted it. The Emperor told the Florentines, at the christening, that this Prince was their's ; and the Elder, his ; and he has often declared his intention of not marrying ; grounded on a spirit of Œconomy, and on the inutility

of it, as his Brother has a child every year ; and as
Princes cannot be biassed by a personal choice, it is
thought that he will not trust again to that of others
for an Empress.    His Mother has wrote a very
gracious letter to Dr. Ingenhause, telling him that
" after God, she owed her three sons to *him.*"    This
was accompanied by a present of two thousand
zecchins' (about a thousand pounds).    'Many have
been inoculated from the Great Duke, and all are in a
good way.    Many others about the town have under-
gone the same operation with equal success.'

The prominent figures among the English in Italy
this year were not many.    The chief was the fallen
Minister, Lord Bute, ill in health, reserved in manner.
In Naples, Rome, and in Florence, he lived in the
most private fashion ; never received visits, never
wore his Garter, and returned cards 'under the name of
Murray ; ' in some places, 'under the name of Stuart.'
He told Mann that if he visited Sicily, he would
certainly write to Mr. Walpole ('who was always his
friend') from Otranto, 'the scene,' says Mann, 'of
your charming novel,'—to which intimation the ruffled
author tartly rejoined, that 'Otranto is in the Kingdom
of Naples.'    Perhaps the most illustrious stranger
was Paoli, the patriot, on his way from Corsica to
England.    He kept stricter incognito than any other
traveller ; and the modest, brave man had only the
homage of a few, but those the best, as he passed.
Paoli's brother and fellow-soldier, the Monk Clemente,
was at Leghorn, 'with many of his friends.    Clemente
is a most extraordinary character ; so zealous of the
liberty of his country ! and so devout, that whenever

he took aim at an invader of it' (and Clemente was a famous shot) 'he recommended that invader's soul to God !   He is now seeking a retreat, either at Val Ombrosa, the Vernia, or some devout Dungeon.'

Mann himself had no worse grievance to chronicle than the serious one, that the expenses of supporting his dignity, reputation, and national honour, considerably exceeded his income ; but he looked for succour from the government.   His long residence in Italy was not without effect upon his opinions.   The infernal audacity of Wilkes, he suggests, would have been crushed by clapping him into prison ; and when he hears from Walpole an account of the follies of an unruly married English beauty, he exclaims: 'Such an abuse of liberty almost makes one an Advocate for Convents, or places where an Husband, with the consent of his relations on both sides, can either prevent or conceal the dishonour that a thoughtless young Creature may, with her own ruin too, bring upon them all !'   But the scandalous chronicle of Florence scarcely warranted the efficacy of the remedy for preventing or concealing the follies of 'unruly beauty !'

## 1770.

Since the Young Chevalier, on his knees before the Pope, in 1767, was contemptuously bidden to 'get up,' there is no further notice of the humiliated Prince till the August of 1770, in which year his figure stands out prominently in a brief scene, the most striking perhaps of the whole year ; and which may therefore claim precedence.

*August* 21*st.*—' My ministerial attention is exerted to its full strength in observing the motions of a person who, since I deprived him of " Majesty," has no constant name.   Baron Douglas ; Count Renfrew ; and now, in the tour he is making, Count Albany. He came here, on Thursday last, from Senigaglia, and is lodged at a publick Inn ; not that of the English, as you will easily believe.   He wears the Garter, with the Cross of St. Andrew at his button-hole.   The Government shows him no distinction, but the Nobility of both Sexes visit him, and he returns the attention.   He goes to the Casino, and to the Theater ; and makes visits to the Ladies in their Boxes.   The one which he makes use of is contiguous to mine. He says that he intends to stay at Pisa some time, to make use of the Baths in that neighbourhood. . . .'

'. . . Saturday morning, early.   Having written so far last night, I went late to the Theater, where I received an invitation from the Lucchese Envoy, to go late this Evening to a Concert at his house, which he gives to a Roman Lady, for whom I had made two Conversazioni.   I was dubious whether I should accept the Invitation, not doubting but Count Albany would be there ; and He, supposing the same with regard to me, ordered a Count Spada, who is with him, to desire a Lady to fish out of me whether I actually intended to go or not.   She used no mystery, but told me plainly that if I went, *he* certainly would not ; and that he was impatient to know my answer. I therefore desired her to say, that being uncertain whether my presence might be indifferent to him, I would abstain from going.   Did I do right ?   I don't

know whether the English gentlemen and ladies who
are here will follow my example—though that is very
indifferent.'

Of a King *de facto*—the King of Spain—Mann
gives a curious detail.  Walpole had alluded to him
as one who on leaving a room which was lined with
tapestry, among the figures on which was that of a
horse, always raised his leg, as if he were about to
ride.  'Long ago, when he was at Florence, as
Great Prince of Tuscany, and lodged in the Palazzo,
he amused himself by shooting with a bow and
arrow at the Birds in the fine Tapestry-hangings
of his rooms, and was become so very dextrous
that he seldom missed the Eye he aimed at.  John
Gaston' (the Grand Duke) 'was much displeased
when he was told how sadly his precious meubles
of the Gobelins were treated by the expertness
of his Pupil; so that, the first time the young
Prince went out, orders were given to remove the
Tapestry and to put up Damask with gold fringe and
lace in the place of it.  When the young Sportsman
returned home, both he and his Spanish Court were
surprised and even offended to see so great an alteration; but John Gaston sent him word that, as the
weather was growing warmer, he was fearful that the
Prince's health might have suffered by the heat of
the winter furniture.  He was forced to accept of the
excuse, but lamented much the loss of his amusement.
He had recourse to another invention whilst he lay
in bed, with the small-pox, at Leghorn.  His Pages
used to fix little hooks to fine threads or wires that
hung down unobserved in different parts of the

room, which were all fastened to a sort of a bell
rope within his bed; which hooks, when properly
baited by the sly Pages, with the wigs of his
Courtiers, he with a sudden jerk, drew them up
to the top of the room. Mr. Skinner, then Consul
there — the most rediculous dressing creature I
ever saw—was often served so. He commonly wore
his own hair, which was black; but on very great
occasions, he put on a white wig, with four tails and
a vast deal of powder over his black locks.'

Assuredly, the Bourbon Kings and Princes of
that day had strange ideas of amusement. 'The last
letters from Naples,' says the Envoy, 'brought the
Great Duke and the Publick an account of a most
wanton piece of cruelty that the King of Naples had
caused to be exercised on two Florentine Cavalieri,
and personally very deserving men, by tossing them in
a blanket, at his Camp at Portici, in the presence of
the whole Court and thousands of spectators. Bonechi,
the Great Duke's Agent there, has asserted in his
letter, that he was to have been served so too, but
luckily, he was not there. This is worse than shooting tapestry birds, or thrashing tapestry horses.'

Florence afforded no such lively amusements.
Mann, referring to the occasional dull Court balls
given usually for the Nobility, notes, as seemingly an
incident of noble balls only, that there was 'a Supper
for the *whole* company; after which, they dance
again, as long as the Great Duke chuses, for when
he retires the whole is at an end. The Great Dutchess
is only a Spectator. . . . She is not permitted to
dance. In this situation, she has been to every

Carnival since her marriage, by which she promises
to provide a numerous succession for the House of
Austria. This circumstance and many personal good
qualities make her the idol of that family.' Among
the guests occasionally was Count Orloff, 'a very
principal agent in the late Revolution at Petersburg.
. . . He positively asserts that the catastrophe of it
was not brought about by violent means, but that
Peter the 3rd died of despair and drink.' With equal
positiveness, the officers of the Russian fleet in the
Mediterranean, whom Mann encountered and entertained at Leghorn or Florence, asserted, with an
uniformity which seemed made to order, that there
was nothing in the alleged murder of Peter, but what
was perfectly natural, quiet, and proper.

The Great Ducal Court was vastly amused this
year by an illustration of the power of Spain in a
matter of etiquette. 'The King of Naples gives great
Balls at Caserta, and to eat, too; but as, by a most
rigorous order from Spain, he cannot admit people to
his Table; he has no Table at all. He and his Queen,
as well as the whole company, eat off their knees; a
strange and very slovenly way of serving a great
supper. His sister, at Pisa, and the Great Duke
there, are not under the same control on Ball Nights.
They admit as many as their Tables will hold; the
rest of the Company sit at another.'

'The Great Duchess, here, still holds out; she is
very impatient to be brought to bed, that she may
be in time to be at Venice, for the Assention, in her
way to Vienna.' The annual domestic incident not
coming off as was expected, 'The Great Duke and

Dutchess,' we are told, in June, 'set out for Vienna, on Sunday evening. The Emperor has taught them so well to despise grandeur on these occasions, that they really travelled *en Bourgeois*; none but their own Coach, with two servants on the Coach-box, and a single man on horseback, to announce them at the Post-houses. Just as they were setting out, the Accoucheur had orders to attend, and he followed after in a two-wheel, two-horsed chaise, and must, with the help only of the Grande Maitresse, have administered any assistance that had been necessary.'

Florence was left without its rulers till November, and then 'the Court returned here and surprized everybody in their beds. They arrived at break of day, though they had ordered their supper late. Two days after, being the Great Duke's birthday, there was a *Baciamano* and a Gala, for that and their return; since which everything has fallen into its usual channel.'

At Rome, too, everything was in its usual channel. Clement XIV. is described as 'cunning and temporizing,' but Ganganelli made one step towards a desired and salutary end. 'His Holiness' (February 20th), 'has given the Jesuits a strong mark of his displeasure, and his little inclination to support the Society, by depriving them of the direction of a Great Seminary at Frescati, worth a few hundred crowns a year; but more valuable for the number of youths it yearly attached to their Society; and what fell out unlucky for them was, that the Pope addressed his Bull for this purpose to Cardinal Yorke, Bishop of Frescati, hitherto their greatest friend and protector,

who for many years past, has, out of charity, given
them five hundred crowns a month.'

*May* 12*th.*—'The Bourbon Ministers at Rome
begin to awaken again from their slumber. Their
Courts only meant to give the Pope time to look
about him ; but they now suspect that he has interpreted their complaisance as a mark of desisting from
their pretension. They have therefore begun their
attack again. The King of Spain has lately wrote to
the Pope in harsh terms, and says that it is the last
time he will write to him on the subject. Cardinals
Orsini, Bernis, and Almada have all renewed the
demands of their Courts to suppress the Order of
Jesuits. The Pope's whole behaviour has justified
your opinion that he would never willingly consent
to part with the Jannisaries of the Church. He is
cunning, and might hope, by protracting it, to ward
off the blow ; and that, by some fit of Devotion, the
Princes might be satisfied by some considerable reformation of the Order. The conduct he receives from
the whole College of Cardinals for his total want of
confidence in any of them, makes him perceive that he
has carried the neglect of them too far ; in short, he
is made uneasy on all parts ; he has lost his rest
and appetite, for the recovery of which he was
blooded a few days ago.'

In this year, when Sir John Dick, the Consul at
Leghorn, had some hopes of being appointed a Com-
missioner of Trade, and of returning home, Mann
says, with a touch of natural melancholy, '*I* have
no such hopes. I know nobody there, excepting
you ; nor can I flatter myself that anybody else would

wish to see me there.  I should be quite a stranger
even in my own family ; and I have always been
treated by them as such.   Then, the length of the
journey, the great expenses of it, the change of
climate at my age, and the danger of being looked
upon as a superannuated creature for whom a small
pension might be thought more proper, in order to
make room for the son of some necessary man !
These reflections terrify me ; though I must still own
that the Amor Patriae will not permit me totally to
lay aside the thought of seeing it again.'

With one exception, there is little to be said of the
English this year, who came within what Mann, as
British Envoy, called his jurisdiction.   ' We have,' he
says, ' a quondam Beauty here, Lady Hesket, a relation of Lord Cowper, and like him inclined to make a
long stay.   Lord and Lady Sudley have been the
winter at Pisa, and lately here.   She was a favourite
with the Dutchess, and her companion at Whist ;
though she left off when she pleased, and even
refused the Royal invitation when engaged to another
party.'

The British subject of exceptional note was Smollett.
The author of 'Roderick Random,' stricken by mortal
illness, and yet eager to live, was then lodged at Pisa
before he took up his dwelling on the slopes near
Leghorn, which looked on to the sea, from the sight
and air of which he hoped to catch some straw of
comfort if not of hope.   All the less amiable qualities
of the able but impracticable man had died before
him.   The once fierce spirit of the struggler in the
battle for life had been quenched ; and in a chastened

mood, Smollett, as he sat in the cheering spring sun, finished the last and, in many respects, perhaps the best of his novels,—which are anything but works of fiction,—that immortal 'Humphrey Clinker,' the story of which is told in a succession of letters, to not one of which is there an answer.—Mann had just read the then famous pamphlet, 'The False Alarm.' Our Envoy thought that in its moderation and just reasoning there was to be found 'the best method to confute the seditious Junius, and to destroy the effects of his daring Insolence with everybody but the Mob, who cannot be reclaimed by what they cannot read.'

'I was at Pisa,' adds Mann, 'when that paper came in. I sent to Smollett, the author, who is settled there for his health. He approved much of both the stile and the method of treating the subject. He seemed persuaded that Johnson was the author of it. I know how delicate a point the Liberty of the Press is thought to be in England, therefore, with all possible diffidence, I ask whether the licentious abuse that is now made of it would not justify a law which would prohibit the publication of anything without the name of the author. Everything really meant for the good of the Publick might still be conveyed to it—Calumny and Sedition only would be excluded.'

'An Italianized Englishman is worse than the devil!' so says the Italian proverb. Mann was somewhat Italianized. The Florentines were astounded when they heard of the impunity of Wilkes; and Mann agreed with them, that the squinting tribune of the

people deserved to be put out of sight in a dungeon.
The true English sentiment, however, keenly survived in him. Junius, who, safe under a pseudonym,
assailed the foremost men of his day, and probably the
man who had been his benefactor, above all, was, in
Mann's eyes, the most odious of cowards. Referring
to the mutual recriminatory publications of Wilkes
and Horne Tooke, Mann remarks:—' I like, however,
their setting their names to their accusations, recrimi-
nations, and invectives, and heartily wish that the
Liberty of the Press was reduced to the exclusion
of everything that the authors have not courage to
avow.'

## 1771.

Mann opens this year with a long letter from Pisa,
January 14th, in which he puts a great disaster into
a postscript. ' I left Florence,' he says, ' the day of
a severe shock of an earthquake, which was so
transitory that it did not give time to the people
to be much frightened ; but all last week at Leghorn,
frequent shocks have been felt which have so terrified
the inhabitants that few remain in the town; thousands have gone into the country ; many on board
the ships in the Mole, others sleep in boats on the
canals, and many in their coaches upon the Place.
The most essential damage will probably arise from
the hurt people will receive in their healths, for the
buildings have suffered very little as yet ; but, as
formerly in London, a Trooper prophesied the total
ruin of the Town, so an old woeman has announced the

fall of Leghorn as this day. I am now listening to
hear the Crash. It is astonishing to see the different
effects of fear ; and nothing is so sure as that Reason
never avails but when every other passion subsides.
Patroles were stationed in the streets to prevent some
outrageous rogues from robbing the houses that have
been abandoned. I have at last induced Sir John and
Lady Dick to leave such a scene of horror, where they
were surrounded by objects that inspired terror. They
are now here with many others. Hitherto we, at
Pisa, have not felt any Earthquake, but we are in
danger of being drowned by the incessant rains that
have ruined the whole country.'

The year was one of acute distress in Italy as in
England and great part of Europe. 'This winter,'
says Mann, in February, 'all France, Germany, and
Italy have been under water. It is calculated that
a fifth part of Tuscany, this year, on that account,
remains uncultivated.' Mann complains, later, of the
setting severely in of the Italian spring, as Walpole
does of the English summer. 'I write to you from
the fireside,' is his April account from Florence, 'and
yet I am cold ; never did Italy see such weather, so
late in the year. Pisa was fully as bad the last week.
The snow covered the streets, and I was covered with
it, till showers of hail washed it off, the whole journey
from thence.'

Mann was not so cold in February but he could
speak warmly of Patch, the English artist at Florence,
who has been already noticed by Sir Horace. 'He is
really a genius, and all his productions have merit.
In his youth he studied Chemistry, and lived some

time with Dr. Mead. About twenty years ago, he came a-foot in Italy, with Dalton, who is since grown so great a man.' . . . 'Patch went directly to Rome and studied painting under Vernet, whose manner he imitates very well; a specimen of which I will send you in *Due Sopraporte*, if you give me the measure, or chuse any particular view of Florence. He left Rome many years ago, on account of some indiscretion about Religion; but nevertheless, he brought the strongest letters of recommendation hither, from the unprejudiced Prelate Piccolomini, then Governor of Rome, and since Cardinal. I took much to him, and tho' he does not live in my house, he is never out of it a whole day. He has an excellent turn for *Caricatura*, in which the young English often employ him to make Conversation-pieces of any number, for which they then draw lots; but Patch is so prudent as never to caricature any body without his consent and a full liberty to exert his talents.'

'Many of Patch's Conversation-pieces are in England, but the most conspicuous is one he did by the Duke of York's command, the subject of which was the Duke's departure from my house. I am told that it is now at Gloucester House; it is very large, and every figure, both noble and ignoble, is from life (and by the Duke's order), a list of whom is in the hands of a Publick Cryer (who is supposed to be pub-lishing a Proclamation), with the numbers referred to (in small) under each figure. But a picture of this kind must necessarily loose its principal merit, by the persons being unknown. A year or two ago, Patch

took to engraving, of himself, without the least assistance, and by a sort of a Careless manner, is allowed
by everybody here to enter into the character of the
Author.   He was always an adorer of the heads of
Masaccio in Carmine, and both drew them and
engraved them himself; and well he did it in time,
for about a fortnight ago, the Church was almost consumed by fire, and those paintings so much damaged,
that I believe none remain entire.   The Church had
been three years repairing, and, as there were Gilders
and other workmen, the accident must have been
owing to their negligence, tho' it is not yet known.   The
body of St. Andrea Corsini, which laid in a very fine
Chappel of that family, was saved at the risk of the life
of a servant who rescued it from the flames.   All the
Sepulchres took fire and burnt for many days.   What
pestilential air do the devout breathe in Churches! but
the loss of Masaccio's paintings will in some measure
be repaired by a work Patch has in hand, in which
there will be the celebrated pictures of Fra Bartolomeo,
at St. Mark's, with others of Michel Angelo, Andrea
del Sarto, etc., etc., to make up the number of 24.
This is now in hand, and your · encouraging and
recommending it would be very advantageous to him.
It will be distributed by his Brother, Mr. James Patch,
Surgeon, in Norfolk Street, who sells his Masaccio,
but he believes they are all disposed of.'

   Mann believed in the power of English Artists, as
he did in the long-living beauty of English women.
The latter fact reminds him of a pretty compliment
which Voltaire paid to a lady, on her hundredth
birthday.

' Nos Ayeux vous ont vu belle,
  Vous plaisez à cent ans ;
  Vous meritiez d'épouser Fontenelle ;
  Et de le survivre long temps.'

' None of our Italian Ladies merit, after the flower of their youth, such compliments. It is astonishing how soon they are excluded from all Society but that of their Maids and Priests. Even the Suares, whom you may remember handsome, is now horrible. No single trace of that extreme beauty which enamoured such a succession of our Countrymen, which I suppose may account for such a total alteration.'

On the other hand the claims of ' our Countrymen' to take rank at the Courts of Italy, were very stringently examined before they were allowed. This was more particularly the case at Venice, whose magnates refused to receive any ambassador who came without proofs of his nobility. ' That haughty Republick absolutely rejected Mr. Stanhope, Lord Chesterfield's natural son, for a Resident, and at the present King's accession, insisted on a Peer of England being sent thither as Ambassador, instead of a Commoner of much higher birth, who had been named.'

The little Court of Tuscany was bound to observe severe rules of etiquette by the law in force at Vienna, but the two brothers, Emperor and Grand Duke, equally hated the constraint ; and loved to shake it off. Half the year Leopold and his Duchess spent at Pisa, and the foreign envoys had to follow them. ' He fancies that he enjoys his liberty more there, and he

has likewise a view of recovering this part of his Dutchy
from the abject poverty it has so long grovelled under,
by spending part of his money here ; and indeed the
Inhabitants seize his idea perfectly well, for everything
is more than one third dearer than at Florence.    I am
quite ruined in double house rent, and many other
additional expenses.    More is expected of the Foreign
Ministers, in a publick way, than at Florence, and I
am now returning there to feast the English.'

In the absence from Florence of the Grand Ducal
couple, Prince Corsini (who had succeeded Count
Rosenberg, the successor of Richecourt and Botta),
remained in Florence, 'doing the honours of the
Court ; that is, to keep a table on Gala Days, and to
entertain strangers ; for which article he has a separate
allowance of six thousand crowns, besides his appointments of Maggior Domo Maggiore of the Great
Dutchess.    Count Rosenberg has left great debts,
which I believe he expected the Empress would pay,
because she had done it twice before, in Denmark and
Spain, but she was not so disposed now, so that the
Sale of his Effects (Plate and Jewels included) must
suffice as far as it will go, to satisfy the Butcher and
Baker and other such Creditors to the amount, they
say, of $\frac{m}{24}$ crowns.'

One item of Mann's expenses came under the
head of 'presents' to Court Ladies of his acquaintance,
on their marriage.    Here is an instance.    'Will you
give me leave to trouble you with a Commission to
buy four fans for me to give to a very great and
fine young Lady who is going to be married to the
Lucchese Envoy here ?    She is the daughter of my

Cicisbea, Madame Minabelli. The Envoy has given a commission to Sir John Dick, to send for four fans, Indian, or such as are called so in England, by all means; but I think he has limited the price of the best to 4 zecchins . . . . and the others, inferior; now, I must outdo his; therefore, must have them of the newest fashion, as well as the handsomest that can be had of the sort I am speaking of.' Much writing to and fro had to be done before this commission was happily executed, and the beautiful so-called Indian fans were in the hands of the delighted bride. From such elegant trifles, our Envoy's attention was soon diverted to the inexplicable doings of ' Count d'Albany,' — one of the names under which the humiliated and degraded Charles Edward kept the very small dignity which he was able to sustain.

The once young Chevalier mystified those who thought him still worth watching, by ' an elopement.' ' On the 12th of August, a packet of letters was delivered to him, to set out that afternoon; though it is supposed that he did not confide the secret to any one but his old Valet de Chambre; and to disguise it the better, he went out of the town of Siena (where, since he had quitted Pisa, he had resided for some weeks) in his own Coach, and at the distance of half a mile, a common two wheel chaise was waiting for him, in which he went to the first Post, from whence he sent orders to his people at Siena to return to Rome. He changed his Cloaths and arrived at the Gates of Florence, at midnight, gave the name of Smith there, changed horses at the Post House without getting out of his Chaise, and proceeded to Bologna, where, to avoid being known, whilst he changed horses, he kept a Handkerchief constantly at his mouth, tho' he was detained a long while, and was in some danger of being hurt by the Shaft horse falling three times. Still, he never got out, for fear of being known. He proceeded to Modena, but that decided nothing as to the road he was to take. The general conjecture is, though no kind of proof or authority is quoted for it, that he is going to Poland (at the instance of the Confederates), to be a Pretender to that Crown, too. To give some colour to this conjecture, it is supposed that Princess Jablonowsky, a Polish Jacobite, who was two years ago sent into England by the Confederates (though she was refused an audience as their Ambassadress), settled all this matter last year with him, at Rome.'

'This elopement may excite a curiosity in England but, I think, cannot give any alarm; as it is not at all probable that any great Power interests itself at present for him, or would quarrel with England on his account. Neither can any one well suppose that he himself would at his time of life, and almost lethargic by wine, enter on so boisterous a scene as that of disputing the Crown of Poland,—at a time too that, in all probability, the Confederates will not be able to hold out long, for want of support from the Turks.'

*September* 17*th*.—'You will laugh at me perhaps for being solicitous about so pitifull an object as the Pretender now is, but though advanced in years, and either drunk or fast asleep, he still may be made use of to do mischief. He was traced to the foot of the Alps, since which we have had no notice of him. It is still uncertain whether he is gone into France or, to put up for King in Poland. The latter is still the favourite opinion in these parts. It is certain that the Cardinal, his Brother, evaded the question that was made to him by another great Porporato, by saying, "God prosper him! but he should have taken this resolution last year." This, like all other oracles, only serves to give an air of importance and to increase the doubt. Cardinal Bernis, at Rome, and the other French Ministers in these parts, speak of this journey with a seeming frankness, and declare their ignorance of the object of it; and indeed one cannot well suspect that France, at so critical a juncture in her domestic concerns, when their King is so near fixing an absolute despotism, would enter into any Imbroils that might imped the execution of his design.'

In October, the projectless Wanderer was in Genoa, where the Duke of Gloucester was then temporarily residing. 'The Duke of Gloucester and the Count d'Albany met "full Butt" in the streets of Genoa. They bowed most graciously to each other. The latter is returned to Rome where, not only by the Cardinals and Nobility, but even by the common people, he was hooted at, for having made much mystery of so insignificant a journey.' Mann ends the painful record, in December, by saying:—'The Pretender is now in Rome, getting drunk every day, and quarrelling with the new companions he brought

with him from France.  His personal character contributes as much as anything else to a total neglect
of him.  The Polanders could never make anything
of such a log as this, though their Minister at Rome
liberally sent an Express to Warsaw, to warn that
unhappy King' (Stanislaus II.) 'of his being gone
thither.  The Pope has sent a most cordial invitation
to the Duke of Gloucester to go to Rome, and has
ordered his Nuncio to be assiduous in paying his
Court to him here in Florence.'

The Duke of Gloucester, brother of George the
Third, was then 'on his travels,' accompanied by his
wife (ex-dowager Lady Waldegrave), who was not
yet acknowledged as such by her husband.  The
Duke was then thirty-two years of age ; he was a
brave soldier, without military talent, and a good
man, without any ostentation of goodness.  On his
way towards Florence, he was taken alarmingly ill
at Leghorn.  Mann hastened thither to perform what
service might be required of him.  The British Envoy
writes page after page of unpleasant diagnosis.  Not
a symptom escapes him.  The lengthy details are
extremely nasty, but the princely sufferer maintained
his own dignity by his uncomplaining endurance of
terrible suffering.  He thought so little of life, which
seemed every moment about to leave him, that he
said, it was a matter of indifference whether, as
Mann puts it, 'he lived or dyed.'  When death seemed
not to cast so cold a shadow over him, Mann was
admitted to kiss the Duke's hand, as he lay in bed ;
but the bed was so curtained and the room was so
dark that the Envoy could not see the Duke's face ;

and the Duke himself was so exhausted that the few words he attempted to utter were inaudible to the obsequious listener. The Grand Duke was ceaseless in courteous offers which the Duke of Gloucester was too prostrated to understand, even if they could have been communicated to him. Chains were drawn across the entrance to the street in which he lay, apparently dying, and soldiers were stationed to keep disturbers and disturbances at a distance. After a long season of what seemed hopeless agony, the Duke rallied, and with some difficulty, not unattended by danger, his friends contrived to bring him to Mann's hospitable house in Pisa.

The Grand Duke sent 'a proper message' to compliment him, and 'there was a little omission in the Duke of Gloucester not admitting to his presence the officer whom the Great Duke sent with the first message. I told him it would offend, but it was late, and he was playing at vingt-un with his family. I received the message and returned the answer in the Hall, so that the blame, though it was only whispered, was laid upon me, and like a good courtier, I let it rest there. But the next morning I made full amends by inducing H. R. H. to receive Count Thurm (the Grand Maitre) in his night-gown, rather than not hear the message the Count was charged with from the Great Duke.' Then followed State visits, State dinners, playings at loo with the Grand Duchess, a flying trip to Florence, to hear Tenducci, the singer, 'whom,' says Mann, 'you despised so long in England, but who shines extraordinarily, and intends upon this recruit of reputation, to return to England, for double the pay he had before.'

The details of the Duke's visit are not more interesting than similar records in a fashionable journal ;
there is more interest in what Mann says of him
personally :—' I think he has lost ground ; he is very
pale, and they say his legs swell. . . . I observe a
languor that denotes decay ; he has had no violent
attack of his Asthma, but is never quite free from it,
and now and then coughs ill and hollow, and seems
to train his steps.  He has discontinued riding some
days, which is attributed to his not being able to
bear the fatigue of it, tho' he says nothing ; he is
naturally reserved and seems to have no confidence
in the principal people about him ; and, to say the
truth, I am not surprized at it. . . . Nothing can
exceed the attentions which the G. Duke and Dutchess
shew him, but his want of spirits makes him incapable
of enjoying them and of making a proper return.  I
sometimes fear that they do not make just allowances
for that apparent coldness.'

*Pisa, December* 13*th*.—' Dr. Jebb and Mr. Adair,
who have been sent by the King to attend the Duke
of Gloucester, expected to find him in a much better
condition.  They have not scrupled to say that they
think him in a bad way.  They have forbid his
departure for Rome till they see him better able to
bear the journey.  I have heard it doubted whether
it will ever be allowed at all.  He is not allowed to
assist at Balls or Suppers in the Theater.  He now
makes little excursions in the morning into the
country, and then stays at home for the rest of the
day. . . . . Lord Cholmondely has totally attached
himself to the Duke, and a Mr. Lee has totally

attached himself to Lord Cholmondely. Never was
there so strong example of the young men of the
present times. Their manners, their language, everything they do or say is new; and I constantly afford
them mirth, by not understanding the most senseless
jargon, which, they say, is the *Bon Ton*, but as yet,
it makes the most miserable figure, translated into
Italian. . . . The Duke never communes with the
senseless people about him; he is too wise for that.'

At the end of the year the Duke's life was considered in great peril by the medical men, native and
English; but there was a naval surgeon, with a name
'something like Mike,' who protested that the Duke
was not seriously ill, and would certainly recover. As
'H. R. H.' did recover and live above thirty years after
this illness, in Italy, it may be taken that the 'something like Mike,' knew something about his profession.
The Duke, indeed, according to irreverend scoffers,
had the better chance of life, from the fact that each
of his medical attendants disagreed from all the others
as to the remedies that were most fit for their patient;
and each, when he had the opportunity, flung the
drugs which he had not prescribed out of the window.
The Duke of Gloucester resigned himself to this treatment, got well, and took nothing away with him but
his incurable asthma, and an unjust conviction (forced
upon him by his suite, who turned Mann's house upside
down, and behaved with an insolence that an inn-
keeper would not have allowed), that the British
Envoy, who had no refuge but his own garret, had
not put himself out of the way, for the benefit of the
Duke, or the 'comfort of his attendants.'

## CHAPTER X.

### 1772.

THE Duke's unjust appreciation of Mann's generous and unselfish sacrifices, is the never-ending theme of the letters of 1772. The iteration is wearisome, and the complaining often puerile. The joyousness of the Duke's progress through Italy, on his return from Naples, was checked by the news of the death of his mother, the Princess of Wales. He of course declined all invitations, but he could not resist a dinner given in his honour, by the notorious Cardinal Bernis. 'Nobody,' says Mann, 'since Cardinal Aquaviva, has lived with such magnificence as this French Eminence. It is said that he spends $\frac{m}{30}$ a year. The Duke saw the Pope in the Café house in the Garden at Monte Cavallo. It was a prepared surprize. They were quite alone for about twenty minutes; and we may suppose that the *most interesting* conversation passed between them; of which H. R. H. only can give an account to his Royal Brother. Upon the whole, I am persuaded that both He and the Pope will be well satisfied with each other. . . . After the Duke left, the Pope was much pleased with a large quantity of chirurgical instruments which the Duke sent to the principal hospital in Rome.'

Of the Grand Ducal court there is a repetition of the usual details. The Grand Duchess continued to afford the same reasons as every year before for not being present at interesting national fêtes, namely,` her own interesting situation—probable, actual, interrupted, or just got over. The Grand Duke had a little diplomatic affair to settle, not unlike some of wider seriousness in later times. 'The Great Duke has received instructions from his Mother, to go to Parma, to preach submission and œconomy to the Dutchess, his Sister (Maria Amelia, married to Don Ferdinand, Duke of Parma). Everything, but particularly the finances, are in the greatest disorder there. She doubts (and it is said generally, with good reason), of her husband's capacity to govern; and everybody is convinced of the impossibility of their finances answering the profusion she makes of them. She is as generous as the Empress ; France and Spain complain of it, but their remonstrances have had no effect. The G. Duke does not expect much better success ; so, has remonstrated against the Commission, but has not yet received a remission from Vienna.'

Rome, Naples, Pisa, Parma, and Florence 'swarmed' with travelling or established English families. 'Lord Plymouth' (Other Hickman Windsor, the 5th Earl), 'who succeeded to the title in 1771, is still here; the most sweet temper and fat body I ever knew. What a sad prospect at his age, of being immovable before he is thirty ! but he does not care,

his indolence already makes him prefer a bed and
elbow chair to all other amusements, yet, he is a
cheerful and good-natured . . . . What did the Duke
of Newcastle say to his son's being so great a Dupe
to a proud prostitute and a set of sharpers ? He
had literally once lost to them forty-four thousand
zecchins' (about half that number of pounds sterling),
' but, after supper, he was let to win two Cards, one
of 18, the other of 16 thousand, and then thought
himself happy to leave off with a debt of eleven
hundred, for which he has given his Obligations,
besides, a thousand in presents to the Girl.'

' . . . We have two Platagenets here, the Dutchess
of Beaufort, with her amiable daughter, and Lord
Huntingdon. They are greatly distinguished by the
Court. We have besides many other English, and
more expected. . . . Sir William and Lady Hamilton
arrived here lately, and after a week's stay, set out
for Rome and Naples. She has suffered much in the
journey from Vienna. He is sadly embroiled with
a good for nothing fellow, D'Hanceville, who published the two first volumes of his Tuscan Vases and
had received from Sir William 1000*l.* to carry on the
work in two other volumes ; but that idle adventurer
undertook a wild scheme to furnish Tuscany with
fish, and obtained a Patent from the G. Duke to
carry it into execution, if he could, tho' it was
plain to all the world here, that his only view in
procuring it was, the appearance he would have of
countenance and protection, to seduce some incautious
people to lend him money.' This sample in a small
way of the modern gigantic and too often supremely

rascal race of Promoters or Floaters, 'did nothing
but pocket the money of his dupes, and they, seeing
no disposition made for executing his plan, seized all
his effects' (a righteous law permitted them), 'among
which were the copper-plates for the two last volumes,
though even these were in pawn for the weight of
copper ; and he narrowly escaped to a convent, where
he still amused his creditors with the assurance of
Sir Wm. Hamilton's furnishing him with large sums
of money to satisfy them ; but this too failing him,
they are now devising the means to sell everything
and to divide the produce among them.' Now-a-days,
it is, for the most part, the scoundrel Promoters who
divide amongst them the money of their ruined
dupes.

The most important event in this year's record
is the marriage of Charles Edward, now fifty-two
years of age, with Louisa Maximiliana Carolina,
Princess of Stolberg Gadern, then in her twentieth
year. Her mother, Charlotte Maria, married to the
Prince of Horne, was a daughter of the ultra-Jacobite
Earl of Ailesbury.

'The first news of the Pretender's marriage was
from France. It reached us before he could have
completed the marriage, under the sanction of the
Madonna di Loreto, whither he went to meet his
Bride. He first conducted her to a Villa of Cardinal
Maregorchi (?) at Macerata, and thence to Rome.
The same day, he notified to the Cardinal Secretary
of State, and to the *Maestro di Camera*, his return
"colla Regina sua Consorte." These words, "with the
Queen, his Consort," gave offence, and his Messenger

was told that no such person could be in Rome. She
is pitied, as his insisting on her taking the stile and
dignity of Queen, was contrary to her own and the
Cardinal's earnest entreaties. She will be condemned
to live alone with him; for he is drunk half the day,
and mad the other half. She is the Sacrifize, but, as
Madame de Caylus says, "Ce sera un beau mariage
d'ici à cent ans pour sa famille."'

The above was written in May; by August, the
parties had sunk under neglect. To Walpole, who
had asked Mann to send him prints of their portraits,
the Envoy replies:—'I have written to Rome; but
there is no print, either good or bad, of the drunken
Chevalier, nor has any been made of his wife. The
answer that I literally received was, "they are not of
consequence enough for that,"' and Mann leaves the
subject, to state that Zoffany is in Florence, charmed
with the genius of the English artist, whom Mann
loved and admired—Patch. He adds:—'Zoffany has
been sent here by a great Personage' (George III.)
'to make a perspective view of the *Tribuna*, with
small figures (portraits) as Spectators. This, it seems,
is his stile, and it is said, he is excellent in it. From
hence, he is to go to Rome, to do something of the
same kind.'

## 1773.

On Rome the eyes of the world were just then fixed
with intense interest, watching the course which the
Pope would take with respect to the Jesuits. The
subject is largely discussed in all the letters of the

year from April to November.  The details gathered
together thus tell the eventful story :—

*April 24th.* —' The Fate of the Jesuits is at last
decided ; at least, till another Catholick King, less
obstinate than this, should reinstate them.  One great
obstacle to this would be in the restitution of the
wealth they have been stript of by the Bourbons and
His most faithful Majesty.  In the course of the next
week, the Pope is to pronounce the sentence, the sub-.
stance of which is, as follows :—Their General to be
dismissed and all his Army to be disbanded.  That is
to say, it is to be distributed in small congregations,
in the different parts of the Ecclesiastical States,
totally under the command of the Bishops in the
districts where they reside.  The Novices to be dismissed and no new Recruits to be enlisted for the
future.  None of the old Jesuits to remain in Rome.
The Pope permits foreign Princes to dispose of them
in their own States, as they please ; but they too are
to be under the direction of the respective Bishops.
What do you think the Empress and her Son will do
with their's who possess, in the Austrian dominions
alone, fifty millions of Florins ?  This will afford an
easy pension to the incumbents, for life, who will be
no longer loaded with the expence of bribing Royal
mistresses or courtiers, for the future.'

*May 4th.*—' The Pope has disappointed the expectations of everybody, in not making known his
determination last week with regard to the Jesuits.
It cannot be deferred long; unless the Court of Vienna,
which has hitherto obstructed the great Reformation
which the Pope consented to make, should now, as it

is asserted, insist on a total suppression which, for the reasons I mentioned in my last letter, would be much more convenient.'

*June 8th.*—' Nothing is talked of in Florence but the Imprisonment of the Director of the Jesuit College at Bologna, for refusing to disband his Students and to send them home, unless Cardinal Malvezzi produced the Papal order to him for that purpose. The Students likewise have been confined in a Villa. Nobody can guess why the Pope defers to put an end to this affair by publishing his Brief to suppress the Society.'

*June 19th.*—' We have nothing new in these parts. The Pope continues to teaze the Jesuits, but has not courage to suppress the Society.'

*July 13th.*—' The mysterious manner in which the Pope protracts the dissolution of the Jesuits, keeps everybody in suspence. The motive seems to be that of regulating the disposal of the resources of the Society in his own and other States. Those ' (the funds) ' in the Legation of Bologna he gave last week to that City, but placing them under the arbitration of the Cardinal Archbishop Malvezzi. Modena receives all the young Jesuits and their Students who take refuge there. In Florence, as yet, they are permitted to live quietly ; but their revenues are very small.'

*August 14th.*—' The Jesuits are teazed and tormented before their total suppression. No week passes without some instances of it; but as these tormentings do not come up to martyrdom, they can only make a merit of the mendicity to which, in many places, they are reduced ; and this excites the charity of all their partisans. Most of their Colleges, with all their revenues, in all the Pope's States, have been seized and appropriated to the Apostolical Chamber. Our G. Duke has long* been at variance with the Papal Court; and, in no one instance, has yielded to it. The Bishoprick of Arezzo, the most considerable in this State, being worth near 12,000 crowns (annually), remains vacant, because the G. D. would not permit the Pope, as usual, to assign a pension upon it. Disputes were carried high. At last, the former very wisely put an end to them, not as you will imagine, by consecrating a Bishop, but by putting the whole revenue under administration ; assigning one third for any future Bishop, one third for the repairs of the Churches in all that Province, and another for the Poor,—which has been much approved of. He still went further last week, by suppressing, of his own authority, an Abbey at Pisa, without consulting Rome. It was worth above 2000 Crowns a year, the disposal of which is not yet known. These are bold strokes for one so near Rome ; and what is still worse for that Court is, the general approbation which these instances of such contempt for it meet with.'

*August* 24*th*.—' You would never believe that the Pope would disband his Jannisaries ; but you did not, perhaps, reflect on the inflexible obstinacy of the King of Spain. . . . After some years' struggle, the Pope has been obliged to give up that mighty body. The Bull to suppress the Society was notified to them on Monday ; and, to insure their pacific submission, detachments of the Corsican Guard were sent to all their Colleges and Houses, with Notaries and others deputed to carry this affair into Execution. Everything passed

without the least opposition within doors, or disturbance from the populace without.  All their Archives,
Plate, and other valuable Effects, were seized and
sealed up.  The soldiers were left to guard them,
to prevent any Jesuit from going out, or anybody
having access to them.  Three only of their Churches
were opened the next morning, in which the Capuchins and other Franciscans officiated.  The Bull is
of an enormous size, too big for this letter. . . . Many
pages are employed, to show with what unlimited
authority the Pope's predecessors have established,
suppressed, and reformed abuses in some Orders, and
totally suppressed others.  This historical account of
the exertion of the Papal power was thought necessary, to silence those who assert that the Pope, of his
own authority, could not suppress the Jesuits.  Ganganelli ' (Clement XIV.) ' then proceeds to enumerate
many disorders the Jesuits have committed in diverse
parts of the world, and the heavy complaints that
have been made against them by four great Kings,—
Spain, France, Portugal, and Naples ; all which has
obliged Him, after the most fervent supplications to
Heaven to enlighten him (which we may naturally
suppose, has not interposed in favour of the Jesuits),
to suppress the Order, as pernicious to Religion, etc.,
etc.  Eight days were assigned them to quit the
habit and to declare their total submission.  At the
same time, a prohibition to say Mass, to hear Confessions, and in short, to perform any Act of Priest-
hood was notified to them.  They may live as Secular
Priests, with a Pension that will be assigned to them,
or may pass into any other Order.  This will be dif-

ficult, as all other Orders hate them. Those who refuse any of these favours are to be banished from the Pope's States, and are to be excommunicated. This is making the affair compleat.'

'The Bull was presented to the Great Duke the day before yesterday by the Nuncio, but hitherto no steps have been taken in consequence of it ; and the Jesuits all yesterday continued to officiate in their Churches as usual. Their Revenues in this State are very small, out of which, it is said, that 80 crowns a year are to be assigned to each for his maintenance, which makes $3\frac{1}{2}$ zecchins a month, or 35 Shillings sterling !'

*September 7th.*—'The Tuscan Jesuits have submitted to their Fate with the utmost resignation. The Great Duke has taken possession of all their Lands and Effects, as all other Princes have done, or will do ; but he has behaved kindly to them. To each he has given twenty crowns to buy another dress, and other douceurs, to defray the expense of removing to other habitations. He has invited any of the Learned of the Order to come into Tuscany, and he will imploy them. Those of them who assisted at weighing their silver (when a Saint was put into one scale without any of his merits in the opposite one) winced and showed the utmost agitation; but the whole did not amount to more than 400lb. w$^t$. At Rome it was quite otherwise. The Plate, except what has been left in their Churches, for others to officiate with, amounted to 64,000lb. w$^t$., exclusive of the Statue of St. Ignatius, and the various changes of Jewels that adorned him on particular days. Padre Ricci, the late General, is closely confined, and undergoes strict examinations every day; but he commonly answers, that the whole affair has so agitated his mind, that he remembers nothing of what they speak to him about; so that, as yet no discoveries have been made where their Treasure has been deposited, which is the great object of their Inquiries.'

*September* 21*st.*—' The Pope is still perplexed in the search after the riches of the Jesuits. Something considerable, they say, has been found, in money and jewels. Some more of their agents have been sent to Castel St. Angelo; but whether the Pope gets at any more of their petty cash or not, he may console himself with what is more substantial, their Inheritance, which is said to amount to four millions of Crowns, in the Ecclesiastical States.'

*September* 28*th.*—' The consequences of the suppression of the Jesuits still continue to amuse the publick. The Pope has been greatly exasperated by the discoveries that have been made from their Papers. Counter-Briefs, in the name of their General, have been found, which annul all that the Pope has authorized against their Order, denying not only his Authority, but even the Legality of his Election! This provoked him much, and was the cause of the very close confinement of the General. Many Letters have appeared at the Post House addressed to him, but in Cypher; and he swears that he has neither Cypher nor Decypher; and when he is questioned about anything, he repeats that the whole affair has so agitated his mind, he remembers nothing. A report prevails that, among their papers, a Plan and Direc-

tions for our Gunpowder Plot has been found.  Hitherto,
I have not been able to  get  any information about it,
nor can judge whether there is any ground for the
report ; but you will easily imagine that I will exert
every means in my power to get some light into it.'

*November 9th.*—' The Pope is returned to Rome
from his Villegiatura at Castel Gandolfo, whither he
went to show he was not afraid ; though in his airings
he never outrode his Guards on horseback, as he used to
do; and they were more numerous than usual.  He was
received at Rome with the greatest acclamations ; so
that it is plain there were no Jesuits among the crowd.
Their late General and some others are strictly guarded
in the Castel of St. Angelo.  He affects imbecility, and
gives no direct answer to any question made to him by
his Examiners.  I am quite certain of the existence of
the Papers ' (the plan for the Gunpowder Plot) ' which
I mentioned in a former letter. It is said that a French
Jesuit, now in prison, has been convicted of being the
author of a Book which touched the Pope to the quick :
" De Electione Simoniaca Clementis XIV." The King
of Spain certainly threatened to publish the Letter
which Ganganelli wrote when he was Cardinal, containing a conditional promise to suppress the Society.
It was never flatly denied, but evaded by saying
that the King put a stronger construction upon the
Cardinal's words than was meant. Nevertheless, the
Pope was afraid to refer the construction of them to
the Publick.  He has not, however, obtained all the
fruits he expected from his compliance.  There is
no talk of the restoration of either Benevento or
Avignon.'

Thus passed this great affair, under pressure from France and Spain, the kings of which countries had, some years previously, suppressed the Order, expelled the members, and confiscated their property. The exact date of the suppression of the Society, by Clement XIV., was the 21st of July, 1773. On the 7th of August, 1814, the Order was restored by Pope Pius VI.

Of the religious knowledge and practice in Italy at this agitated period, Sir Horace Mann gives the following instance:—

'You may have heard how much, of late, the *gout* of the Italians for all sorts of theatrical amusements is encreased. I can't tell you how many Theaters are now open in Florence and in every small village. The highest price at the Great Opera is three Pauls' (equal to 1*s*. 6*d*.) ; 'the lowest at more humble performances is two *Crazie*' (about three halfpence), 'the fourth part of a Paul. One of these Managers, having succeeded very well, presented a Memorial to the Great Duke to have leave, during Lent, to represent "Le Commedie della Passione di Nostro Signore." H. R. H. observed, that at least the Manager might have stiled them *Tragedie*, but he rejected the Memorial ; possibly, not to interfere with the other Companies who represent those Tragedies in all the Churches and Convents in Italy. A young Painter, not long ago, had a commission to paint the Trinity for an Altar piece. He made his sketch and carried it to Patch for his advice. The picture consisted of the Father, the Son, and the Madonna! and it was with great difficulty that Patch perswaded him of his Error; which

I am the less surprised at since, as I have asked fifty common people, and they have all answered that the Trinity was composed as above!'

In another letter, Mann breaks off from some weary details on obscure politics, to refer to another painter:—'You will laugh when I tell you that Mr. Zoffany is now waiting for me in the next room, to put my portrait into the Picture which the King sent him hither to make, of the *Tribuna* of the Gallery. It is a most curious and laborious undertaking!' The *Tribuna* was the famous octagon room in which not only the Dancing Fawn and the Wrestlers challenged admiration, but where the three Venuses compelled it; namely, the Venus Victrix, the Venus Urania, and the Venus de' Medici. This triad of sculptured beauty was only surpassed by the beauty limned by Titian. *His* two Venuses are the counterfeit presentments of two beautiful women, such too is the Venus de' Medici; and little traditionary scandal says that, in one, you see Titian's wife; and in the other, Titian's mistress! 'The first,' says Dr. Moore, 'is the most beautiful portrait I ever saw, except the second.' This was the scene which Zoffany had to fill with portraits of living persons then in Florence. George the Third made him the bearer of a letter to the Grand Duke, who gave the artist every facility for his work. All the English then in the Tuscan capital were eager to appear in this picture which was to hand them down to posterity. Zoffany painted them in, and when they left Florence, rubbed them out; for the artist's *Tribuna* got too crowded, and he had more than once to give air to his Octagon and to send some of his

minor spectators away.    Such of the English who
cared for the distinction of standing permanently in
Zoffany's picture, were very careful not to offend the
great man.    On small provocation, the painter avenged
himself by wiping the offender out of the canvas.
Mann probably did not care about the matter; or
why should he suppose that Walpole would laugh at
the idea of his sitting for the purpose?    It was very
proper that King George's Minister should appear in
the *Tribuna;* and there Sir Horace may still be seen,
in the picture which now hangs in the Gallery at
Windsor.

There were living Venuses among the English
women then in Florence.    Mann names one, in Mrs.
Pitt.    ' I saw enough of her,' he says, ' to admire her
beyond all the woemen I ever saw ; and to pity her
as much.'    (The fascinator was deaf.)    ' The elegancy
of her beauty struck everybody; and a certain sagacity
in explaining what people meant, supplied the want of
hearing, and made her neither troublesome, or at a loss,
in company.    Neither did I perceive the least decay
of her sight.    I saw her thread a small needle by
candle-light, at the Duchess of Beaufort's, to mend a
ruffle, before she went to a *Bal masqué* at the Theater;
where she danced a minuet with all the grace imaginable, at the Great Dutchess's request.    She only uses
a Glass, there ; or to look at pictures at a distance.
As to the other Lady,—she spoke so much of you,
and showed us so many of her own works, and so
much practice in pictures, that she was thought very
cleaver in those points here, and gained at the Gallery,
the reputation of a Connoisseuse.'    The ' other Lady '

was Anne Pitt, sister of Lord Chatham.   The deaf
Mrs. Pitt was the wife of George Pitt (afterwards
Lord Rivers).   Walpole describes him as ' her brutal,
half mad husband, with whom she is still not out
of love, and who has heaped on her every possible
cruelty and provoking outrage ; will not suffer her to
see, or even hear from, one of her children.'   Some
Englishmen, resident in Florence, preferred Italian to
English beauty.   ' What do they say in England,'
writes Mann, ' of Lord Cowper's disposition to marry
a Florentine Lady.'   The negotiation was broken
off, on Lord Cowper's insisting that if there were
children of such marriage, they should be brought
up as Protestants.   Negotiations were subsequently
resumed.   ' The report of this, and of greater concessions than, he says, he ever made, have been
publick here, and consequently must have been wrote
home.   I had lately a long conversation with him on
the subject ; and I believe I made him sensible of all
the inconveniences that would attend such a step ;
nay, that even the report of it was prejudicial to him.
He replyed, that he looked upon it as all over, as he
had heard no more of it, for some time.   Thus,' said
Mann, ' it still depends upon *them*, that is to say, her
family.   He said : " *No !* "   " If that is the case, give
me leave to quote your word of honour to Lord
Rochford, that it is all over, and that you will think
no more of it.   Such an assurance would probably
make your family easy, and would please the King."
He promised to give me an answer in a day or two.
More than ten have passed without any ; and yet it is
asserted about the town, and by the young Lady's

Relations, that all Treaty is broke off, on account of
Religion.   I will not interfere any more.'

Walpole had announced to Mann the possible
arrival in Florence of two somewhat embarrassing
personages, the Duke of Cumberland and his Duchess,
—Anne Luttrell, daughter of the Earl of Carhampton,
and widow of a Derbyshire 'squire, Christopher Horton.
The marriage with the Duke had taken place in 1771,
when his Royal Highness was seven and twenty, and
the widow much older.   The King was more offended
by this union than by that of his other brother, the
Duke of Gloucester, with the beautiful widow, Lady
Waldegrave.   Mann was ' quite alarmed' at the announcement that the Duke and Duchess of Cumberland were likely to arrive in Florence.

' I think it will be very difficult to know how to
behave properly to the Travellers whom you announce.
Their departure from England must be a signal for
me to apply for directions, as their approach might
make it too late.   I beg therefore to be informed as
early as possible of that.   A Great Dame ' (the Grand
Duchess) ' has spoken to me of them, and asked—
what could be done with *her?*   No doubt, that the
same question will be proposed at Vienna, and that
the answer will be, *Nothing!* which will serve for a
Rule everywhere.   The remembrance of the wretched
return on a less embarrassing occasion ' (the Duke of
Gloucester's visit to Florence) ' will make *people*'
(Mann, himself) ' glad of so good an excuse for that
*Nothing!*   At Rome, probably, it may be worse,
where that motive may operate more powerfully, both
from the character of the Dames there, and as the

provocations were greater. Upon the whole, I foresee great inconveniences.'

Throughout the letters of this year, there is repeated evidence that Mann was beginning to feel the burthen of life, the weight of his years. It was the same with Walpole. Each communicates to the other the greater frequency and the longer continuance of their old enemy, the gout. Mann, as Pope says, ' grew sick and damned the climate, like a Lord.' At the beginning of April the climate kept him in bed, sick and suffering. 'We have actually a third Winter. It now snows upon the mountains around. The climate of Florence has quite lost its reputation with all the Tramontanes here.' Walpole found that of England quite as trying, and he kept within doors. He preferred having his climate 'framed and glazed.' Constantly too, in the letters of this year, Mann refers to all amusements with a bitter melancholy. He thinks they have lost all good quality, when, in fact, it is he who has lost all taste for them. One quality the British Envoy certainly had *not* lost,—his unselfish hospitality. The master of the feast might be worn and weary ; but he never allowed his guests to suspect it.

Next to the public question of the Jesuits, the private one of the condition of young Lord Orford, Walpole's nephew, occupies most space. Walpole has told in his letters the disgrace and ruin which that profligate Lord had brought upon his house and estate, and the insanity and peril of death which threatened himself. Mann, on his side, writes of Lord Orford's mother, the once gay and extravagant Lady Walpole, who made even Italy stare in profound astonishment at her, her lovers, and her audacity.

'His mother is now in Florence,' he writes in March. 'She has been detained by the purchase of her own Villa, at Fiesole, which, about a year ago, had been bought over her own head. . . . Cavalier Mozzi, her messenger, told me that she had commissioned him to desire that I would inform you that, if her age and ill health permitted, she would hasten to England, though she does not see in what shape she could be useful to her son. . . . She intreats you and Sir Edward' (Walpole's brother) 'to take all the care of him that his situation will admit of.' When the new's of her son's condition was more alarming in its purport, 'She came over to me, and expressed both her concern and her embarrassment, saying, she was too old and infirm to take such a journey, nor could see of what use she could be to him if she was there. . . . She set out yesterday for Naples, I believe, to bring away all her furniture, in order to fix in Tuscany. . . . She has bought the villa at Fiesole . . . and people are looking out for a house in town for her. During this Winter, she makes use of Lord Tylney's, which he is coming back to inhabit himself.'

Later in the year, the reports becoming still graver, and Lady Orford being urged to go over to her unhappy son, she again pleaded infirmity, and also 'a complete ignorance of her son's affairs, to which she added the fear of involving herself in difficulties that might embarrass her much. This latter expression may carry a very extensive meaning, but as she has not explained it to me, I have no right to do it.' In

June, when her excuses were backed up by the announcement of her resolution not to go to England,
desperate as was her son's condition, Mann writes:—
'You know her situation and will easily perceive that
stronger motives than those which she alledges, of her
age and health, will make her repugnance to return to
England insurmountable; therefore, in my opinion, it
will be vain to insist upon it.' Insistence, however,
being attempted, in a visit which Mann made to her
in June, she observed that 'her ill health made it
impossible for her to stay many weeks in England,
or to sleep a single night in London. . . .' Besides,
when Mann again tried to impress upon her the
propriety of her being near her son, she observed,
that the King had continued to him the income
of the places, the duties of which he was unable
to fulfil, and therefore, as far as that son's affairs
were concerned, she might be easy. . . . 'I hear it
whispered,' says Mann, in September, 'that she has
a vast claim upon the Estate, for a deficiency in her
Joynter ever since the late Lord Orford's death. As to
Lady Orford's health . . . she rides for some hours
every morning, and is in continual motion the rest
of the day, by which she maintains a vivacity not
common at her age.'

Walpole's Letters may be consulted for the sequel
to this affair. Lord Orford, who was bad and mad,
through his mother, recovered from his mental infirmity, and lived, a ruined man in body and estate,
till 1791. Walpole then succeeded to his nephew's
titles; but, as he remarked, to call Horace Walpole
'Lord Orford,' was like calling him names. So, the

dowager Lady Orford remained in Italy, where her
vivacity, past or present, excited no comment among
Florentine or even English ladies. But both these
classes of ladies were much more given to pass smart
judgments on the Grand Duchess who, in Dr. Moore's
words, 'is of a domestic turn, and lives much in
the country with her children, of which she has a
comfortable number.' The most remarkable British
lady in Florence, at the close of the year, was Lady
Mary Coke, widow of a son of the Earl of Leicester,
which son died in his father's lifetime. The lady, a
daughter of the Duke of Argyle, was familiarly known
as 'the Scotch Princess,' from certain affectations of
belonging to, and being a worshipper of, all that was
Royal or Imperial. She came to Florence from Vienna
in a 'huff.' 'She has talked to me for hours of the
good, and, latterly, of the bad usage, nay affronts,
which she had received from the Empress, which, she
supposes, influenced the Arch-Duchess at Parma, to
whom, though Lady Mary demeaned herself by offering
to defer her departure, she never could get admittance.
She was afraid of something of the same kind here,
though, in the days of her favour, the Empress had
often told her that she had recommended her to
the G. Dutchess, who received her with cold civility.
The G. Duke never receives Ladies, so that she has
not, nor probably will see him, as there are, at
present, no dancing rooms nor table at Court; which
circumstance must prevent the growth of any familiar
acquaintance there, as other great Ladies, and some
very inferior to Lady Mary, have had. This neglect
she sometimes complains of as an injustice to her

birth; at others, she attributes it to the persecution, as she calls it, from the Empress, whom alternately she abuses and adores. She may have many good qualities, but hitherto she has not given many proofs of them. I began by shewing her great attentions, and saved her the mortification of being cited, and being obliged by the publick tribunals to do justice to her servants. The height and violence of her temper exposed her to being summoned before the tribunals. In thus saving her, I was forced to make use of means which, were she informed of them, would appear an unpardonable crime,—unless œconomy should step in to disarm her anger.' (Mann probably hinted that Lady Mary Coke was mad). 'Notwithstanding all this, she dines here frequently, and passes her evenings here at cards. She seems to be coming about again . . . I have told her how much you interested yourself for her ; to which she seemed sensible, and has bid me make her compliments.'

Lady Mary Coke, who contrived to amaze the Florentines, was not disgusted with matrimony though her husband and father-in-law had locked her up and the laws alone had compelled them to release her. The Campbells were naturally excessively indignant that a daughter of the Great Duke of Argyle (Maccullommore !) should be subjected to cruel dignity at the hands of the Cokes. Her husband died in 1753, and she survived him fifty-eight years. Walpole greatly admired her, and he even wrote verses ' On the St. Anthony's Fire, in Lady Mary's Cheek.' Just ten years before her appearance in Florence, Lady Temple had written of her :—

'She sometimes laughs, but never loud ;
　She's handsome too, but somewhat proud ;
　At Court, she bears away the bell ;
　She dresses fine, and figures well ;
　With decency, she's gay and airy ;
　Who can this be but Lady Mary ? '

Walpole called the Duchess of Grafton and Lady Mary, his 'Polly and Lucy,' he being their platonic Macheath. There was, at least, great eccentricity about the daughter of Argyle. 'She sentimentally attached herself to Edward, Duke of York, and with such mad conviction of a certain reality about it, that after his death, she appeared in public in widow's weeds.' Walpole tells in what guise he met her, in 1765, travelling near Amiens, in a coach and four, with a French equipage and a couple of *suivantes.* The lady was in pea green and silver, with a smart hat and feather. Walpole's reason, he says, induced him to take her for the Archbishop's concubine ; but his heart whispered him that she must be Lady Mary Coke. In this year, 1773, he writes of the daughter of the Campbells, her eccentricities in Vienna and Florence, and the coolness with which Empress, Grand Duchess, and Archduchess (Parma) had met her advances :—'I have heard of some of Lady Mary Coke's mortifications. I have regard and esteem for her good qualities, which are many ; but I doubt her genius will never allow her to be quite happy. As she will not take the Psalmist's advice of not putting trust, I am sure she would not follow mine ; for, with all her piety, King David is the only royal person she will not listen to ; and therefore I forbear my sweet counsel . . . She has a frenzy for Royalty and will fall in love with, and at the feet of, the Great Duke and Duchess, especially the former ; for, next to being an Empress herself, she adores the Empress Queen, or did, for perhaps that passion, not being quite so reciprocal, may have waned. However, bating every English person's madness, for every English person must have their madness, Lady Mary has a thousand virtues and good qualities. She is noble, generous, high-spirited, undauntable ; is most friendly, sincere, affectionate, and above any mean action. She loves attention, and I wish you to pay it, even for my sake, for I would do anything to serve her. I have often tried to laugh her out of her weakness ; but as she is very serious, she was so in that ; and if all the sovereigns in Europe combined to slight her, she still would put her trust in the next generation of Princes. Her heart is excellent, and deserves and would become a Crown, and that is the best of all excuses for desiring one! . . . It is a very good heart, with a head singularly awry ; in short, an extraordinary character, even in this soil of phenomena. With her pretensions and profound gravity she has made herself ridiculous at home, and delighted " de promener sa folie par toute l'Europe." '

With this light, Mann's report of Lady Mary's sayings and doings in Florence, in the year 1774, will be rendered all the more intelligible. It was a year of much gaiety in Florence, disturbed by the great thunderclap that came from Rome.

# CHAPTER XI.

## 1774.

FIRST, it is to be observed that the reports alluded to in the last chapter travelled very slowly, as did Walpole's letters from England. Writing on January 11th, Sir Horace says :—

'Your letter dated 21st Decem$^r$ arrived here 9th Jan$^y$, so it has been 21 days on the road, and at this time of the year I don't think they can come sooner, when the posts even are quite regular, but they sometimes fail, that is, the English do not come forward, supposed to be owing to the retardure of the Packet boat at Ostend, in which case it frequently happens that we receive two or more posts together, this was precisely the case the day before yesterday, three posts arrived at the same time, but your letter bore the same date as the freshest newspaper, which is a proof that it was not retarded by anybody's curiosity, nor have I ever observed any marks of their having been opened.'

Next, after many trivialities in the same letter, Mann refers to his friend's friend, Lady Mary :—

'Your Scotch Princess is quite mad upon the article of Empresses and their Descendants, whose

Emissaries, from their first Ministers and Courtiers
down to the lowest of the servants, lay traps for her
and persecute her every hour of the day, which she,
poor creature, who cannot (as she says) be in the
wrong, is forced to submit to not knowing how to get
away.   Turin, as the least under the influence of her
great Persecutrix, is her object, but Parma and Milan
lay in the way, to the latter there are two objections,
while the travelling Court is there, on which subject
she has quarrelled with L^d Huntington beyond all
accommodation.   I am upon a very good footing
with her, I attend her to the theaters and allot her
the first places in my Boxes, she frequently dines and
plays at Cards here, though this subjects me to hear
her lamentations.   She now however lets me contradict her and show her the delusion of her dreams,
but as she tells her story to many she always adds
that I could answer for the truth of every instance
and word if I would but speak.   Some strange pretentions must have been started by the travelling Court
both in other places and at Milan, which have produced a second circular letter to *us*.   I am not
informed of their future motions.'

*January* 18*th.*—' Oh, my dear Sir, how well you
know the Lady who was the subject of my last letter!
and still her extravagance has exceeded even the
large bounds which a favourite fully requires.   I was
forced to combat with it, in a thousand shapes, but
could never subdue it ; nevertheless, we lived together
and parted upon the best terms ; insomuch that,
latterly, she declared she did not think herself safe
when I did not accompany her ; and though, seeing

the necessity, she said, to leave a country under the
persecuting influence of the great Lady' (Maria
Theresa) 'she once adored, she took a servant at my
recommendation to conduct her to Turin, she nevertheless endeavoured to persuade me that a large sum
of money had been given to him, to use her ill on
the road. She set out by *voiture*, yesterday morning,
towards Lirici, where she must risk her life by sea,
to Genoa, to avoid greater dangers by passing through
the Empress's dominions, to Turin, where all her
persecution is to end. I wish her folly may there end
too, but I doubt it much; for nothing is so difficult
as to eradicate an error from a reasoning mind.'

*February* 19*th.*—'I have already acquainted you
that Lady Mary Coke has left Florence. I was in
hopes that her folly was attached to this soil only,
as being under the influence of the Empress, but she
has committed a thousand follies on the road; at
Lirici the weather was too bad to put to sea, but
she interpreted the refusal of the Boatmen as a signal
that she was to be murdered there; she even pitched
upon a Marquis Botta, whom she saw from her
window, as her executioner, declaring that she had
seen him at the theater here, and consequently that
he must have been sent after her for that purpose—
however she got safe to Genoa, where she turned
away the servant whom we had given her to
conduct her to Turin, declaring that she heard
that he had received a large sum of money here
to treat her ill, and on his accidently naming the
Great Duke, she cried out, "Oh, name him not,
thence comes all my persecution," and she dismissed

him there.   At Turin, she made great complaint of
the treatment she had met with at Court here, and
told such strange stories that Sir W<sup>m.</sup> Lynch wrote to
me for an explanation of them.   From thence she has
answered a letter that I wrote to her to convey one
that I had received for her from the Princess Amelia,
in that answer she only signs Mary ; I really believe
she is more to be pitied than blamed, for she has
since wrote to the Consul at Genoa, that all her terror
had been removed by seeing in the same house a man
whom she had known at Vienna, who must have been
sent from them by the Empress, so that it was plain
that the same persecution was never to cease.   I was
tormented with all this when she was here, for she
declared she never thought herself safe out of my
company, tho' at times she was very angry with
me, but it now excites my compassion, and I should
not be surprised to hear it had produced very serious
consequences.   She proposes to stay at Turin about
two months, and then to return to England to lay the
whole story before Princess Amelia.   Lord Huntingdon will have a great share in it, as he has most
innocently incurred her indignation.'

Another lady, as mad as Lady Mary, but with a
difference, next appears on the scene.

*March* 12*th.*—' The Dutchess of Kingston is at
Rome, but receives nobody, she is expected here in a
few days, I will make an attempt to see her.   I knew
her when she was a child, and lived at Chelsea, but
that is an Epoque I will not remind her of.   The
English travelling ladies have published her history
to the Italians ; they say she is learning the Russian

language in order to make a visit to that Empress,
the other would probably treat her worse than Lady
Mary says she treated her.'

*March* 29*th.*—' The Dutchess whom you mention
has not been here, she is still at Rome, where she lives
most privately ; possibly she may have adopted this
method not to appear to feel the omission of many
English ladies there who had determined not to
visit her ; she is employed in choosing a house there,
which is to be fitted up for next winter, in the mean
time she proposes to return to England. I have not
heard that she has a band of musick, but she acts the
great inconsolable Dutchess Dowager, and, for the
same reasons that a greater Dutchess now at Rome '
(Duchess of Cumberland) ' has laid down, will avoid
courts, not to insist on the *tabouret.*'

*April* 23*rd*—' The Dutchess of Kingston is expected here after she has settled the conditions for the
purchase, it is said (tho' I can't believe it), of the Villa
Negroni at Rome, that of Sixtus quintus ; a courier
passed by a few days for Genoa to treat with the
Negroni family about it. She *has* a band of musick,
which I did not know when I wrote last. She went
into no company nor received any. The Dutchess of
Beaufort writes me that she was conscious no one
would go to see her, therefore very prudently took that
resolution. The Italian ladies won't be so squeamish
when she is fixed in her noble villa and gives them
entertainments.'

*May* 17*th.*—' The Dutchess dined here yesterday,
and I afterwards carried her to the Casino, which
delighted her much, till their resemblance to some of

her own parks where she had passed such delicious
hours with the Duke produced a flood of tears.    Mrs.
Pitt says she is now representing Andromache under a
crowd of veils, as she formerly by her no dress thought
she represented Iphigenia.    I left her before she set out
to write a few lines to the Pope, who showed her every
mark of attention, and desired to be her agent in the
purchase which she again wishes to make of the Villa
Negroni at Rome, about which she wishes to resume
the treaty with that family as she passes at Genoa.
Should that take place she proposes to take her own
ship with the furniture of two or three of her Villas
in England to furnish the Casino which Sixtus
Quintus inhabited, and by that means to add to the
noble monuments of antiquity (which she is to purchase too) that adorn that extensive Villa, all the
elegance and convenience of English modern furniture.
Mrs. Pitt did not see her Grace, but civil messages
passed between them . . . . This court is still en
retraite at the Imperiale on account of the inocculation
of the young Princess, tho' it is happily over, and for
which Dr. Gatti received a present yesterday of a
thousand zecchins from the Empress and four hundred
in a gold box from the Great Duke, but notwithstanding this retreat the Dutchess of Kingston sent a
respectfull message thither; the honour the Emperor
showed her somewhere, and the connection with the
Electress of Saxony, made her think it an indispensable
duty.    She set out this morning.'

Sir Horace was more interested in the Mrs. Pitt
named above than in the notorious Duchess of Kingston ; especially as that lady was Walpole's friend.

*March* 29*th.*—'The instant I received your letter I wrote to Mrs. Pitt, who a few days before was arrived at Pisa ; I told her that I took that liberty in consequence of the interest which you took in what relates to her, and that I begged to be honoured with any of her commands if she thought I could contribute in any shape to her conveniency in these parts. She took this very kindly both in you and me, and I am now expecting her reply to a second letter, in which I traced out a plan for her summer residence here as she desired. I fancy we shall be good friends ; I love an elderly sensible woman, they are the only part of their sex that I can claim any merit with, and I hope you will look on this beginning as a pledge for my shewing her every mark of attention in my power for the future.'

*April* 25*th.*—' You little think, my dear Sir, at this instant how great the intimacy between Mrs. Pitt and me is become. Since I began this letter she is come hither, and actually occupies an appartment in my house. I had taken one for her (that in which you found me on your arrival at Florence), but it was to be ready only for the beginning of next month; the Baths at Pisa not aggreeing with her, she took a sudden resolution to come hither, and very obligingly accepted of the offer I made her of an appartment till her own can be got ready ; the few hours I have passed with her have convinced me of all you have said of her merit, which she has augmented with me by the esteem and regard she expresses for you—I told you I should take much to her—well I must go and see how she has slept, and that she has her milk and chocolate for her breakfast.'

' Mrs. Pitt has delighted me with a description of a Fête she gave at her house in town, where for want of room she contrived certain Pearches, as she called them, for part of her guests, not indeed to sit upon but to lean against for repose ; she says that you assisted at this Fairy entertainment, and could witness to her reception of more people than her house could hold, and that you often called for the wand that produced the Entertainment.'

*May 17th.*—' I am charmed, my Dear Sir, with Mrs. Pitt, she is a character I had not met with in any of our countrywomen ; she often puts me in mind a little of our late delicate friend the Princess Craon, tho' Mrs. Pitt has not the least grain of her *minauderies* and abounds in good sense, for which the other great Lady was not much renowned, et s'était dispensée, for many years before we knew, de lire et d'écrire (as she wrote to you in a line or two to thank you for the elegant Chinese present), but still with all this material difference, Mrs. Pitt would not, I think, be quite what she is if she had not lived in France, and frequented people of that town. Her conversation is most lively and entertaining, but her vivacity often exhausts her strength, as particularly to-day. She has wrote me two polite notes to tell me that her nerves are so weak that she cannot talk or go out with me to take our usual airing, but must sit tranquilly on the charming *Terras*, where you found me when you first came to Florence, tho' she says she is impatient to have an account of the addolorata Principessa (Dutchess of Kingston) with whom I passed all yesterday.'

*May 28th.*—'The more I love Mrs. Pitt, and was charmed with her society, the less I can abstain from bewailing my disappointment; know then that at the very instant I was writing to you by the last post and boasting of the agreeable hours I daily passed with her, and hoped to continue for some months, she was forming a plan to leave Florence in a few days, and announced it to me as an irrevocable resolution, forbidding me from the kindest motive to touch on that subject the first time we should meet. I cannot express to you my surprise, as she often said how much she was satisfied with her situation here. Unluckily, I think, for her, she heard talk of the waters at Abano near Padua, and fancied they would do her good; I heartily wish she may not be mistaken, but she is so extremely weak and emaciated that tranquillity in a better air than Abano seems to be more proper for her. She set out on Monday. However, I obtained a promise from her to return hither immediately if she found that these waters did not agree with her.'

With ordinary visitors, Mann got on exceedingly well; but his serenity was somewhat disturbed when he heard that the Duke and Duchess of Cumberland were really in Italy. 'That travelling court,' he writes, 'now at Milan, has fixed its departure for the 25th instant, for Genoa, if the proposal that had been made to get one of that Republick's galleys to convey him to Civita Vecchia takes place; the answer was to be sent as last Saturday. General Provost has quitted him under pretence of going to Switzerland to see his relations, but a total disapprobation from England of his conduct seems to be the cause of his dismission.'

The above was written in February. In the following month, Sir Horace says :—

'The travelling Court lately at Milan is now at Rome ; the strangest things happened at the former place by the disorders and profusion in the family, which totally exhausted their finances ; the female nobility there were greatly offended and have communicated their complaints to those of Rome, much prouder and more *exigeantes* than they were, so they are prepared for their arrival. It is said that the Dutchess of Cumberland has resolved neither to receive or to go into company, which I believe will be the only means to avoid *tracasserie*. The Pope was prepared to show the greatest attentions to both, but that would avail little in other respects. H. R. H. proposes to stay there the Holy week—thence to go to Venice for the Ascension, and then to return to England thro' France. Hitherto the excursion does not seem to have answered either in regard to amusement or œconomy.'

*April* 23rd.—'The Royal Traveller set out from Rome last week ; by all accounts his behaviour has been very proper the whole time he staid there, I mean as to his receiving and returning the attentions that were paid to him, but I should doubt whether his prudence in a political light will be approved of in accepting one of the Pope's Frigates to carry him to Toulon ; the Pope seems happy in having had this opportunity to be employed, and has done everything nobly ; the vessel was crammed with all sorts of pro-

visions. New liveries were made for the Bargemen,
and before he left Rome a royal present was made to
him of a picture in Mosaick, another of Tapestry,
and 27 Volumes in folio, richly bound, of all the best
stamps, and works of Piranzi; how is the King to
requite all this generosity ? or the nobility of Rome
to have a return for the festa they gave his Brother ?
he at least thanked them kindly, very different from
the other Brother who insulted them. A story is
current among the English who come from Rome,
that the present Duke asked Mr. Grenville whether
he did not think that the match he had made was
very indiscreet ; extremely so, replied the other, to
which the D. is said to have answered that he was
much obliged to him for his frankness, tho' he believed
he was the only man who would have told him so,
he liked him the better for it, and hoped to keep up
a friendship with him in England. I am the more
inclined to give credit to this as I have been assured
that at Milan he had let drop many expressions of his
repentance.'

'. . . The Pope is showing the Duke all royal
honours. St. Peter's is to be illuminated for him, and
other royal honours are to be shown him. That Prince
has desired the Republick of Genoa to send one of
their Gallies to Civita Vecchia, by the 8th of April ;
but no application could be made to the Senate for
this purpose, because its members are retired to convents and other holy Retreats, and suffer none but
their spiritual Directors to speak to them.'

The Duke and Duchess went on their homeward
way, and Sir Horace was not half-beggared and ill-

thanked, by having to entertain that couple at his official residence in Florence. Of a little scene at court there, he gives the following description :—

'Durini, the late Nuncio at Warsaw, the cruel enemy of the Polish Dissidents, who out of zeal for his religion did so much mischief there, passed by two days ago on his way to Avignon, which he is to govern. I had a great curiosity to see him, and found a pretence to intrude into the room at Court, where he was waiting for an audience. Civilities passed between us, but as I had no murder to commit or any conspiracy to engage in, I did not ask his benediction.'

The chronicle of the second half of this year is more important, and nobody figures more conspicuously therein than the Pope, who had suppressed the Society of Jesus, and who was not forgiven for it by the Jesuits.

Rome, the Pope, and the Jesuits are subjects which most occupied Mann's attention towards the close of the year. Rightly or wrongly, there seems to have been an accepted idea, that the Jesuits would avenge themselves on the supreme Pontiff for his suppression of the Society. The idea appears to have disturbed the serenity of Ganganelli himself. Mann writes in August :—

'The Pope's health is much impaired. The tranquility of his mind is greatly disturbed by Prophecies of his death. A Devout *Pitonessa* and her Spiritual Director have been put in prison for publishing their dreams ; and one of the officers of the Inquisition has been sent to Monte Fiascone to examine the Madonna di Valentino, who has been busy in this mysterious affair !'

A month later, September 20th, Mann writes:—
'The poor Pope has had the mortification to see
that his crowned Sons have not shown him that gratitude which he expected for his compliance with their
demands, which has drawn upon him such crouds of
publick and private Enemies that make him tremble,
day and night. This, with an habitual disorder of an
inveterate Scurvy (with other diseases) has reduced
him to almost a deplorable state of health, and for
some time past to a total incapacity of attention to
any busyness.'

'Crouds of Bishops from other parts are attending
at Rome, to receive their Miters, but the Pope has not
strength to put them on the prelates' heads. Many
Cardinals in *petto* are, with equal impatience, awaiting
for their Hats. He was to go to his Villegiatura on
the 12th; but his Physicians will not permit him as
yet. In short, he is to be pitied. The disorder of his
body and mind makes his recovery very dubious. The
Prophecies of his dying soon have made the deepest
impression upon him; and a Process is actually still
going on at Monte Fiascone by two officers of the
Inquisition to examine the Madonna di Valentino
there. I don't understand how that is to be done, but
they are at Monte Fiascone for that purpose.'

Nine days later, Mann resumes the subject:—
'The accounts which I gave you, by the last Post, of
the Pope's situation will have prepared you for the
news of his being quite a Lunatick—or, of his death.
The latter has luckily prevented that horrible impu-
tation (unheard of among the Successors of St. Peter)
of an *Infallibilita Pazza*—an insane Infallibility. He

died last Wednesday night ;—hurried out of the world by the Prophecies of some old women ' (this is the first time Mann spells this word correctly), ' the supposed Instruments of the Jesuits, in which diabolical affair, the Madonna at Monte Fiascone has been dabbling ; on which account, a Process was actually carrying on against her, on the spot, by two Officers of the Inquisition, from Rome ! '

*October 1st.*—' Never was Poison more manifestly proved than in the case of the late Pope ; for, though the dissection of his Body was made the same day he died ' (the last word spelt, for the first time, accurately), ' the putrefaction of it was so great that the Surgeons had great difficulty to perform that operation.  As soon as they touched his head, all the hair and all his teeth fell out.  All the bones of his body wasted away ; and the flesh, upon the least touch of the knife, did not divide, but came away in pieces.  They were forced to embalm the body twice, in order to transport it to the Vatican ; but his face was so disfigured that it was necessary to cover it with a mask of wax.  At the dissection, his bowels were put into a large, strong, earthen pan, but the fermentation of them was so great that it broke it.  The body was deposited the first night in a private Chappel, in order to be consigned, in form, the next morning, to the great Chapter of St. Peter's ; but, on the removal of it for that purpose, the head detached itself from the body ! '

' It is supposed that a slow poison was given to him in the last Holy Week.  His Confectioner was taken ill at the same time with all the symptoms that

accompanied the Pope's illness; and, when the last
Letters came away, that servant was at the point of
death.    It has been remarked that, for some months
past, a great number of ex-Jesuits resorted to Rome ;
and that many Letters from Germany and France
have been received at Rome, to inquire if the Pope
had been poisoned, and in what state of health he was
then in.'

*October 8th.*—'The murder of the Pope has been
proved on the clearest evidence.  A slow poison was
given him by his own innocent *Credenziera*, in a dish
of chocolate, last Holy Thursday, at the Vatican,
where his Holiness assisted at the ceremonies of that
day.  It is surprising that he who, from the beginning
of his Pontificate, had taken every precaution to
avoid what he always feared, should persist in drinking the Chocolate, though, from the first sup of it,
he told the servant that it had a bad taste.  Nevertheless, they both continued to swallow their death.
A few days after, they both fell ill, and, during the
whole interval, till they expired, the symptoms were
the same, and the *Credenziera* died a few days after
His Holiness.'

'This circumstance shocked the Romans much
and silenced those few who still affected to have some
doubts of the cause of the Pope's death.  They
asserted the Prophecies and interpreted them as a just
vengeance from Heaven, for his having suppressed
the Jesuits.  They might well give credit to them, for
such predictions are never divulged till the authors of
them have secured the means of their completion.
The Pope was personally hated by the People ; and he

had offended all the Cardinals by the contempt with
which he treated them, in never taking their advice,
or communicating to them anything relating to his
Government. Padre Buontempi, a Friar of his Order,
and as ignorant as himself in matters of that nature,
was his sole Confidant, so that everything was in confusion ; and a general contempt for the Pope's person
has operated a total neglect to investigate the authors
of his death. Nothing more is said of it at Rome,
where the Cardinals are shut up in the Conclave, to
make another Pope, who may be treated as the last
was, if he should confirm the Suppression, or draw
upon himself the vengeance of all the Great Catholic
crowns, if he refuses to do it. A Great Lady here'
(the Grand Duchess) 'is under much agitation on
account of her father,' (Charles III. of Spain) 'whose
death likewise was prophesied at the same time.
What horror do these ex-Jesuits and their partizans
(who are of both sexes) spread all over Europe.'

'The late Chancellor Maupeou is suspected to
have been deeply concerned in the late tragedy ; but
part of the reports are too extravagant to give credit
to.'

*November 22nd.* — 'We have no news of the
Conclave, other than that there is a perpetual war
among the Cardinals, and that never was more art
and cuñing made use of to defeat the Cabals of each
party ; but the Holy Ghost will soon put an end to
this, when each party has collected its whole force,
and the rigour of the season makes the confinement
dangerous to the Electors.'

*December 27th.*—'You ask me what the Cardinals

are doing. Why, exactly nothing, but quarrelling and
cabaling ; each party being only strong enough to
defeat the intrigues of the other. How long they
may go on so is as uncertain as it was a month ago.
Poor Cardinal de Solis, after a most fatiguing journey,
arrived, at Death's door,—at Rome ; but he bid Death
come another time, and in the interval escaped into
the Conclave, where he can give his vote as well
as the stoutest Cardinal there ; but, if they should
come to blows (as the famous *Drama* makes them do),
de Solis will soon be crushed. He is not above four
feet high ; a dryed, blackish parchment only covers his
little bones, and altogether, he is the most ridiculous
little Mummy you ever saw.'

' I am very desirous you should see that Satyr'
(the *Drama*). ' It cost the Conclave 500 crowns to
discover the author ; and he was soon put into
Prison ; but, when they came to his trial in order to
hang him, it turned out that he was not the author,
and that it was wrote in the Conclave ; in which the
Holy Ghost is hovering about and must, of consequence, have been privy to it. This stopped all
perquisitions within those sacred walls. The first
manuscript that was sent hither, to Florence, was
printed by sovereign connivance, and a thousand
copies of it were soon distributed. The Nuncio here
complained of it, and obtained a severe prohibition to
print, sell, or keep any copy of it. The Sbirri were
sent to all the printers where it was known there
were no copies to be found ! This is the satisfaction
which the Court of Rome must now o' days be contented with. A thousand more copies were printed

off to supply the great demand for it from abroad, —so that the prohibition had only excited a greater curiosity, and it has furnished the Printer with a pretence for doubling the price of it. I must send you one enclosed; however angry they may be for swelling the Packet.'

Contrasted with the death of Ganganelli and the election of his successor, other incidents appear almost trivial. 'A little Arch-Duke, of seven months,' says Mann, referring to one of the Grand Duchess's 'failures,' 'died here three days ago. A formal circular letter was wrote to all the foreign Ministers, to give them notice of it,—I suppose that he may be erased out of the Kalendar, that no young Princess of the same age may depend upon him, for an husband, twenty years hence;—but everything that relates to Arch-Dukes is carried very high. The foolish old Marshal Botta used frequently to say, to exalt their dignity: "Eh, je vous assure qu'un Archi-Duc n'est pas une Canaille."'

When the death of the great Lord Clive was mentioned at the Tuscan Court, the Grand Duke had a pretty euphemism for 'suicide.' Mann expressed a feeling of pity for him 'for ending his life so early when he had obtained every means, excepting that of health, to make a long life happy. . . . The Great Duke spoke of him yesterday, when he made use of a gentle expression on the occasion, saying, "qu'il avoit entendu dire qu'il était mort bien vite." I understood him, but replyed, that his constitution was quite broken, and that the violent pains he constantly had in his stomach had obliged his Physician to have recourse to Lodanham, which is supposed to have hurt him.  The G. Duke understood me, too.'

Mann notices rather rudely the progress of Zoffany :—'The one-eyed German, Zoffany, who was sent by the King to paint a perspective view of the Tribune in the Gallery, has succeeded amazingly in many parts of that, and in many portraits he has made here.  The former is too much crouded with (for the most part) Portraits of English travellers then here.'

It was at this time that Mann was disposed to introduce into Florence the newly invented 'double-plated dish-covers,' as not being distinguishable from silver, or less lasting in looking like the purer metal.  Our Envoy wrote to 'Mr. Munro, of Birmingham' on the subject.  Walpole affected to be shocked at what he thought such lack of taste ; and Mann was in the depths of despair at appearing so vulgar in the eyes of so fine a gentleman and so dear a friend.  Among quires of details about nothing, such a paragraph as the following occasionally presents itself :—' Lord Cowper has declared his intention to marry the youngest daughter of Mr. Gore, of Lincolnshire, who, with his family, has been here some months.  She is very young and pretty.'  Lord Cowper carried out his intention, but in 1781 he sent the Countess and her children to England, remaining, himself, an Italianized Englishman, in, or near, Florence.  In September, Mann tells Walpole :—'The Dutchess of Kingston is daily expected here to receive some attentions from the Great Dutchess, whose Aunt of Saxony has strongly recommended her Grace to her.—Sir Wm. Duncan, they

say, is dead at Naples, and has left to Lady Mary all
he had, only recommending his nephew to her. Did
you ever hear that it was rigorously a Platonic
Matrimony ? '

## CHAPTER XII.

### 1775.

THE Grand-Ducal City of Florence was now interested
in graver matters than even deaths of popes or
marriages of peers ; and those matters were connected
with the revolt of the English colonies in America, the
ultimate success of which, accomplished by timely
French succour, turned out so beneficially for the
' rebels,' and proved to be not less beneficial to the
old mother country.   May peace be within the walls
and palaces of both parties !   Mann had said that ' no
nation would part from such possessions without a
struggle.'   He thus writes, April 8th :—

'I can easily conceive that the agitation in both
Houses of Parliament on the American affairs must be
very great ; from thence it descends to the Coffee-
houses and Taverns, and then the Populace is so
violent over a pot of Beer ! but I suppose all this will
subside till the re-echo gets back from the most Sturdy
Colonies.   I have seen here, last week, two very
violent American Patriots who landed at Leghorn,
directly from thence.   They seemed to think and
wish that all the late healing concessions may avail

nothing.   If all their countrymen are as furious as
they are, I should despair of it too.'   In May, Mann
and the English colony in Florence had less hopes
than ever ; but he endeavoured to console himself and
others ' by the persuasion that half what we see in our
publick papers is not true.   I am leaving Politicks to
my nephew.'   In June it is worse still : ' What a
dreadful scene is opened in America ; the consequence
of which, at all Events, must be terrible.'   When
news reached Florence of the Act of Perpetual Union
between the States having been agreed upon, our
Envoy seems to have been struck dumb.   There is not
another allusion to America in any letter throughout
the year.

There were two unfortunate princes in Italy to
whom the course of events in America was a source of
much comfort and congratulation, namely, the Chevalier, or Count Albany, in Florence, and the Cardinal
York, in Rome.   Charles Edward had a distaste for
Rome, where he was not recognised by a kingly title ;
and, by the aid of the Cardinal, he. lived decently in
Florence.   Some of our countrymen, according to Dr.
Moore, made the humble state to which he was reduced ' a frequent theme of ridicule, and who, as
often as they saw him in public, affected to pass by
with an air of sneering insult.'   ' Base, abject, and
unmanly,' are the epithets which the Doctor justly
applies to such ill-bred and no-hearted persons.   On
one occasion, Moore and the Duke of Hamilton (with
whom he was travelling as physician) encountered
Charles Edward and his young wife in one of the
avenues of a public walk near the city.   ' . . . We

observed,' he says, 'two men and two ladies, followed
by four servants in livery.   One of the men wore the
insignia of the Garter.   We were told this was the
Count Albany, and that the lady next to him was the
Countess.   We yielded the walk, and pulled off our
hats.   The gentleman along with them was the Envoy
of the King of Prussia to the Court of Turin.   He
whispered the Count who, returning the salutation,
looked very earnestly at the Duke of Hamilton.   We
have seen them almost every evening since, either at
the Opera, or on the public walk.   His Grace does not
affect to shun the avenue in which they happen to
be ; and, as often as we pass near them, the Count
fixes his eyes in a most impressive manner on the
Duke, as if he meant to say,—our ancestors were
better acquainted.'   Dr. Moore says of the Countess :
' She is a beautiful woman, much beloved by those who
know her, who universally describe her as lively, intelligent, and agreeable.'

Mann does not paint the Chevalier in such pleasant
colours.   'The Pretender,' he writes, July 28th, 'whom
we call here Count Albani, is in a bad state of health ;
he has long had a sore leg, which occasioned a great
Discharge ;  this stoped not long ago, and a slow fever
ensued, with many other bad symptoms ; the beginning of the week they alarmed his people much.   The
bad leg is still closed, and the good one has threatened
an opening, which was to be desired, but it has not
happened yet.'

Mann is not too courteous with regard to the lady.
Referring to a match having been concluded ' between
a Mr. Danby, son of a rich Yorkshire Gentleman, and

the eldest Miss Seymour,' he adds: ' Her Farther had made all his dispositions for staying here this summer, but this affair will break through them, how much so ever it may displease the Comtesse d'Albani, for whom he has the strongest *attachment,* with the approbation of her husband, but with such vigilant attention, he says, as at all events, not to render the legitimacy of an Heir to his Crown dubious. This occasions much mirth here.'

' When the Chevalier was looking out for a house in Florence, where he and the Countess might be permanently established, the Countess employed Marquis di Barbantani (French Minister) to ask my leave (not exactly in those terms) to take one of the English Publick houses all to themselves, to which you will easily imagine I made no objection, but on further examination, it did not suit them. He is in a very dubious state of health. The discharge from his legs, which was supposed to keep him alive, by defeating the bad effects of drunkenness, is closed, and his legs are vastly swelled. . . . nevertheless, they say, he may go on for many more years than his young, amiable wife may wish, though she behaves to him with all the attention, nay tenderness, that is possible. He never quits her.'

In the letters of the early part of this year, none are to be found with any reference to the election of the new supreme Pontiff. Angelo Braschi was elected Pope on the 15th of February. He is known in history as that Pius the Sixth whom Bonaparte dethroned; who was expelled from Rome and deposed in February, 1798; and who died, in August of the

following year, at Valence. Mann's first notice of him
is in a letter of May 31st :—

'I can only talk to you of a pompous simple Pope,
who is in his heart a Jesuit ; and who, by degrees,
will restore them to a great part of what they were
formerly. They are to be re-instated in their colleges,
and live in Society. They are to say Mass publickly,
and, it is said, will be permitted to receive Confessions:
the rest may be safely left to their own Industry. The
King of Spain has, hitherto, been the only great
Enemy to that Society, from a motive of fear for his
own life. The Pope has many means to persuade him
that an unchristian perseverance in his Enmity may
hazard his life in this world and in the world to come.
Give only time to the Church of Rome and she will at
last attain her end.'

'The very moment of the Pope's Election, he wrote
a letter with his own hand, to his Unkle, the Bishop
at Casena, with orders to give portions to a number of
the prettiest girls, "*le piu vestose*," and to cloath them
from head to foot. Every part of their dress he
described ; and, to finish, he ordered each girl should
have a *Battasie*, a term which his holyness invented
on the occasion, by which he meant what the French
call a " Couvre-Salope." He has now published an
Edict for the dress of Priests ; describing the manner
of wearing their hair ; prohibiting powder as highly
odious to God, and destructive of their future Salvation. What will smart Priests and Abbés in France
say to this ? They will all be banished from the
polite Toilettes at Paris. They will stink like Goats
or Capuchins, and their wit will flag for want of

opportunities to exert it.    In short, this poor man
employs his whole time in matters of this importance;
not reflecting that he may destroy his own work, and
that the Eye has a considerable share in the propaga-
tion of his Religion.    I formerly knew a Lady Howe
in England who, being upbraided by her female friends
for becoming a Catholick.    " What could be your
Ladyship's motive ? "—" Why really, Madam, you
must allow that the Roman Catholick Religion is
much more entertaining ! "    To this there was no
reply.'

How resolute Spain was in active hostility against
the Society of Jesus may be seen in a paragraph of a
letter, dated June 27th, at which time there were
several Jesuits, prisoners in the Castle of St. Angelo.

'. . . The Pope was secretly disposed in their
favour, and intended to set them at liberty ; but the
vigilant Monino' (ambassador of Spain, in Rome)
' advised his master of it, who by the return of the
Post, ordered him to tell the Pope, that the moment
*that* should happen, he was to leave Rome, with all the
Spaniards who were there.    This menace struck the
Pope extremely, and, it is supposed, will decide the
fate of those poor devils, for their lives.    The Pope
is turned out a simple man ; and though he has
not many much wiser than himself to deal with,
obstinacy on the part of the King of Spain will,
on this occasion, defeat all his holynesses purposes.'

One present purpose was the ceremonious carrying
out of the 'Possesso,' in reference to which Mann writes,
October 28th :—' . . . The great show at Rome of
the Pope's taking possession, attracts many strangers.

Crouds arrive here daily on their way thither, for the 19th of next month, when all the pomp of that Court will be displayed. The Pretender will not assist at it.'

In the last century the 'Possesso,' was a very magnificent affair. Our Minister was not present on this occasion; but the Duke of Hamilton's physician was, and he has fully described it in one of his gossiping letters from Rome, from which a few passages may be appropriately taken, by way of supplement to Mann.

'On this occasion the Pope goes to the Basilica of St. John Lateran, and, as the phrase is, takes possession of it. This church, they tell you, is the most ancient of all the churches in Rome, and the mother of all the churches in Christendom. When he has got possession of this, therefore, he *must* be the real head of the Christian church, and Christ's vice-gerent upon Earth. From St. John Lateran's he proceeds to the Capitol and receives the keys of the fortress; after which, it is equally clear that as an earthly prince, he thought, like the ancient possessors of the Capitol, to have a supremacy over all kings.'

Dr. Moore saw the procession from the senator's house in the Capitol, by favour of Prince Giustiniani.

'On arriving, we were surprized to find the main body of the Palace, as well as the Palazzo de' Conservatori and the Museum, which form the two wings, all hung with crimson silk laced with gold. The bases and capitals of the pillars and pilasters, where the silk could not be accurately applied, were gilt. Only imagine what a figure the Farnesan Hercules would make, dressed in a silk suit, like a

French petit-maître. To cover the noble simplicity of Michael Angelo's architecture with such frippery by way of ornament, is, in my mind, a piece of refinement equally laudable.'

'We were led to a balcony, where a number of ladies of the first distinction in Rome were assembled. There were no men, excepting a very few strangers; most part of the Roman noblemen have some function in the procession. The instant of his Holiness's departure from the Vatican was announced by a discharge of cannon from the castle of St. Angelo; on the top of which the standard of the church had been flying ever since morning. We had a full view of the cavalcade, on its return from the church, as it ascended to the Capitol. The officers of the Pope's horse-guards were dressed in a style equally rich and becoming. It was something between the Hungarian and Spanish dress. I do not know whether the King of Prussia would approve of the great amount of plumage they wore in their hats, but it is picturesque; and showy qualities are the most essential to the guards of his Holiness. The Swiss guards were, on this occasion, dressed with less propriety; their uniforms were real coats of mail, with iron helmets on their heads, as if they had been to take the Capitol by storm, and expected a vigorous resistance. Their appearance was strongly contrasted with that of the Roman Barons, who were on horseback, without boots, and in full dress; each of them was preceded by four pages, their hair hanging in regular ringlets to the middle of their backs. They were followed by a number of servants in rich liveries.

Bishops and other Ecclesiastics succeeded the Barons,
and then came the Cardinals on horseback, in their
purple robes, which covered every part of the horses
except the head. You may be sure that the horses
employed at such ceremonies are the gentlest that
can be found ; for if they were at all unruly, they
might not only injure the surrounding crowd but
throw their Eminences, who are not celebrated for
their skill in horsemanship. Last of all came the
Pope himself, mounted on a milk white mule, distributing blessings with an unsparing hand among the
multitude who followed him with acclamations of
" Viva il Santo Padre!" and, prostrating themselves
on the ground before his mule, " Benedizione, Santo
Padre ! " The Holy Father took particular care to
wave his hand in the form of the Cross, that the
blessings he pronounced at the same instant might
have the greater efficacy. As his Holiness is employed
in this manner during the whole of the procession, he
cannot be supposed to give the least attention to his
mule, the bridle of which is held by two persons who
walk by his side, with some others, to catch the
*infallible* father of the Church, in case the mule
should stumble.'

'At the entrance of the Capitol, he was met by
the Senator of Rome who, falling on his knees,
delivered the keys into the hands of his Holiness,
who pronounced a blessing over him, and restored
him the keys. Proceeding from the Capitol, the
Pope was met by a deputation of Jews, soon after
he had passed through the Arch of Titus. They
were headed by the Chief Rabbi, who presented

him with a long scroll of parchment on which is
written the whole law of Moses in Hebrew. His
Holiness received the parchment in a very gracious
manner, telling the Rabbi, at the same time, that
he accepted his present out of respect to the law
itself, but entirely rejected his interpretation ; for
the ancient law having been fulfilled by the coming
of the Messiah, was no longer in force. As this
was not a convenient time or place for the Rabbi
to enter into a controversy upon the subject, he
bowed his head in silence, and retired with his
countrymen, in the full conviction, that the false-
hood of the Pope's assertion would be made manifest
to the whole Universe in due time. His Holiness,
meanwhile, proceeded in triumph, through the
principal streets to the Vatican.'

Moore's opinion of the new Pope, Pius the Sixth,
is of rather a higher quality than Mann's ; while his
judgment on Clement the Fourteenth, is in some
respects more severe than that of Mann. Under
Clement, there was a relaxation of church discipline. That Pope could not bear the ostentatious
parade of his station, without giving evidence of his
distaste. He was moderate in his views, tolerant
of those of others, and held a great many things
as trivial which, by others, were accounted of importance. Ganganelli had a heart for better things.
'He did all in his power,' says Moore, 'to revive trade
and to encourage manufactures and industry of every
kind. He built no churches, but he repaired the
roads all over the ecclesiastical state.' As he hated
bigotry, and could even esteem a virtuous heretic,

the Jesuits whom he suppressed, stigmatized him
as 'the Protestant Pope.' Of Ganganelli's being
poisoned by those Jesuits, Moore says nothing. The
Scottish physician states that this Pontiff was of a too
easy-going disposition to suit either the religious
ideas or the political sentiments of the age, and it
was because of such easiness in the head of the
Church having begot general relaxation in the
members, that the conclave was induced to fix upon
Cardinal Braschi to be Pope ;—'from the same
motive that the Roman Senate sometimes chose a
Dictator to restore and enforce the ancient discipline.'

What men generally thought of the new Pontiff
was comprehensively expressed in the popular saying
in Rome, Florence, and indeed all over Italy : ' He has
teeth made for biting, and a nose for smelling !' What
orthodox and tender-hearted women thought of the
nobly-born, good-looking, and ultra-Catholic Pius,
was quite as clearly expressed by them, when, as
the gracefully majestic Pope passed through admiring
crowds, the women declared ' Tanto è bello quanto è
santo !'—He is as holy as he is handsome.

Mann brings into singular association with the
Pope, the notorious Duchess of Kingston. 'The
Dutchess,' he says, March 11th, ' arrived here' (from
Rome) 'late last night, in obedience to a summons from
the Ecclesiastical Court to be at Paris on such a day, to
answer to some questions that the agents of that Court
(who are to meet her there), are to propose to her,
concerning her first marriage. She has left all her
jewels and rich furniture at Rome, and under the
immediate care of the Pope, who has promised not

to deliver them to anybody, without her order attested by a Notary Publick. She says that she is resolved to stand to any trial, and seems persuaded that she shall defeat, at last, all the efforts of her persecutors. The world does not seem to be of that opinion.'

On the 8th of April, there is complication in the lady's affairs. ' Poor Lord Bristol,' Sir Horace writes, ' I see, is dead and gone. The Countess ' (as Mann calls her from the accession of her first husband to the Earldom of Bristol) ' is I suppose in Paris, where she was to meet people from England, to talk over her affairs, and, as she said, to bring them to some conclusion. The present Earl seems to be more interested in it than ever ; especially if he should be obliged to take his wife again, or sue for a divorce to get rid of her. How lucky it would have been for both, had they taken that short method before she married the Duke ! '

On April 22nd, Mann asks :—' What is become of the widdow Dutchess or the new Countesse ? I suppose she is at Paris negotiating a peace with her antagonists on the other side of the water. Whatever the event may be in regard to her title and her pecuniary affairs, the publicity of her story will always be prejudicial to her in Italy, especially among the great Ladies at Rome, who neglected her much the last time she was there.'

In June, there is news of her. Mann, styling her ' the late Dutchess of Kingston,' adds :—' She has wrote to her friend, the Marquise de los Balberos, to tell her that the Ecclesiastical Court acknowledges

her as Dutchess of Kingston; the House of Peers,
as Countess.  She chuses therefore to abide by the
former, and will probably be a Dutchess among the
Romans.  But I cannot persuade myself she will go
to Rome, while a part of the Royal Family ' (the
Duke, with the Duchess, of Gloucester) 'is there, to
discountenance her.'

The 'part of the Royal Family,' referred to above,
is noticed, with the Duchess, in the same paragraph
of a letter of August 12th.  'We hear that a great
personage is coming from your parts ; that he and
his family are to stay some time in Swizserland,
and to pass the winter at Rome, I do not augure
well of the latter part.  Neither his own appearance
there formerly, or his Brother's since, has left good
impressions there.  The great Ladies there are proud
and saucy, and are glad of having any pretext to
neglect their supporters.'

The Duke and Walpole's niece had not arrived at
Michaelmas.  'I hear,' says the Minister, September
30th, 'that the Duke of Gloucester is still at Venice, or
by this time, perhaps, on his way to Rome.  It is said
that the Dutchess is four months gone with child, a circumstance which I had not heard of before.  You seem
to disapprove of the air of Rome for the Duke's health;
but he is so prepossessed in favour of it that I believe
it will be difficult to disswade him from fixing there,
for the winter.  Siena I should not think proper for
him.  The cold is very severe there, and the vicinity
of the *Maremma* renders the air less wholesome than
in many parts of Tuscany.'

'I have not heard that any of the King's Ministers

in Italy have received instructions for their behaviour
—though I should think it very probable that they
themselves may avoid the places where any such
reside ; and not only on their account, but on that
of the Prince of the Country who would be embarrassed about the Dutchess. As to myself, I had
at all events laid down the rule you advise ; and
whether at a distance or present, shall endeavour to
show to both all possible respect, or find some method
to convey the assurance of it to them, without
transgressing any positive order that may be prescribed to me.'

After the Duke and Duchess were fairly established
in Rome, Mann had to take many precautions when
making notes of their daily life. ' I see,' he writes
to Walpole, December 30th, ' you do not receive such
minute accounts of the Duke and Dutchess as the
tender interest which you take in their welfare gives
you a just title to expect. I am cautious of making
too much enquiry, for fear of giving offence, but I
hear the Duke is well in his health, has been at some
of the Roman Assemblies, and uses proper exercise.
On a day appointed, all the English travellers were
admitted to kiss his hand ; and were graciously
received. My nephew was of the number, but he
had not any opportunity to execute the commission
I had most particularly charged him with, to lay me
at H. R. H.'s feet, and to say every thing that might
convince him of my dutiful respect. He therefore,
according to his instructions, intended to speak to
Col. Haywood, the next day ; and to convey the
same message to the Duke, by him ; but as the

Post set out before my nephew could inform me of the issue of it, or of his audience of the Dutchess (for which a day had been appointed), I must wait for my nephew's first letter from Naples, as likewise to hear from Lady Orford how she was received by the Dutchess. Lady Orford proposed to stop two or three days at Rome, and to ask an audience, if there should be any probability of obtaining it before she proceeded to Naples.'

'The Princess Falconieri is appointed by the Pope to attend the Dutchess, and notice had been given to the Roman Ladies that she would receive them on a day named; but this did not take place, on account of some slight indisposition ; and this displeased those haughty Dames, whose pretensions encrease in proportion to the superior rank of those whom they ought to respect. I fear however that everything will not turn out to their Satisfaction. A strict incognito would have made all easy, but I must own that I have never (except by very inferior Princes) seen it thoroughly adopted. The late Duke of York went the nearest to it of anybody, so did the Electress-Dowager of Saxony ; but the Margravine of Bareith ' (the King of Prussia's sister) ' received all the Ladies in Florence, sitting up on a Couch, and she only permitted a stool or two to be in the room, as a mark that a few might sit. The Elector Palatine, though under the title of Count, made the Great Duke the first visit at his inn. The Cadets of inferior sovereign houses are more tractable, they return visits and accept of invitations. Many have done me that honour. Two days' ago I entertained two Princes of the House of Darmstadt. The Margrave of Anspach Bareith is daily expected. These are very expensive guests, as all the Grandees of the Court must be invited on such occasions, both male and female.'

'. . . . I have never heard the Gabrielli in a Theater, but often in a private room, when she sang divinely; but she must be coaxed into good humour. It is said that she is often subject to some female indisposition, during which she cannot sing; but that she rather chuses to pass for capricious than disclose the cause of her impotency. This is very artfull! The first, it is supposed, may be bought off, but the other would be a prejudice to her in many other respects. She is like the Roman Ladies,—always offends where most respect is due.'

Only a few of the great English ladies flit now across the scene: Lady Mary Duncan rather retired from it. 'She is here, the most afflicted widow I have ever heard of. We went to see her; but her grief broke out into such showers of tears, that would not permit her to stay in the room, so we retired too. . . . I have made an acquaintance with another of your female friends, Lady Cecilia Johnston, who has lately been here for a few days, during which, there was, as she called it, a great "flirtation" between us. In short, I showed her all the attentions in my power. Not a wry word passed between us.' Of Mrs. Pitt, Mann speaks as 'the former great Beauty, who still retains "les plus beaux restes;" but she is so deaf that her society has become very troublesome.' After this un-gallant comment on a lady to whom he had delighted to pay court, he makes an insinuation against 'my

good old friend, Mrs. Anne Pitt. . . . She lately
wrote to me from Geneva, from whence she was going
to Nanci in Lorraine, in search of health, but I fear
that she has one great obstacle within herself, that
will defeat her views. We have crouds of English
females, and many more are expected.'

It was during this year that Mann had the offer to
which he directs Walpole's attention, in these words:—
' The last time Count Orlow was here, and alone with
me in my coach, he, with great expressions of friendship, desired to know what mark of the Russian
Empress's sensibility of the services I had rendered to
her people here' (he had been civil to the Russian
officers at Leghorn while their fleet was there) ' would
be agreeable to me. I answered that though I was
highly sensible and grateful for so gracious a disposition of H. I. Majesty, I was conscious that I had not
had any opportunity to merit such an honour (though
nothing was mentioned) and, after a civil contrast of
modesty on my side, and perseverance on his, an
awkward silence ensued of a few moments, and then
the affair ended. Pray don't think that I wish to
revive it.'

All foreigners of great rank brought letters of
recommendation to Mann, ' which,' says our Minister,
' cost me much money and time. . . . The Prince,
and his brother, Count Orlow, have been often here of
late. The former is gone to Spa for his health, and
from thence proposes to go to England. Shan't you
be curious to see a man who has set a great Princess
on a throne, and has despotically governed her and
her whole Empire so long, now sent to foreign parts to

recover his vigour ? Poor humanity ! Why has not
Nature made a more equal division of its faculties ? If
you should doubt of those of his youth, see the loads
of Diamonds he carries in proof of it. The Count, his
brother, the *fléau* of the Turks at sea, having finished
and made up all his accounts with Sir John Dick '
(Consul at Leghorn), ' and Mr. Rutherford, of the
many millions that have passed through their hands
for five years past, set out two days ago for Petersburg, highly satisfied with the conduct of his above-
mentioned agents. Sir John will next appear in
England, with his new decoration of the Order of St.
Anne of Holstein, which he has deferred putting on
till he can quit the abject name of Consul.'

The great event of the year for Sir Horace himself was the coming to his house of the nephew whom
he had never seen (Horace Mann) and his fair and
fragile wife, Lady Lucy. ' I am already charmed
with their behaviour,' he writes, May 2nd. ' The
sight of him has renewed all my affection for his
father ' (Galfridus), ' whose memory will be ever dear
to me. I can trace in him all that cheerfulness, good
nature, and sweetness of temper that *he* enjoyed in the
first part of his life,—for, from a motive of affection,
he always concealed from me, everything that he
knew must give me affliction. Lady Lucy is a most
amiable woman. They seem to adore each other; but
even this contributes to lessen their happiness. The
bad situation of her health deprives her of every
amusement that might even contribute to her recovery. She has not been able yet to dine at table, or
to receive any visits, though half the Town has called

upon her. Time and great tranquility seem to be the
only remedy. They have a charming little girl who
takes up her whole attention.'

About three weeks later Mann pursues the theme :
' I am charmed with my nephew, having found him
exactly such as you have often described him to be.
The sweetness of his temper reminds me every hour
(with sighs) of what his father was. His great good
sense, his easy behaviour, with the most amiable disposition to please, but above all his Respect and love
for you, will ever endear him to me. It is not partiality, nor even your approbation that blinds me. I
have compared him with all the young English who
have passed by during a long course of years, and
have not met with one so exactly to my own mind as
he is. He has all the amiable vivacity and activity
that one likes in a young man, but not a grain of
that rough jollity that makes those young English
so insupportable.'

' Lady Lucy is of a sweet temper, sensible, gentle,
compliant with every thing that her weak constitution
will admit. For the first ten days she was so much
out of order that I seldom saw her ; for I have strictly
complied with the conditions we had settled, that she
was to do exactly what she pleased and not to attempt
anything out of complaisance to others. This method
has produced a wonderful effect. She now comes to
table, and for the two last evenings has come out of
her appartment, I can't say, to receive, but to associate
with the Ladies who were there ; and she has been
once at the Burletta. These are great strides towards
the recovery of her health. They have a sweet babe

with them, whose education occupies all her mother's attention.'

*May 31st.*—' I am charmed with him, every day, more and more ; and I hope he is contented with me. Lady Lucy seems a good deal improved in her health. *He* has promised not to obstruct her total recovery.' On June the 18th, Mann's tone is not so hopeful :— ' Lady Lucy's illness which, with great grief, I fear will soon come to a fatal end, keeps my nephew abroad at a time that our joint affairs require his presence in England. The last accounts of her give room to suspect that her Physician has mistaken her case ; as he now owns that it is a dropsy in her Breast ; but whether it was originally so, or became such in the course of her illness, it is dubious whether a Sea voyage, which was supposed might be beneficial in a consumption, would be proper now. A consultation was to be held on this point by Dr. Drummond and the Physicians of the Country, on the result of which the sea voyage was to depend. The ship was not ready, so that no time would be lost by that precaution.'

'My Sister, who died lately, was quite a child when I left England ; and I have never had any connections with her. One cannot, however, be insensible to such accidents, as they commonly occasion disturbances in families.'

In July, young Sir Horace and his younger wife left Florence for the baths of Valdagno. ' The great heat obliged Lady Lucy to travel very slowly, so that they did not get thither till the 20th. My nephew's plan seems to be to see all the north part of Italy, before he returns hither, on his way to Rome and

Naples, for the winter.' The physician at the Baths
promised the invalid a perfect restoration to health,
and, in September, she was again a welcome guest
in Mann's house,—at least, much improved in condition. ' We have great hopes that a winter at Naples
may compleat her recovery, and enable her to give the
proof of it which we are most desirous of.' Mann
affected to have no family pride ; but he was anxious
that his family should not become extinct in the male
line. In the autumn, Lady Lucy, after recovering
from a relapse, set out for Rome, with her husband.
Mann saw them depart with heaviness of heart. His
house was cheerless to him ; his own health was
failing ; and the world seemed out of gear,—for he
saw a young Republic rising beyond the Atlantic, and
the old monarchy about to tumble to pieces in France.

## CHAPTER XIII.

### 1776.

FEW and brief, and contemptuous, are the scattered
notices of Charles Edward, Count of Albany, in
Mann's letters written in 1776.   'The Pretender, poor
man, behaves well, when he is not drunk.   He has
gained his cause in a Court of Justice, against Lord
Cowper, about a house, and has hired it for five years.
Don't mention Lord Cowper's name.   His good nature
was imposed on when he entered into that dispute.'
The remaining notices of this unfortunate prince are
of melancholy interest.

'Is it possible that I should have omitted in the
frequent course of my letters, to make mention of
a Personage here whom I contributed so much to
reduce to the state of a Private Gentleman ?   Oh !
what am I saying ?   I fear you do not approve of  my
determining the Pope not to acknowledge his Royal
Titles, on his father's death, which, at the beginning
of the present reign drove him from Rome hither;
though the Pope still allows him the pension which his
father had from the Apostolick Chamber of twelve
thousand crowns.'

' He is very ill in his health from eating, and more

from excessive drinking. His legs are much swelled, and one is commonly open, the discharge from which is supposed to be necessary for his existence. Whenever that ceases, he is ill indeed. That is his case at present; but he will not stay at home. He goes every evening to the theater, where he sits in the corner of his box, in a drowsy posture, but is frequently obliged, by sickness at his stomach, to retire to the common and much frequented corridore. I have seen him in that condition, assisted by two servants, all the others that attend there fly from such a nuisance.'

'Two days ago, a couch was made for his Box, for him to lay at full length; on this he slept the greater part of yesterday evening. Visitors, however, to his wife go thither, as usual. He is jealous to such a degree that neither there or at home, she is ever out of his sight. All the avenues to her room, excepting through his own, are barricaded. The reason he gives for this is, that the succession may never be dubious. He has frequent epileptick fits which, his Physician has told me, must end in apoplexy; and that he does not think it distant.'

'His quarrel with Lord Cowper was wrongly represented in our Gazzettes. Poor creature! He never thought of getting justice by his sword, which is grown too rusty. The quarrel was about a house, which he wanted to buy; but some Obstacles obstructed the conclusion of the bargain. In the mean time Lady Cowper wanted a more proper house than her own, to lay in; and proposals were made to the proprietor, to have it for a certain number of months; and he inclined to let it to Lord Cowper.

This displeased the Comte Albanie, and the dispute was carried to a publick Tribunal, which decided in the Comte's favour. This displeased the Great Duke, who favoured the Cowpers. In short, the whole town took part in it, but I dissuaded my Lord from making an appeal to another court, so that the Albanies now reside in it; though the contract heightened the price considerably. What the Comte complained of most was, that he should meet with so rebellious an opposition from one of his own subjects. The Ladies' (Countess of Albany and Countess Cowper) 'still vye with each other in beauty, so that they can never more be friends.'

Lady Cowper has a triumph over the wife of Charles Edward in another matter:—

'Lord Cowper has obtained the honour from the King to be God-father to the child of which Lady Cowper is pregnant; and His Majesty has conferred that upon me of being His Proxy. Now, I am quite ignorant of what is required of me on such an occasion, and must have recourse to you, my Dear Sir, for information. . . . Is any particular formality or show in dress necessary? Am I to give money to the Nurse, Accoucheur, or Servants? I know that the King makes a present to the Mother or Child, but exclusive of that (which, I suppose, is all that the Court does), whether a Proxy gives anything himself. This, I believe, may be exactly known, as the King seldom assists in person at such ceremonies.' 'The King,' says Walpole in reply, 'gives plate to his god-children; you, I dare to say, are to give nothing, and indubitably have no particular dress. Here, I think, the

lord or lady who represents, rides backwards and alone
in a royal coach; as your own is a representative of
the King's, no doubt, it will do.'   Walpole adds, in a
postcript: 'I saw Lady Holdernesse' (Lady of the
Bedchamber to the Queen) 'to-night, and consulted
her, and found that I had been right in all my directions.   *You* can give nothing, unless you are ordered;
and as you cannot possibly go in one of the King's
coaches, need not ride backwards in your own.'

This selection of a godfather in May for a possible
event which did not occur till August, was an illustration of 'taking time by the forelock.'   How mother,
father, child, and proxies rather astonished the Florentines is thus related :—

'The absence of our Court,' Mann writes, in one of
his August letters, 'adds to the common sterility of
anything interesting here; but a private event, in
which all ranks of people have taken some part, is still
the object of conversation.   Lady Cowper's delivery of
a son has diffused a riotous joy among the common
people, who have expressed it for three evenings by
little Bon-fires and lights at their paper windows.
Lord Cowper's generosity has always made him very
popular; but on this occasion he has displayed a
Royal Magnificence, by distributing a large quantity
of bread to the poor of two Parishes, and other Acts of
Charity.   My Lady, too, has received a noble mark of
his Generosity, in a Diamond Necklace, valued at
£1500; and five hundred zecchins' (about £250) 'for
her Pocket.'

'The Florentine Dames stare at such profusion,
and reproach their Lords with Niggardliness on such

occasions. Perhaps you may remember,—I know it
excited our Mirth when you was here,—that one of our
first Tuscan peeresses was regaled by her husband, for
a Son and Heir, with a *Coupon* of the best black
velvet for a Gown, and fifty zecchins, all in new ten
paul pieces! The Christening is to be performed
next week, with as much Pomp as only the interven-
tion of the English can make. Sir John Dick (who
with his wife has been with me for some time) is to be
the other proxy for Lord Spencer; and *she'* (Lady
Dick) 'for Lady Dowager Cowper.'

In September says Mann: 'The Christening went
off very well, and my proxyhood made a pompous
article in the Italian Gazettes; but the common people
who posted themselves in the street, to see me pass,
were much disappointed, expecting to see a coach and
six, instead of a pair of horses! but, as to the rest, the
Gazetteer allowed it to be a *sfarzosa Gala.* I had
added some lace to my Gala liveries. The other
Sponsors were Lord Spencer and Lady Dowager
Cowper, represented by Sir John and Lady Dick, who
are since gone to Leghorne to break up house, and
leave that place. He put on, on that occasion, his order
of St. Anne of Holstein. Before they go to Rome for
the winter, he has been busy in packing up his things
for England; but he has been much disappointed by
a refusal he received last week, to admit them there,
duty free; so that he is now busy again in unpacking
them for sale.'

In another September letter our Minister incident-
ally alludes to an unamiable quality in Italian manners:—'We have here the Duke of Ostrogothia, a very

affable and good-natured Prince, whom you will see in
England in the course of the Winter. We are in a
suite of great dinners for him; mine was on Sunday
—don't think that the Italians contribute to them.
There is not one of them who ever invites, though
many are ambitious of partaking of those we give.'

A more celebrated visitor than the Swedish Duke
is thus hit off:—'The Dutchess of Chartres is flying
through Italy. She allowed five days for Rome, three
for Naples, etc. She has taken in Italy. The *caricata
caricatura* of her head excites laughter. She wears
17 large plumes; more than Alexander in an Opera!'
Other foreigners figured at the Tuscan Court this year.
'We have now here the Margrave of Anspach, to whom
I pay great court. He is extremely affable and gracious
to me as he was twenty years ago. I entertained him
yesterday at a dinner *de* 24 *couverts;* at which your
amiable friend and my old acquaintance, Baron Glechin,
assisted. We had talked an hour the day before about
England, which he adores. . . . I asked the Margrave
if he knew you. He broke out in raptures, and said
how happy he had been in that particular; that his
first acquaintance with you was made at Paris, at
your charming old blind friend's house; that he had
cultivated it in England, and that he had all the
reason to flatter himself, "qu'il m'honore de son
amitié."'

Some of the English lady visitors were to the full
as eccentric as the Duchess of Chartres. 'We have a
crowd of English of both sexes. The females don't do
us much honour. One of them made her entry on
horseback, with a vis à vis behind for a nurse and her

child, drawn by her own pair of Nags, driven by an old English coachman. That is her town equipage too, without a servant, so that the old fellow is forced to get off his box, to knock at a door or let her out. She came to dinner and to a large assembly here of our greatest court Ladies in a *pet en l'air* (farthingale) but with a yard of feathers and trumpery on her head. Surely our Nation produces more originals than any other. To compensate and to draw off the Eyes from this oddity, we have a charming American lass of sixteen. They are all to be here this evening.'

In a letter of May the 14th, Mann tells his correspondent with regard to these visitors:—' I have but a slender remembrance of the Lady who has recorded me in her works. I certainly did not do much to secure such an honour, as I do not recollect her. Such travelling searchers after reputation often boast of civilities from a Minister, which they interpret as a Homage paid to their Merit! I must therefore rank Mrs. Miller in that class.' (She was the famous bluestocking lady of Bath Easton). 'I have often regretted the not having kept a list of my countrymen and women' (last word now spelt correctly for the first time) ' who have passed here in my time, with some private notes about them. The perusal of it would still have amused me. We have very lately had a remarkable couple, a Mr. Hewett and his wife, both of a certain age, which she endeavoured to conceal with *rouge*, and the most fantastical dress, which he too liked. They seemed fond in company, but were always fighting when alone! He beat her in Boboli' (part of the Grand Ducal gardens) ' till a

sentinel separated them.　Some days after, the noise
of his chastisement, in their room, was so great as to
alarm the servants, who broke open the door.　They
found her on the floor in a dismal condition.　He said
they were acting a Tragedy, which appeared too true,
by the Lady's black eye and bruises.'

To Mann's announcement that Mrs. Pitt had
returned to Pisa, from whence she had been · driven
' by the riot and noise of building the scaffold for
their ridiculous Battle of the Bridge, after Easter,'
Walpole replies :—' Who thought of Mrs. Pitt rising
again at Pisa ? . . . But who can calculate the notions
of such eccentric heads as the English ?　My dear
country men and women are—very sensible ! '

Amongst the latter was the Duchess of Kingston
who has been previously mentioned.　She occupies
as much space in Mann's letters of this year as in
Walpole's.　It may be as well to mention here that
when she was Miss Chudleigh, and Maid of Honour to
the Princess of Wales, she was privately married in
1744 to the gallant Augustus Hervey, and she continued
to act as Maid of Honour, after this marriage—which
was never acknowledged by either party.　In 1766
she was publicly married to the Duke of Kingston,
who is said to have bought, with money, the collusion
of the first husband.　The Duke died in 1773, leaving
his widow his whole estate, of £17,000 a year, the
landed property for life ; and the personals absolutely.
The natural and legal heirs opposed her succession, on
the ground that her marriage with the Duke was null
and void, being an act of bigamy.　The Ecclesiastical
Court ignored the first marriage. The House of Lords,

before whom she was tried this year, undid the second
by pronouncing her thereby guilty of bigamy. She
withdrew to the continent before any penalty (which
included burning in the hand) could be pronounced;
and as her first husband, who was then in Italy, had
succeeded to the Earldom of Bristol, she was said to
have been reduced to the rank of Countess. Previous
to the trial, Mann wrote :—

' I see no way for the Dutchess of Kingston to get
out of the terrible Laberinth she is in ; nor how she
will be able even to stand the trial. What is the Pope
to do with the treasure he has taken charge of, upon
a solemn promise never to deliver it up, without an
order from her, well authenticated. Lord Bristol ' (the
first husband) ' is at Nice. He must be vastly mortified if he reads the printed papers ; and more so,
probably, by the prospect of the very serious consequences.'

In April, after the trial was over, the English
in Italy made free comments upon the illustrious
convict. ' Mrs. Pitt says, she is persuaded that the
Dutchess, herself, so far from being humbled, was
mightily pleased in having assembled so august a
Senate, and such a full house ! '

*May* 14*th.*—' Lord Cowper has a letter which says
that she was landed at Calais ; I suppose, on her way
to Rome, to secure the treasure she left there ; and
that she will pass through Florence ; but after all,
who can tell that she does not mean to repair to
her first Lord, who has laid hidden, for many months,
at Nice, waiting the issue of a cause, in which he
was so much concerned. This whole affair has most

extraordinarily employed Mrs. Pitt, who proposed a doubt that neither could solve. "Suppose," said she "that a Son had been produced from this marriage, contracted under the sanction of a sentence of the Ecclesiastical Court, whose authority had never been disputed, would the Peers have declared the child a Bastard?" Probably, *yes*, I say, for the same reason that a man may forfeit an estate which he has purchased under a false title. Both are very hard cases. Mrs. Pitt was particularly shocked at the Dutchess's indecency in quoting the indulgence of the Princess' (of Wales) 'and by that means, loading her unhappy memory with part of her guilt. Mrs. Pitt bids me tell you that she thinks you will not attribute her feelings on this subject to any cause of partiality . . . The Dutchess is about 55, not more. We took to each other here as old acquaintances.' Mann and Walpole had played with her, when all three were young, at Chelsea, where Sir Robert Walpole had a house, and where the young lady's father, Colonel Chudleigh, was Governor of Chelsea Military Hospital.

*August* 13*th.*—'I cannot help pitying the poor hunted Dutchess. What will become of her, if she survives the various persecutions of her Enemies? Are not her Counsellers ashamed of having involved her into so many difficulties? The only wise step, and which she probably took without consulting them, was to secure her portable treasure under St. Peter's key, which his Vicar has promised not to give up, but by her order, well authenticated that no constraint has been used to extort it from her. How will all this end?'

The Vicar of St. Peter, as Mann calls Pius the

Sixth, does not seem to have been a personage much to be feared at this time. ' The Pope,' says Sir Horace, ' has a very serious quarrel upon his hands, with the Venetians, whom he has threatened with an Interdiction,—but that does not frighten them at all.' Indeed, the Pontiff himself was less concerned about the Venetians than he was with George the Third's brother, the Duke of Gloucester, and his Duchess (Walpole's niece, the illegitimate daughter of his brother Edward, and the widow of Earl Waldegrave), who had been for some time, in Rome, objects of kindly interest to Pope Pius. From January to October, Mann chronicles the doings of those illustrious visitors, and begins with one of some importance.

*January 23rd.*—' The Dutchess of Gloucester was happily brought to bed of a Prince, the 15th; and, at the departure of the letters, they were both as well as could be wished.' (This Prince, whose grandmother, Sir Edward Walpole's mistress, was a milliner, was the really honest man who married George the Third's youngest daughter, the Princess Mary.) '. . . The Nuncio has just now told me that great ceremony had been observed on this occasion, to authenticate the birth of this Prince. I said, that they were necessary, as he was in succession to the Crown. I shall be attentive to everything that relates to the Dutchess's health, in order to remove the anxiety you may be under on her account.'

*March 2nd.*—' I am afraid of inquiring into what passes at Rome. All that I know is that their three Royal Highnesses are well, and that the young Prince

was christened with as much *eclat* as a private house
could admit of, and that all the English at Rome
assisted at the ceremony ; but still, I don't know his
name' (William Frederick) ' or his Godfathers, excepting the Margrave of Bareith.'

*March 9th.*—' All goes on well at Rome. The
Dutchess goes abroad. I am glad to see that you
have recovered the favour of your Royal nephew. I
too have received a *mark* of his condescention.'

*April 13th.*—' The Duke and Dutchess of Gloucester are well pleased with their situation and the
attentions that are shown to them by the Pope, the
Nobility of the country, and by all the English who
pass or reside there. Everything went off properly
between them and the Arch-Dutchess Christine, who
only met at publick places. The Villa the Duke and
Dutchess are going to belongs to the Aldobrandini
family, and is in a very wholesome situation.' Similar
brief notices are scattered through some exceedingly
dry letters, till in one of October the 12th, Mann
writes to Walpole :—' Relating to your family at Rome,
I have some reason to hope that *He* ' (the Duke) ' is
altered in regard to me from what he was in Pisa.
Some very respectful attentions which I have luckily
had in my power to shew to both, have drawn the
most gracious acknowledgements from them, by
frequently condescending, both by Colonel Heywood's
letters, and messages by travellers, to express their
acceptance of them. I took the opportunity of con-
veying your letter to the Dutchess by one of the Prince
of Sweden's officers, to enclose it in a few respectful
lines to her. It was to be delivered as yesterday ; so

that I shall not know the result of it till Tuesday, in case she should do me the honour to acknowledge the receipt of it. I have been very cautious in making any inquiries, but I have heard that everything goes on tolerably well, though they were not equally well pleased with all the great Ladies at Rome, yet many had shewn proper respect to the Dutchess. She stays much at home and receives all the English with much affability. They are returned to town, from a Villa which Cardinal Albani has lent them, for the hot months. This is all I know, or that I can add by this slow conveyance.'

In the letters of this year there are few descriptions of incidents at Court, from which, indeed, Mann was beginning to absent himself. The first refers to Maria Theresa. 'This little Court has received an invitation from the Empress Queen to meet her at Gorizia, with five of their children; the 25th and 26th of April are appointed for the departure of the two Caravans. The Empress wished much to come on hither, but they frightened her by telling her she was too old to come on so far;—but the real truth is supposed to be that they would not allow her such an opportunity to squander her Treasures.'

*May 4th.*—'This Court has fixed a day for their departure for Gorizia (and all their baggage was sent thither to meet the Empress, who has set her mind on seeing as many of her Grand-children as could be carried thither); but a Courier arrived here two days ago to acquaint the G. Duke that the Empress's age and state of health would not permit her to make that journey. The disappointment is very visible here, and so much the more, as it is suspected that other reasons were more prevalent than those that were alleged ! '

The son, daughter-in-law, and grandchildren of Maria Theresa accordingly went to Vienna to gratify the aged Empress.   On October 19th, Mann writes:— ' This Court is returned from Vienna, but is still *en retraite.*   We are to be admitted to-morrow, and each Minister is to present his travelling countrymen.  Lord John Clinton is to be at the head of those I am to carry.   He asked me, on his arrival, whether you had announced him to me ; and I said, *yes,* supposing it had escaped your memory.'

Throughout the letters of this year there is a tone of despondency whenever the writer refers to himself. A cause for this is found in Mann's declining health, and in vexations arising out of deaths of his kindred, and disputed rights to property, in which he had little personal interest ; and in the long and iterated and re-iterated details, in which readers of the present day would find none at all.  When there was some idea that these family troubles might require his presence in England, the old Minister, so far from being glad, was affrighted at the prospect of once more seeing his native country.   ' Consider, I beg you, my age, and all the inconveniences attending such a journey, the difference of the climate,  and the different manner of living.   Retirement (from office) I abhor, being conscious I have not resources enough in myself to make it supportable, nor complyance sufficient to live in the country with any of my relations, as formerly my Brother proposed to me, saying that if at any time I should chuse to go home or should be removed from

hence, he would order an Appartment to be properly
fitted up at Linton for me.  What should I ever do
in the great town of London, without employment or
pursuit of any kind, and without health or strength to
partake of the fatiguing amusements of it ?  I have no
friend but you.'

Walpole used to laugh at the Italianized Englishmen, like Chute and Whithead, who thought it 'horrid'
to live in London, in a house that was not between a
courtyard and a garden.  Mann looked to ending his
own career in his own Italian house, so situate, in Italy.
' I shall be more at my ease in the great decline of my
life.  I have hitherto struggled with Œconomy to
support myself with decency here, and to lay by a
small pittance to support me in case I had been removed from here, and had been deprived of my right.'

Walpole longed to see his old friend in England.
'Surely,' he said, 'you can think of nothing else.
Old Knight, the cashier' (of the swindling South
Sea Company), 'used to come once a year to Calais,
to look at the cliffs of England.  You are not
banished as he was, but have been much longer
absent.  . . . I am almost afraid to frighten you
with an account of our winter ; but this is such a
winter as I never saw.  I was with you in Florence,
in 1741, and those, ever since, have been springs and
sometimes summers.  This was made for the North
Pole, has lasted three weeks, and, every day, grows
worse and worse.'  To this, Mann replies : — 'The
example you quote me of old Knight does not exactly
*quadre* with my situation ; he left England much
later in life than I did, and though he might once

a year go to Calais to see our Cliffs, he no sooner got leave to return to them than he repented of changing climates and died a few months after. How could I expect a better fate at my age and with so feeble a constitution, that I was sent in a ship to Naples, in my younger days, with my coffin by my side. I should be unwilling now to want another, at least for a few years.' In succeeding letters, Mann still dwells on age, ill-health, and indifference to return to the native scenes of his youth. Walpole ultimately felt that there would be something inexpressibly sad in a meeting of the two friends after so many years, and under circumstances which indicated that they only met to bid each other farewell.

Sir Horace Mann's failing health did not diminish his active kindness towards his countrymen. 'The hospitality and politeness of the British Minister,' says Dr. Moore, in his 'View of Society and Manners in Italy,' 'afford his countrymen frequent opportunities of forming an acquaintance with the best company in Florence. This gentleman has been here about thirty years' (seven and thirty) 'and is greatly esteemed by the Florentines. It is probably owing to this circumstance, and to the magnificent style in which some English Noblemen live, who have long resided here, that the English in general are favourites in this place. Lord Cowper's conduct and disposition confirm them in the opinion they long have had of the good nature and integrity of the nation to which he belongs. His lady is of an amiable character and affords them a very favourable specimen of an English beauty.'

Mann occasionally refers to his visits to the Casino, a 'society,' says Moore, 'which is pretty much on the same footing with the clubs in London. . . . There is one essential difference, however, between this and the English clubs,—that women as well as men are members;' and he adds : ' The company of both sexes behave with more frankness and familiarity to strangers, as well as to each other, than is customary in public assemblies in other parts of Italy.'

Mann also occasionally speaks of a Lady as his Cicisbea, meaning thereby one whom he visited for the sake of an hour's gossip, and no doubt, Baretti was right in his statement that Cicisbeo and Cicisbea denoted a Platonic admirer of either sex. Dr. Moore's description of the system in 1776 differs a little from that given many years before by the Earl of Cork and Orrery. In the Earl's time, when Mann was young in Florence, there seems to have been three sorts of Cicisbei : the honorary, the actual cavaliere servente, and the lover. Dr. Lalande affirms that a Cicisbeo served his lady as a brother would his sister; but he allows that there were Cicisbeos of love as well as Cicisbeos of convenience.

Lord Cork's experience led him to a statement substantially to this effect. The system was an old-established one, and when a couple were about to marry, the Cicisbeo who was to wait on her, was often previously elected, and his name inscribed, and his duties laid down, in the marriage contract. In a week after marriage, at all events, she was never seen abroad with her husband, or without her Cicisbeo.

Husband and wife dined together invariably; the
presence of the Cicisbeo then would have been an
anachronism. But the faithful cavaliere servente
presented himself when the lady had shaken off sleep
and the husband was gone on the service of Cicisbeo-
ship to some other man's wife. Then, he presented
her chocolate, set her slippers in nice order to be met
by her dainty feet, and next disappeared till she was
ready to arrange with him the programme for the
day's occupations and diversions. If she went abroad,
he accompanied her to the public promenade or to
private visits. If she remained at home to receive
visitors, the Cicisbeo was at her side; and at evening
parties, the Cicisbeo helped his Cicisbea to receive
her guests, and was at her elbow, ready for any errand
or service, during the whole evening. He was discreet
as well as assiduous, and if the lady showed any
disposition to converse with a gentleman, the Cicisbeo
left them to their devices, and amused himself by
playing with her lapdog or in teaching the macaw to
speak Italian.

Moore's theory as to the origin of Cicisbeism is
that it sprung out of the resistance of woman against
the sort of solitary imprisonment, and the implied distrust which they once endured at the hands of their
jealous husbands. 'From the custom of secluding
the wife from all mankind but her husband, it
became the fashion that she should never be seen
with her husband, and yet always have a man at
her elbow.' This man, the proto-Cicisbeo, was a
friend, who could be trusted by the husband, and who
was not disagreeable to the wife. ' It was stipulated

that the lady, while abroad under his care, should converse with no other man but in his presence and with his approbation.   He was to be her guardian, her friend, and her gentleman-usher.'   This grew into a species of tyranny which neither party expected.   'In 1776,' says Moore, 'even where there is the greatest harmony and love between the husband and wife, and although each would prefer the other's company to any other, still, such is the tyranny of fashion, they must separate every evening; he, to play the cavaliero servente to another woman, and she to be led about by another man. . . .'

'The Cicisbeo, in many instances, is a poor relation, or humble friend who, not being in circumstances to support an equipage, is happy to be admitted into all the societies, and to be carried about to public diversions, as an appendage to the lady. . . . The humble and timid air which many of them betray in the presence of the ladies, and the perseverance with which they continue their services, notwithstanding the contemptuous stile in which they are treated, is equally unlike the haughtiness natural to favoured lovers, and the indifference of men satiated with enjoyment.'   That men could be found with leisure and inclination to be the mere servants of idle and supercilious women, is thus accounted for:—
'The Italian nobility dare not intermeddle in politics ; can find no employment in the army or navy, and there are no such amusements in the country as hunting or drinking.'   It was only among the upper and idle ranks that the system ever existed.   The middle and lower ranks had no leisure for such

unmanly trifling; the married men were engaged in
their respective trades or professions, and their leisure
hours were passed in company with their wives and
children.' In the descriptions of the Earl of Cork
and Doctor Moore, Cicisbeism is represented as it
existed in Mann's time. At present it has no existence at all, and the Italian husband may say, as was
once said for Italy, *farà da se!*

But the one lady who most occupied Mann's
thoughts, was the 'Lady Lucy,' the wife of his
nephew Horace, or Horatio Mann. She was the sixth
of the ten daughters of Baptist Noel, fourth Earl of
Gainsborough; and she was the sister of the fifth and
sixth Earls. Mann's interest in her was founded on
a little family pride as well as sincere affection. His
fervent hope was that, through her, his family name
would be continued, that on the little family estate
at Linton, son would succeed to father; and that
the name of Mann would go down to succeeding
generations. In dwelling on this subject, he goes into
somewhat lengthened details, with copious remarks on
both nephew and niece. The latter had begun to show
symptoms of consumption; but that painless disease
did not affect her spirits. She shook off the languor,
and then suffered from the effort. A dance had the
strongest temptation for this charming young person;
but after she had taken part in a minuet, joined in a
cotillon, or had swam through the mazes of a *contre-
danse,* she was sensible that she had shared the perils
of a Dance of Death, and was wiser till she recovered
some degree of her old strength; and then, the
brilliant and accomplished creature glided rather than

flung herself into the vortex of pleasure, but only to issue therefrom more feeble and more irreparably weakened than ever. An hour's sunshine, provided it was not fierce, seemed to revive her. It would tempt her abroad, and the beauty of a treacherous Italian night would allure her to tarry in it, after sundown, whence came chill and cold, which gave permanency to a cruel, killing cough, which had till then only been occasional. Mann's account of these phases of Lady Lucy's health, the expression of his hopes that she would yet be the happy mother of healthy sons, the hearty joy he felt when she seemed to improve, the depression which weighed upon him when the Shadow of Death came upon her, darker and nearer— would fill half this volume. He was never tired of the theme, but the intense interest he had in dwelling on it would scarcely be understood now. The substance of what Mann wrote up to this time, concerning his niece, is contained in the above few lines. After Lady Lucy left Florence, with her husband and little daughter, Sir Horace was painfully eager to have news of the progress made in search of health. In that search she sailed from port to port, drank at healing springs, dwelt in sheltered nooks, bathed in salutiferous waters, and every day, losing nothing of Hope, drew unconsciously nearer and nearer to Death. The old bachelor uncle, who cared so much for a mere name, and for her who, he hoped, would help to perpetuate it in her native land, found sympathy among the Florentine ladies, with whom he conversed freely on that and, indeed, every other subject.

## CHAPTER XIV.

### 1777.

THERE were public events in which the world was
interested at this period, and which occupied our
Minister's mind at Florence, as much as the one
subject connected with his private affairs and the
vitality of his name. The rebellion in the English
Colonies in America was, of course, vigorously and
diversely discussed by Mann and his diplomatic
colleagues in Florence. In the comments of the
British Envoy there was some sorrow, but no anger.
'I was much surprized,' he says, January 7th, 'to
see, in the papers, a diffidence which some pretended
to have conceived of Sir William Howe, grounded on
the civility with which he received the American
Deputies. How could a reconciliation ever be hoped
for, unless he received them and heard their proposals?
For my part, though that conference produced no
decision, I conceived hopes that there were grounds
for an accommodation. If, on the contrary, the Congress meant it only as a feint to conceal their reliance
on France and Spain (which I think is much to be
feared), that conference could produce no harm or
prejudice to us, and the civility shown by Sir William

Howe to those Deputies only confirmed the desire
of England to bring about a happy reconciliation.  I
wish there were better hopes of it now.'

The Prince, who had sold some of his own soldiers
to fight in a quarrel in which they were in no way
concerned, came under Mann's view in Florence :—

*January 25th.*—'The Master of the brave Hessians
passed by here, lately, on his way to Rome, to confirm
his conversion at the Pope's feet.  I made many
attempts, by visits and messages, to pay my court
to him, but his Incognito was so strict that he would
not receive anybody else, nor did any civilities pass
between him and this Court, though he appeared
publickly about the Town and at the Theaters.  He
is now at Rome where, after reciprocal visits *en blanc'*
(leaving cards), 'the Duke of Gloucester went into
his Box at the Opera.  He visited the Pope by the
back-stairs, and was alone with him for over an hour.
What passed, or what language they conversed in,
is not known.  His holyness has not had so polite
an education as his Predecessor Ganganelli.  I believe
that he frequents the Duke's house, but I never
enquire what passes there ; though, I have lately
been told by some English who are come from thence,
that the Duke has frequent small returns of his
disorder.  This may in some measure be attributed to
the rigour of the season, which has been greater all
over Italy than has been known for many years.'

'He' who frequented the Duke of Gloucester's
house, at Rome, was not Pope Pius VI, but 'the
Master of the brave Hessians,' who sold his soldiers.
Nevertheless, the courtesy of the Pontiff towards the

English Prince was never wanting. It was sometimes
carried almost to excess,—as it was on the occasion
when, on a rainy day, the carriages of the Pope and
the Duke entered at the opposite ends of a muddy
street in Rome, at the same moment. When the
vehicles were near each other, the Duke and the Pope
had a lively little contest in civility. Each carriage
was stopt (by order of him who sat therein) that the
other might pass first. The Prince would not accept
or assume this mark of precedence; and the Pontiff
was as stiff-necked in his politeness as the Prince. In
his proud humility, neither would yield; meanwhile,
gaping spectators were enjoying the edifying spectacle,
while others were on their knees in the mud piously
awaiting the pontifical blessing. At length, Pope
Pius bade a messenger inform the Duke, that if his
royal highness did not pass, he, the Pope, would
have to back his carriage out of the street, in which
it could not turn. This finished the punctilious ceremony; while the vehicle bearing the Pope, remained
standing, that of the Duke was driven slowly and
carefully by, so as to avoid the smallest collision.
Each illustrious personage bowed to the other, and
each had reason to feel that he had behaved 'like
a gentleman.'

In April, just as Mann was daily expecting Lady
Lucy and his nephew to resume their old quarters in
his house, there happened what he calls a 'mortifying
circumstance':—'the arrival at Florence next Thursday
of much greater personages' (the Duke and Duchess
of Gloucester), 'to whom I wish to be in a condition to
show all possible respect and attention, having been

well assured that nothing will be required that can expose me to give offence elsewhere. I suppose you have had notice from Rome of their removal to a cooler place for the summer. The Lago di Garda is said to be the spot, if the Venetian Ambassador's house there convenes them. They are to return to Rome, for the winter; for though the Duke has not always been well there, it is supposed to be the place that agrees with him best.'

Later in the month, Mann, in anguish from the gout, wrote from his bed:—'My wretched gout deprives me of all possibility of gratifying my ambition and inclination to show those respectful and personal attentions to the Duke and Dutchess of Gloucester as I wished and had proposed to do. The Duke announced to me his intention of coming here, by a very gracious note from Rome, which I answered. I explained the unfortunate state I was in, which deprived me of all possibility of getting out of bed, but I begged that he would condescend to make use of my Coaches and Boxes at the Theater, and honour me with any commands that my ill health might enable me to obey. So soon as he arrived, and I had sent proper messages to both, the Duke was so gracious as to come to my bedside, and stayed till he was told that his dinner (at past Eight) was ready. After that, he made use of my Coaches to go to the Theater. The Dutchess did not go out. From her I received the most gracious and most obliging messages. The Duke returned here this morning, telling me that Her R. H. would see me and bring her children. I said that, though I had no greater ambition than that

of paying my most respectful duty to Her, yet I could
not presume to expect so great an honour and favour.
However, it is to be so, and I shall think myself happy,
even though the getting up and being rolled in a chair
should cost me a fortnight's more twitchings afterwards. The Dutchess goes to the Theater this evening
where, as last night, my servants will attend with Ice,
refreshments, etc.'

'As soon as the Duke arrived, a proper written
message was sent to the Duke Salviati, the *Grand
Chambellan*, by Colonel Haywood, to enquire after
the G. Duke's and Dutchess's health.' (She had been
brought to bed in the morning). 'This morning a civil
message was sent from the G. Duke, and an Invitation
to go to Court at noon. Everything there passed off
properly, and after dinner, He returned the visit and
was received by both their R. H.'s. The Dss. has
likewise received the ladies. Everybody is charmed
with her affability. It must be great, when she con-
descends to visit a poor old creature (as she supposes)
in his bed. This I must attribute to you, my Dear
Sir, and am infinitely obliged to you for it. They
have altered their resolution of staying only two days,
and will not set out till Tuesday. They go to Venice,
for the Ascention, and propose to pass the summer at
the Lago di Garda.'

On the 28th, Mann gives this picturesque account
of the Royal visit, at the very thought of which he
was, not too nobly, elated :—

'I must tell you how exceedingly gracious and
obliging your respectable and amiable niece has been.
The Duke told me, she was determined to see me, and

that I should see her children.    Yesterday afternoon
was appointed for her doing me that honour.    I had
not been out of bed for three weeks, but I contrived
to be wheeled into another appartment to receive
them ; and after the first ceremony, of kissing her
hand, was over, she seemed to forget her Rank, and
to consider herself only as your Niece.    She talked
to me of you with great affection ; saying you had
always been her true friend ; and that she had the
greatest esteem and affection for you.    She talked of
Sir Edward' (her father) 'in the tenderest manner.    She
took the little Prince in her arms, and bid me tell you
what I thought of him.    He is really a perfect beauty
and resembles the Dutchess extremely.    I never saw so
fine nor a more healthy child.    The little Princess '
(Sophia of Gloucester, who has lain up at Kensal
Green since many a long year) 'is not quite so well, but
she is lively and entertaining.    I must tell you a trait
that made us all laugh much.    The Dutchess pulled off
her cap to show me her fine hair, which did not please
the child, who snatched it back in disdain, and walked
off, saying,—it was not civil to take off Ladies' caps
before Gentlemen.    Lord and Lady Cowper and all
the Duke's Suite were in the room, but the child's
anger soon passed, on seeing Ice, fruits, and other
things that were presented to her.    They stayed here
two hours, and left me charmed with their great
condescention and affability, by which the Duke has
cancelled all his former unkindness at Pisa, which I
now attribute to bad people He had about him.'
    ' The Great Duke returned H. R. H.'s visit, a few
hours after the latter had been with him, and saw the

Dss. and her children. This gave the Duke an opportunity to express his desire to see the young Arch-
Dukes and Dutchesses. The next morning was appointed for that, at Poggio Imperiale, where the Great
Dutchess had lain in two days before. The G. Duke
was there to receive them. He handed the Dss. of
Gloucester through the Appartments into the G. Dss's
room, where all the children were. This was a
civility without example, and quite unexpected. They
sat at the bedside longer even than they themselves
thought proper, and would have retired, but were
pressed to stay. You will easily imagine how much
this civility and breach of all Royal Etiquettes pleased
our amiable Prince and Princess, especially when you
reflect that this is the first Court that has received the
Dutchess. Don't think me vain when I whisper to
you that the Great Dutchess, upon the report of their
arrival, long ago had declared that she could not see
her, as she was not received at the Court of England ;
—and now, for this extraordinary change, it has been
argued that, seeing the respectful attentions shewn to
the Duke and Dutchess of Gloucester by the K—g's
Minister, this Court thought itself justified. You see,
my dear Sir, how the most insignificant person in
office may influence in things of importance. Neither
the Duke nor Dutchess shall ever know this from me ;
neither should it be mentioned in England. You will
easily believe that I do not write a word in my great
letters' (official despatches) ' of my own behaviour to
them. I had no instructions, therefore ventured to
follow my own inclinations ; neither do I think myself
obliged to accuse myself in order to be excused, as

Mr. Strange at Venice did last year, by long and tedious letters, to which no answer was ever made. Upon the whole, everything passed off as well, nay, better than could be expected; and the Duke and Dutchess are so highly pleased that they have determined to return hither in the autumn, on their way to Rome for the winter.'

In July, the air was so cold in Italy, that the Duke and Duchess of Gloucester preferred remaining in Venice to repairing to their summer quarters at Lago di Garda. 'Some people here,' says Mann, 'have made fires, and most have thought them necessary, but under my roof we have resisted. . . .'

'. . . I wonder I forgot to mention the Dutchess's beauty, for it made the greatest impression upon me; but her affability and condescention excited my adoration, and they will be more lasting. Their children are most amiable. I told you how fine a child the Prince is. The Duke lifted him up in his arms, and put him to my face that I might kiss him. I took his little hand, but the Duke insisted on my embracing him. The little Princess is a charming child, and may amuse him more, but his affection for the Prince is of a different nature. In short, I never saw more fond parents, nor in appearance a more happy couple in regard to each other.'

This happiness was seriously interrupted by the alarming illness of the Duke at Venice. Towards the end of August, Mann writes that, 'His physicians begin to conceive some hopes of his recovery, though at the same time, they had forbidden the Dutchess to depend too much upon them, as his weakness was extreme. It is said that his chief nourishment was woman's Milk, which I fear indicates an apprehension of a Consumption.' Mann adds, in reference to George III., 'Whatever be the event, I should hope that his lingering in so deplorable a state may have excited compassion that may be advantageous to the Dutchess and his Children ; but the latter must be provided for.'

Mann's generous hope was realized. In September he writes :—'The last letters from Venice made mention of the great comfort, nay benefit, which the Duke had received by a kind letter from the King, his brother. It had so immediate a good effect, that He was able to answer it with his own hand. I begin to glory in my prophecy that the Duke's past sufferings may make a deep impression and be amply rewarded. When he is able to set out, I hope much from gentle motion and change of air. When he was here, he told me he was convinced that for a weak constitution nothing was so proper, and that he had always found benefit by it. I am persuaded he will therefore seize the first opportunity to put it in execution ; and firmly hope that by the Dutchess's tender care, the ability of his Physicians, and his own spirits, he will be able to perform the journey happily.'

While the Duke was recovering the health which appears to have been seriously injured by that air of Rome which has stricken so many, and mortally too, with Roman fever,—which often attacks them after they have left the infected city,—there was consternation in Naples. 'A Courier from Naples passed by two days ago, for Madrid, with the news of the death of the

First Prince' (who had been set aside from the succession) ' of the Small Pox. This accident has frightened that whole Court into their senses. As neither the King nor his children have had it, the Queen wrote by that Courier, to Dr. Gatti, with her own hand, ordering him to set out immediately to perform that operation' (Inoculation), ' she does not say on whom, before the King of Spain can forbid it. His aversion is grounded on Religion, so, he thinks, that even success cannot justify the commission of so great a crime. Gatti is at Naples by this time. The Great Dutchess gave him a chaise and a Courier to expedite his journey, which he proposed to perform in less than sixty hours.'

The King of Spain's wrath was, however, directed against a more important matter than inoculation. The matter in question shows in what a strangely high-handed manner our officers exercised their authority. ' An ugly affair has happened between our ships and the Spaniards off Gibraltar, which will offend their Monarch much. A Spanish man-o'-war, with a small ship, which our people took for an American Privateer, were (*sic*) seen off that Port, and a ship, or perhaps more, was sent out to seize it. As the boats advanced the Spaniards bid them keep off, with threatenings which they showed themselves in a posture to put into execution, but which our people despised. The small vessel ran ashore, under a Fort, and they found it to be not an American, but an English vessel that had escaped from Cadiz, with twenty five thousand cobs (*sic*) on board. *Our people carried off the money, though they perceived their mistake.* Some on both sides were killed. This is the substance of the account sent to Leghorn by one of our officers who assisted in the Fray. Judge what the Spaniards will make of it.'

Mann contrasts the tranquillity of Tuscany with the disturbed and anxious state of England with respect to the revolutionary war in America, and especially the uncertainty which prevailed for want of trustworthy information on the part of those who had entrusted to them the honour of our arms. 'I cannot conceive how our Generals can justify such disattention ?' He then draws this picture :—'All is tranquility in these parts. The Great Duke rides round his own grounds and gives his orders in every corner of his Estate, as a private country gentleman might do. In the beginning of the Autumn, he visited all the part of Tuscany towards the Romagna and Modenese, and returned by Arezzo, an excursion in which he imployed near two months. After this, he amused himself for a month with the masks at the Theaters during the Carnevalino ; and last week he set out again on another excursion to Siena and the Seacoasts, where he must see with regret the vast sums of money that his late Father and He have spent in useless attempts to drain that great tract of land which their predecessors, the Medici, had found impracticable.'

'The Pope is now engaged in an undertaking of the same kind to drain the Palude Pontine, from which no better success is expected, as *his* predecessors too, the Romans, after various attempts, it is said, abandoned. His new Sagristy for St. Peter's is a very long and expensive undertaking. He there

meets water too, a few feet underground, which will
both enhance the expence and greatly retard the
undertaking. The building is to be very large, as it
is not only to serve for the use of the Church, but to
furnish spacious Appartments for all the Chauvines,
who most certainly, will not be able to live in that bad
air during the summer. For the same reason, all
the Popes have abandoned it, and reside at Monte
Cavallo.'

From the beginning to the end of the year, Mann
seldom omits to notice in his letters, however busi-
ness-like, or devoted to very dry details of family
affairs, some notice of his countrymen abroad. In the
intensely cold weather at the opening of the year,
the English colony suffered miserably. Upon which,
our ministerial Envoy remarks : — 'By what I hear
and see by the practise of our countrymen and
women here, I believe that many disorders are
occasioned by the closeness and excessive heat of
their habitations. I know that they hurt me excessively, though I am often obliged to submit to it,
in my own house, when they are there. We have
more English of both sexes this winter, than usual,
though every thing has contributed to make it the
dullest ever known. All the *Spectacles* have been
miserable, and the bad weather has prevented people
from frequenting them, so that our young countrymen
would have reason to repent passing the Carnival
here, had not the same circumstance prevailed all
over Italy ; at Rome, particularly. At Naples, however, though the publick amusements have been bad,
the Court has supplied something ; but the French

Ambassador and Lord Tylney have contributed much more to the diversion of that City. The latter has a most spacious fine house, and is even to give a publick Ball to-morrow evening, the only day in Lent that it is permitted,—and is called the Burial of Carnival.'

There was one of the resident English, near Florence, who was bent on the acquisition of a foreign title as well as the enjoyment of pleasure,— Earl Cowper. 'I may venture to tell you a secret relating to Lord Cowper,' writes Sir Horace, at the end of April, 'a secret which I was strictly forbid to mention before the King had given his consent,— upon which it depended. The Emperor, without my Lord's seeking, he says, offered to make him a Prince of the Empire, by the title of Prince of Nassau of Over-kerque. The King's answer was retarded, but came most favourable, whilst the Emperor was at Paris.' (This was the Kaiser Joseph's famous visit to his sister, the Queen Marie Antoinette.)  'This may occasion a further delay, if the completion of it must depend on Cæsar's return home; but it is thought that his declaration will suffize, though the Diplomas may require some time.'  *April* 28*th.*—'Lord Cowper's principality must be suspended till the Emperor returns to Vienna. The Investiture will cost him several thousand pounds, and he will never be a farthing the better for it.' The year expired before any further step was made in this curious matter. Meanwhile, one who lived like a Prince is next referred to :—'Lord Tylney, who is a bird of passage, will be here to-morrow' (June 29th), 'or next day. His residence in any place is not indifferent, as he lives in a pompous stile. He has at present with him, Sir James Tylney Long and his wife.'

Lord Tylney, an Irish title which died with its bearer in 1784, had one desire on earth which was not however fulfilled, namely, that an heir might be born to his nephew and niece, Sir James and his wife. But there came of this match only heiresses, one of whom, ultimately sole heiress, and the richest and most unhappy of that envied class;—Catherine Tylney Long had the supreme ill fortune to marry, in 1812, William Pole Wellesley, a man younger than herself, to whom she brought the dowry of an Empress. He became known as William Pole Tylney Long Wellesley.

' Bless every man possessed of aught to give ;

Long may Long Tylney Wellesley Long Pole live!'
say the authors of the ' Rejected Addresses,' of this once notorious personage. He squandered all his wife's property and estates, and, after her death, in 1825, was deprived of the guardianship of his own sons. His second wife, a Paterson by birth, widow of Captain Bligh, and directly descended from one of the royal Plantagenets, was compelled to take refuge in St. George's workhouse ; and William Pole Tylney Long Wellesley, who succeeded to the title of Earl of Mornington in 1845, died in a poor London lodging-house in 1857.

In November Mann writes :—' I am in daily expectation of seeing Mr. Mackenzie and Lady Betty, who are going to Naples, for his health. Sir William and Lady Hamilton have been here for a few days, and are now at Rome. Mrs. Pitt will stay there the whole winter . . . where she has been detained by her compassion for a French female servant who has some chronical disorder; but she proposes soon to go to Naples ; . . . and here I sit,' he adds in December, 'nursing a little attack of the Gout in one foot. The weather is so very bad that I have little hopes of getting well soon. I comfort myself with the reflection that I should not know where to go if I was in health. . . . Crowds of English, both male and female, arrive here weekly, and other foreigners. I am quite ruined by great dinners!'

He was also quite disheartened, as fear prevailed over hope, with regard to the fragile beauty through whom it had been expected that the name of Mann would be continued as that of the master of the estate at Linton. The chronicle of Lady Lucy's progress is one less of living than of dying in Italy. In January, when the invalid was at Nice, her husband 'wrote a letter to his constituents' (at Maidstone) 'to excuse his absence and to offer to resign his seat in Parliament. I suppose this step may be the best means to obtain their further indulgence, for which he is writing with much anxiety, but, at all events, his affection for his wife is so great, and his assistance is so necessary for her preservation, that he has determined not to leave her, till he can do it with safety.'

In February we are told : ' They propose to leave Nice as soon as the weather will permit, and she is able to travel. His attachment to her has made him sacrifize every other consideration to it. . . . His con-

stituents have graciously refused his offer to resign.
This does them both honour.'    There were some faint
hopes of her in February; but in March, Mann
writes:—' They were earnestly bent upon coming here
in the Spring, and I was as desirous of seeing them,
but as the time approaches he seems dubious, and tells
me that unless she grew better than she was at the
time of his writing, he would not hurt my tenderness
for her, by bringing her in that condition.    Another
consideration, I believe, has much weight with him ;
which is, that it would put them out of the way of
the place they might chuse to pass the hot months
at, as both Nice and Florence would not be proper.
So that, at all events, they propose to leave Nice the
beginning of next month.    I shall soon be certain if
it be for Florence.'

They reached Florence in April.    On the day
when Mann had the satisfaction of seeing the Grand
Duchess set an example to all other potentates, by
receiving the Duchess of Gloucester, his nephew and
Lady Lucy arrived at his house.    ' Lady Lucy,' he
writes, ' is in far better health than I expected.    She is
gay and lively, and gives me hopes that she may quite
recover her strength here.    The kind concern you have
often expressed for her, makes it a duty to thank you
in their name, as they have desired me, and to convey
to you my nephew's most sincere respects.'    In May the
report stood thus : ' Lady Lucy seems to improve
every day, but is still weak, and feels the effects of
the least alteration of the weather.    One essential circumstance too is still wanting to give any hopes of her
having any more children.'

At the very end of June Mann writes :—' The weather is so uncommonly cool, that Lady Lucy, who dreads the heat extremely, sees no reason to leave Florence on that account, as my nephew and she had proposed when they first came here. I shall therefore have the satisfaction of their society, till this climate obliges them to go to Nice for the winter. Lady Lucy's health is much improved, but still much is wanting to restore her to such a state as tends to our future views, or even to make her life happy. I am highly pleased with their determination, both for their sake and my own. We live together upon the most easy terms and affectionate footing ; and there is great reason to hope that by a proper method, she may make a greater progress to a perfect re-establishment than by traveling about to seek a cooler place.'

And so they remained with the elder Sir Horace (for his nephew was Sir Horace Mann also) till winter began to frighten them away. In November the uncle writes :—' My nephew and Lady Lucy are still here. The latter, for some days past, has felt the bad effects of the sudden change from warm to very cold weather. Some of the neighbouring mountains are covered with snow. This has alarmed them so that they are hastening to Nice ; and though I shall sensibly feel their departure, I cannot wish to postpone it. They propose to return hither for the Spring.' On December 10th, when Mann was rather prematurely laughing at the attempt of Pope Pius VI. to drain the Pontine Marshes, he made this last addition to the little domestic romance in which his ambition and his affection were alike engaged. ' I have received the first letter from my nephew since his arrival at Nice.

They had a short but a very boisterous passage, (from Leghorn) but it was only attended with great inconvenience for the time, and Lady Lucy was tolerably well. I fear, however, that she will never be perfectly so as to fullfill our wishes.' It is with a sigh at the non-completion of his family views, and a groan at the 'ruin' brought upon him by giving grand dinners to illustrious travellers for whom he had no particular regard, that Mann closes the record of 1777.

## CHAPTER XV.

### 1778.

THE old year ended in sorrow, the new one began
with a lessening of hope.  On January 3rd, Mann
takes up the mournful story by saying : ' My nephew
and niece left me the latter end of November.  She
was then much out of order, and, I hear from Nice,
still continues so.  A good climate may, in the beginning of a disorder, stop its progress ; but I much fear
that none can recover so feeble a constitution as her's
is.  My nephew almost desponds, but endeavours to
conceal his apprehensions, as she likewise hides the
symptoms of her inward decay to him.  It was only
by her Maid and the innocence of the amiable Child
she has with her, that we knew some days before she
went from hence that the violence of her cough had
frequently forced blood from her breast.  This I hear
still continues.  The weather, as all over Italy, has
hitherto been bad at Nice.  We therefore hope that
when that mends, she may find the same benefit that
she has experienced in two former winters there.

'The weather here is extremely bad, which keeps
me much at home.  After a month's confinement, I
thought myself able to perform the ceremonies of the

first of the year, but I paid dearly for it. You know the size and Height of the Palace. I wandered all over it and up to the Garrets, for even the babes in swaddling Cloaths receive homage on such days, so that I have returned to my chair ever since. I assure you that I do not contend with my little Gout, and am so much convinced of the comfort and propriety of an easy chair at my age, that I have sent for one of Merlin's which Lady Betty Mackenzie recommended much to me. It will be my Go-Cart, a play-thing for my second infancy.'

There was, meanwhile, a heavy gloom settling round the British Minister. He was distracted by the public calamity, as well as by his domestic sorrow. His dying niece in Italy, and the expiring authority of Britain in the Colonies, occupied all his thoughts. January passed in sorrow; and February began with abandonment of hope, at least on one point. Walpole had written to Mann:—'Don't trouble your head any longer about Lady Lucy's having a son. They are the happiest who have no children.' Early in this month, the English Resident Minister replied to this cynical remark of Walpole:—'I own that you are in the right, and that it is a folly to regret the loss of all hopes of Lady Lucy's having a son. I am now anxious only for her recovery, which my nephew begins to despair of. Every letter from Nice brings bad accounts of her situation and visible decay. They are both impatient to get back to Florence, and I wish that I may see her here.'

Mann never saw his nephew's young and amiable wife again. On the 24th February he writes:—'The fatal news, my dear Sir, is arrived. I yesterday received an account that my dear Lady Lucy died at Nice the 11th of this month; she had been greatly declining ever since she left Florence; but, for six weeks past, my nephew seemed to have no hopes of her holding out long. I have not received any letter from him. He was incapable of writing; neither would he shock me by letting any of his family' (household) 'write directly to me, but ordered a servant to communicate it to one of mine. Such tender precautions show kindness, but are of little use. I am much afflicted for the loss of so excellent a woman, and for my nephew, who is inconsolable. Time only can procure him relief.'

*March* 14*th.*—'I have been expecting my nephew here, but by his last letter he has informed me that various circumstances had determined him to make a short excursion into Germany, in hopes that the exercise and variety of new objects may contribute to dissipate and attenuate his affliction. I could not disapprove of this resolution. He will see people from whom he neither asks nor expects consolation. Time alone will produce that. His return to England, at present, would increase his distress, by seeing all her relations in affliction. The body is to be sent to Linton, but cannot be there till the summer,—where he likewise would be obliged to reside and entertain his Constituents; a scene which he would not be able to go through; he therefore proposes to return here in June and to go to England in the Autumn. He will then have time to treat his Electors, and to prepare himself for taking his seat in Parliament.'

*May* 30*th.*—' My nephew should have had your letter had he returned to England; but he went from Nice into Germany, not chusing to go home this summer, as he then would not have avoided being at Linton and treating his Maidstone Electors, at the time perhaps that the corpse of Lady Lucy will be sent to be buried there.'

*August* 30*th.*—' My nephew arrived here from Germany last Sunday. I had hopes of seeing him in better spirits; but his affliction is still very great, though he is very reasonable; but Reason avails little till a stronger Passion subsides. I believe that I mentioned in a former letter, that he has agreed with his Constituents, that he is to be in England at the opening of the Parliament. Lady Lucy's corpse is still on board a ship at Gibraltar. He does not know it. It will be terrible to him if it does not arrive at Linton before he is obliged to be there, to carouze with his Electors, which alone he dreads much.'

Walpole closes this domestic story with an observation intended to comfort Mann. ' I have talked to you philosophically on the vanity of being attached to the continuation of families; yet, it is so natural, and I am so susceptible of that vanity, that I look forward to your nephew's marrying again, and having an heir to Linton.'

The two friends had now, however, matters of more general importance to discuss in their letters. ' Our situation,' said Walpole, ' will remove that cloud and fill your mind with others.' He alluded especially to America.

Lord North, by attempting to illegally extort

revenue from the American Colonies, really founded
the American Republic.  The surrender of Burgoyne's
little army, of some hundreds less than six thousand
men, to Gates, at Saratoga, had increased the disgust
which the nation had generally felt and expressed
against this war, but it had not lowered the tone of
the government.  Mann's friend, Lord Stormont, was
our Ambassador at Paris.  Franklin was there too,
one of the about-to-be acknowledged representatives
of the United States Congress.  When the latter
applied to Lord Stormont for an exchange of prisoners,
his lordship felt confident enough to make answer :
' The King's Ambassador receives no application from
rebels unless they come to implore his Majesty's mercy.'
Mann felt no such confidence.  On January 3rd he
writes :—

   'Your kind and instructive letter of Dec. 4th
came modestly into Florence, only three days ago,
but in very riotous company,—the publick Papers of
four weeks ; but, during that long retardure of the
letters from England, France had most minutely
informed us of our misfortunes in America, from the
mouth of Dr. Franklin ; and all the Gazettes dispersed
them all over Italy.  You will easily imagine the
consternation of our little Colony here.  They all
flocked to my house, in hopes of receiving some consolation, but I could only join in bewailing our
common distress ; for, though we had no letters from
England, the accounts from Florence were too circumstantial to leave any hopes of their being false ; and
now that we have an authentic detail from England,
it is but a small satisfaction to find that the others

were exaggerated. I dread the consequence of the annihilation of Burgoyne's army, as it may enable Gates to recover all the Americans had lost in that part of America . . . All this and many other circumstances afford too bad a prospect to dwell upon. I wait with impatience for the arrival of every Post, but dread to open the letters it brings, though, as I have said before, France commonly forestalls all the bad news they can contain.'

In February, Mann says : 'An Irish Officer in the French service brought me a letter yesterday, which he had just then received from his relative and Colonel, to inform him that, in consequence of the notice which that Court had received, that an English Fleet was off Brest, immediate orders had been given for a large body of troops to march thither, among which was this Officer's regiment, forbidding him, at the same time, to proceed further into Italy, as he would probably receive an order by the next French Courier, to hasten to his regiment. Can there be any mistake in all this ? The English letters have arrived since, and neither your's or any that I have seen in the publick Papers make any mention of a Fleet having sailed. I hope that the whole of it is an Irish blunder.'

Mann grew more and more despondent ; and gave endless reasons by way of justification, particularly when referring to the Treaty of defensive alliance, which France was rightly supposed to have entered into with the American States. From this mass, it is only necessary to refer to the parts which are connected with the Court and City of Florence. On

March 14th Mann says:—'We have now here a sensible but busy man, Abbé Niccoli, the Great Duke's Agent at Paris, not in the least our Enemy, who contracted a friendship with Franklin, 'purely to get information from him, and to make a merit with his master, by transmitting it to him. The Abbé has left his nephew at Paris, in his stead, and though he constantly receives letters from him by the French Courier, which he instantly carries to the Great Duke, none of them has made positive mention of that Treaty; but the Abbé, last week, received a letter in an unknown hand and without signature, which informed him that the Treaty had been signed. This, the Abbé told me without any mystery, and could, as he said, account in no other way for his nephew's silence on that article than that Franklin might think it too important to communicate at that time to his nephew, in Paris.'

The Abbé Niccoli continued to give Sir Horace information of what was passing in Paris; and especially, that the French Government was most eager that the Treaty should be ratified by Congress, before the British Commissioners could lay before that Assembly their proposed concessions. It is now well known that Congress, quite as confident as Lord Stormont had been, and with more solid grounds for being so, would receive no conciliatory Commissioners, unless they brought with them an acknowledgment of American Independence.

When Mann was ordered to represent the treachery of France to the Court of Tuscany, he could not help writing to Walpole:—'It is very

humiliating to a great nation to be reduced to
complain, especially to those who won't pity us and,
what I fear is still worse, to many who will not
comply with their engagements to give us assistance
to resent it. *Treaties are the most foolish things
in the world; they only furnish the means of eluding
their own contents.'*

*April* 28*th.*—'The Great Dutchess told Mrs.
Pitt, a few days ago, that her father (the King of
Spain) had wrote to her—that Spain does not
approve of the conduct of France, nor will joyn
with her. It would be idle to make any remarks
on this, or to ask why Spain has kept pace with
France in their dispositions, that have hitherto shown
a perfect intelligence.' Mann adds, with manifest
gladness, to the rather weary details in another letter,
an incident which had spirited up the loyal English
colony in Florence. 'The Empress of Germany has
refused to see Mr. Lee, an American Commissary,
whom the French Ambassadour wanted to present to
her, as a Minister or Agent from the 13 States of
America. She was offended, and sent an angry
message to that ambassadour, that she was surprized
that his Court should have made a Treaty with the
Rebels of another Prince, without the participation
of any other Sovereign.'

Mann's political principles never injuriously
affected his courtesy. When he was well aware
of the designs of France, he tells Walpole:—'Mrs.
Pitt, still at Rome, has addressed a Count and
Countess Tessé to me, whom I believe you have
seen in England. He is Master of the Horse to

the Queen of France, and has Her coaches and horses with him. These great Recommendations are attended with great expense.'

Earl Cowper's foreign title was still delayed. 'Lord Cowper is only Prince *in petto*, yet. He waits for his mother's Pedigree from England, to be inserted in the Imperial Diploma; and then the Earl and his Countess will be Prince and Princess Overkirk.'

On the last day of March, we are told :—'There is another hitch in Lord Cowper's new dignity. The great Nassaus objected to his bearing their name with the title of Prince. The Emperor therefore thought he had found a medium, by substituting Overquerque, but his Cousins of that family have likewise put their negative to that; so that it is now to be reduced to plain Prince Cowper; for which he must pay ten thousand zecchins. (About 500*l.*) The Heralds of the Empire have, like King William, in the cases of Lords Rochford and Grantham, objected to his bearing the arms of Nassau. They don't allow such a right from females ; and more particularly when there is any male branch of the family. Neither the Emperor nor my Lord seems to know what they were about, when it was asked and granted, and I believe that both now repent of it.' At length the doubtful greatness came. May 30th:—'Prince Cowper received the Imperial Diploma which, in Germany, entitles him "Highness," but he does not permit anybody to give him any other than Lord Cowper.'

The Earl was a Nassau through his mother who

is alluded to above ; and he was not the first Nassau who belonged to the Peerage of England. William the Third (in 1698) made of Henry D'Overquerque —an illegitimate descendant of Maurice of Nassau,— an Earl of Grantham, but the King would not allow him to bear the royally distinctive name. Immediately after the King's death, however, the Earl added ' De Nassau' to his surname, placing it before D'Overquerque. He died in 1754, when the title became extinct ; but it was revived in 1761, in the person of Sir Thomas Robinson.

William Henry de Zulcistein, whose father was the natural son of Henry Frederick, Prince of Orange (grandfather of William the Third), was created Earl of Rochford in 1695. Like Lord Grantham, he assumed the name of De Nassau after the King's death, and this name was borne by the four succeeding Earls, till the title became extinct in 1830.

Earl Cowper's mother was Henrietta, youngest daughter and coheir of Henry de Nassau d'Overquerque (or d'Auverquercque), the Earl of Grantham above mentioned, and in that way came the cousinship which is referred to by Sir Horace Mann. ' Surely,' says Walpole, ' an English peerage, with substantial dignity in one's own country, is more dignified than a nominal principality in another ; when it is transferred to a third country, it is still more ridiculous. I wonder Mademoiselle (Ann) Pitt does not beg the Pope to create her Princess Fossani.'

Sir Horace speaks in the highest terms of another peer from England :—'We have here,' he says, (October 27th) ' a most amiable family, Lord and Lady Lucan,

the former an old acquaintance, the latter an adorer
of you, by which she has captivated me; but besides
that motive, she is very clever and has many accom-
plishments and is teaching them to her daughters,
who by their judgment of the pictures and all the
collection in the Gallery are looked upon as progedies
(*sic*) at their age here. I wish they were as handsome
as their cousin Miss Molesworth who is with them,
and whom I cannot blame for refusing the Lord who
wished to marry her, with her figure and fortune.
She won't want younger admirers to chuse from.
We have another renowned lady of quite another
stamp from the Lady Lucan—Lady Berkeley and her
daughter, whom Nugent called Chance, and we call
Lady Louisa.' (Nugent was the Dowager Lady
Berkeley's second husband; and of their two
daughters he disowned the second, whom he named
' Chance.') ' Lady Berkeley seems to be seeking for
a place to abide in, but unluckily she always meets
with English who know her history and Englishwomen who shun her acquaintance. Italy, therefore,
I believe, will not be the place. She is very free,
and told Lord L. the other day that she wished Lord
Nugent could see her daughter, as from her likeness
to him he would be convinced how she once thought
of him. . . . I am going to carry Lady Lucan to
the Opera and to talk of you. . . .'

'. . . The soy-disante Dutchess of Kingston is
arrived at Leghorn, in seventeen days from Calais.
She is going to Rome, to fetch the greater treasure
in Diamonds, Plate, etc., which was deposited there
under the sanction of the late Pope Ganganelli. She

is not to pass here now, and perhaps the rebuff that
she met with at Vienna, will induce her to shun
this Court, hereafter.' It appears that the property
which Mann describes as being in the keeping of
the Pope was really in pawn at the Papal pawn-
broking establishment. '. . . A very bad state of
health did not keep the Dutchess at Leghorn. . . .
So soon as she got to Rome, she removed part of
that treasure from the Monte di Pieta into vessels
to be sent to Leghorn, in order to be sent to Calais
by some Russian ships of war, but they sailed last
week before it arrived. The richest sort of it was
sent off in waggons, which are now on the road to
Leghorn. In a letter in French which she wrote
to me, she signed, "Elizabeth Dss. of Kingston,
Comtesse de la Warth en Baviere," which title, she
says, the late Elector gave her.'—'She is a paltry
mountebank' (was Walpole's rejoinder). 'It is too
ridiculous to have airs after conviction.'

Walpole took care to put Sir Horace on his
guard with respect to some of his visitors who
presented themselves at his house in Florence as
friends of Walpole. Thus, of the Lucans, he writes:
—'I am surprised at the Hibernian family you
mention being arrived at Florence so soon; you are
very welcome to show them as many civilities as
you please, and set them down to my account; but
do not receive every thing they say of me, as coming
from the heart. They know your partiality to me,
and they mean to pass their time everywhere as
agreeably as they can. For the other lady and her
daughter, Chance, be doubly upon your guard against

the mother. . . . There is nothing so black of which she is not capable. Her gallantries are the whitest specks about her.'

One incident of this year may be noticed here as it illustrates character, though not in connection with Italy. Mann had often been employed in buying pictures from Italian collectors, for English amateurs. Walpole, to show what sort of vendor had turned up in England, sent to Mann the following curious letter, which caused some mirth in the Minister's house, near the Ponte della Trinità :—

' Hon^ble. Sir

'I hope you will excuse the Rudeness of a Plebeian in being thus bold to address you, but I was encouraged thereto by the mention of your Goodness, Mr. Grainger makes of you in his Biographical History, as I have in my Possession an original Painting of Seth Ward Bp of Salisbury, which I should be glad to dispose of, and for which I ask Four Guineas, and having read an account of your Curious Collections at Strawberry Hill, which I long to see, thought you might be glad to have it to put with them if you had not got one, so made bold to acquaint you of it being encouraged thereto by the mention the Gent. aforesaid makes of your amiable Disposition, and being at present under the frowns of Divine Providence as being but in the Lowest Class as a Serv^t, and being out of Place at present, or else would not have parted with it, as I have been Curious in collecting some Curiosities Myself having a taste that way tho' Cannot afford to do as I would, but have none worthy of your observation besides, therefore if you please to favour me with a Line, directed for John Simco at Mr. Hiron Stone Mason the Corner of Portpool Lane in Leather Lane Holborn, where and when to wait upon you with it, shall take it as a great favour, hoping your Great Goodness will forgive my present boldness in thus making free with you.

' I remain Hon<sup>ble</sup> Sir

' your very Hble Serv<sup>t</sup>

' To Command

' JOHN SIMCO.'

Aug 17<sup>th</sup> 1778.

### 1779.

Of the Pope there is only thrice mention, and of the Pretender only once, in the letters of 1779. On April 17th, among the chief talk of the town, is noticed—' the Pope's illness, which is thought by his physicians to be very serious. I receive twice a week a diary of it, and by that must think so too. Cabals among the Cardinals are already begun, and the foreign Ministers joyn with them. Cardinal de Bernis speaks publickly of his apprehensions of being shut up in a Conclave, during the hot months ; and indeed with his constitution and extraordinary *embonpoint*, there may be danger of its being fatal to him and some others, as the air of the Vatican is little less than pestiferous in that season.'

A week later comes this record :—' The Pope continues very ill of I do not know what. He had an universal Rhuematism accompanied with a violent heat within, which has given occasion to grave people

to talk about, (what I think a very silly opinion of
an illness which I suppose never existed) an *internal
fire,* by which the Pope's Grandmother is said to have
been carried off in a flash, and totally consumed!
Many other idle stories of the same kind have been
propagated on this occasion.   Others say that he has
taken many antidotes against poyson.   I receive, every
week, a diary of his illness.   The last was very bad.
The Cardinals begin their Cabals, and the foreign
Courts have been advised by their Ministers of his
danger, though it is concealed as much as possible at
Rome.'

*May 5th.*—' The Pope is better, and proposes to
make Cardinals soon in his bedchamber.   He was
much disappointed at the birth of a girl, instead of a
Dauphin, for had the Queen of France brought forth
the latter, his Nephew, who was sent thither, would
have had a noble Benefice, instead of the watches and
other toys that he had brought from thence.'   The
' girl ' here alluded to was ' Madame Royale ' (born in
the previous December), and better remembered as the
unhappy Duchess of Angoulême.

*May 25th.*— Italy was suffering and many disorders reigned, because of the unusual drought.   ' At
Rome, the noble fountains furnish a sufficient supply,
but the country is quite dried up for want of water,
and the prospect of any harvest is very bad.   The
Palude Pontine would almost have been dried up
without the great expense that the Pope is making
there to drain them.   In appearance, that work goes
on well, but still some people are doubtful of the
success, for want of a sufficient declivity.   The Pope

is much better and hopes to make Cardinals and provide for his Nephew the beginning of next month.'

'The Pretender, for you know we always join them together, is in a deplorable state of health. He has a declared Fistula, great sores in his legs, and is insupportable in stench and temper ; neither of which he takes the least pains to disguise to his wife,—whose beauty is vastly faded of late. She has paid dear for the dregs of Royalty. How will his Brother be stiled when he succeeds to his Kingdom ? He is already called at Rome, *Sua Eminenza Reale*, but that will not do *then*. I dare say that he has settled this already in his own mind.'

With drought and disease there was an almost complete stagnation of trade, particularly at Leghorn. 'The trade at Leghorn, where many English vessels were detained,' says Mann, ' is almost annihilated. Nothing can escape from the French Privateers in the Ports of Corsica. So soon as any ship, or even any Bark is ready to sail from Leghorn, the French Consul sends off a fishing boat to give notice of it, and in two days after we hear of its being taken. A fresh instance of which happened last week. Four officers (Ingeneers) who had been sent from England, for Minorca, embarked at Leghorn on board a Venetian vessel, with all the secresy that could be practised ; but the French Consul sent off a boat an hour after them, and I have just now received advice that they were taken by a French frigate that waited for them off Corsica. All this was foreseen and foretold by a friend of yours' (Mann himself) ' who was ordered to draw up a writing about it which was

approved of but not executed. Neither the Great
Duke nor our Merchants ought to forgive those who
let Corsica fall into the hands of the French, or those
who will let it remain so at the time of an accommodation, if we should ever be in a condition to
prescribe the terms of it.'

Occasionally Mann speaks, not admiringly, of the
little vanity of the Grand Duke, whom, by the way, Dr.
Moore says, he would have recognized as a member
of the Imperial Austrian family, by the thick underlip
which belonged to them all. 'A pompous Medal
has been struck here, by the Great Duke's order, in
memory of his reception, last year, of the Embassadour
from the Emperor of Morocco, as Louis the 14th did on
the reception of (as many believed, of a sham) Embassadour from Siam. On one side is the Great Duke's
Bust, with the Exergue,—Leopoldo AA. P. RH. B.
Magno Duci Etruriae Optimo Principi.—On the other
side, the G. Duke is represented at Leghorn, dressed
in Royal Robes, with a crown on his head under a
throne ; the Embassadour in a suppliant posture presents his Credentials; two slaves behind their master
lay prostrate on the ground ; another holds a horse, a
present from the Emperor, on which he himself had
mounted and nobody after him, as is their rule. The
Exergue is : Mauritaniæ obsequium et Fœdus Virtuti
Oblatum :—modest enough. The coin is miserably
bad. It is too heavy to send by the post, but I intend
to enrich your Cabinet with it, by the first opportunity
that offers ; on condition that you send me your
tragedy, of which I have heard such encomium, though
I would never contradict those who said to me,—" to

be sure, you have seen it. Nor would I ask Sir Wm. Hamilton for it, not to give him room to triumph over me on this occasion. I have bid my nephew to ask this favour of you, to bring it to me ; for which I now anticipate my thanks. The Medal is a miserable performance, and so was the event on which it was struck. Poor Florence has now no Benvenuto Cellini.'

The King of France treated the Grand Duke with as little respect as the latter did the Emperor of Morocco. 'The Court of France,' it is written, August 27th, 'has sent an Imperious command to the Great Duke to annull his Edict of Neutrality, by which it was permitted by the Powers at war to purchase ammunition and military stores as merchandize, which that King "ne veut pas permettre," though the Edict that allowed it was communicated to his Ministers and approved of by them as a "modèle à suivre." He now threatens that if his command is not complied with, he will send a fleet to block up Leghorn. This he has done, in effect, for a long time past, by the means of his frigates and Privateers stationed off Corsica, who watch all vessels coming and going from Leghorn, and within these few days past the Tuscan subjects have received advice from Spain too, that all their effects destined for England, on board Tuscan vessels, will be seized and confiscated. The Great Duke is outraged (*sic*) at this treatment and has remonstrated against it, but probably with little Effect.'

But Florence was soon as joyful over the opening of her new theatre, as France was in inaugurating her new opera. 'I am not disposed,' says Mann, who blamed this frivolity, 'to give you an account of the

foolish public shows that are to be exhibited here in
the opening of a new Theater.  The subject is the
return of Amerigo Vespucci from the Conquest of
America, which is to be performed to-morrow, in the
Piazza di Santa Maria Novella, with the greatest pomp
and expense, and to be repeated twice more in the
course of a month.  Adieu ! I fear that scenes of a
quite different nature will be exhibited in England ! '

In November, Mann relates how he had an interview with the Grand Duke, to present to him a letter
from the King, and also Lord Herbert.  'He told me that
the day before he had received a letter from Spain to
inform him that the King had given orders to his fleet
to return into his own Ports, and that the motive that
was alleged for it was the fear that the illness which
raged in the French fleet should be communicated to
*his.*    H.R.H. likewise told me that there had been a
hurricane at Martinico that had destroyed everything ;
that Mons. d'Estaing having carried away a vast
quantity of provisions, the inhabitants were in the
greatest distress, and had sent to France for immediate
relief.    Should the first notice prove true we need no
longer fear an Invasion, and the letter may produce
some good.    It is said that their San Domingo Fleet
had been dispersed by a storm ; and many ships lost.

'I cannot answer for any part of this, but I tell
you my author.  The Marquis de Barbantane ' (the
French ambassador in Tuscany) ' whom I see and converse freely with everywhere, excepting in our own
Houses, does not believe any part of it. As an English
man, I am bound to hope that his next letters may
bring him a confirmation of all that is advantageous to

us. He said, what all the world knows, but what few
Frenchmen could own, that, in regard to our present
quarrel, "France, according to the rules of honesty was
wrong, but according to those of policy, she was right."
"Then," said I, "You allow, Sir, that the basis of your
policy is perfidy!" He was not angry, but desired to
see our "Mémoire Justificatif."' The account ends with
something creditable to Charles Edward. 'The Count
d'Albanie had earnestly asked the same favour of me.
I am told he was highly pleased with it, and that he
fights our cause against all the Frenchmen he meets.'

When the time was drawing near at which 'the
French had fixed for besieging Minorca,' Mann gave
his reason for not believing it :—'I never believed it
unless they were sure of the existence of a Spanish
Fleet ; which likewise I did not believe, and for which
I had the authority of this little Court, which authority
is greater than people may imagine, for their father'
(the King of Spain) 'writes constantly to his Daughter,
and communicates to her both his private sentiments
and what he wishes should be known.' At this little
Court, which had its political news for Mann, there
might be occasionally seen an English Merchant, who,
like Earl Cowper, bore a foreign title. 'The Baron
Rutherford, whom you often meet at Gloucester House,
is a most worthy man, with whom I have lived for
many years in the greatest friendship and who has
great partiality for me. He is of an antient family in
Scotland, of which his nephew is Laird. He was in
business at Leghorn, where he made a small fortune
that satisfied his very moderate ambition; and was re-
tiring, when a favourable opportunity offered of making

a large addition to it, by being made Agent or Commissary of Russia during their war with the Turks, for which Commission (united with Sir John Dick), as the acting man, he gained so much credit and favour with that Empress, that, contrary to his wish, she made him Baron of her Empire, after he had positively refused the Order which Sir John wears. She also sent him a fine box with her picture ornamented with jewels. He is a most worthy and sensible man, for whom I have the greatest Regard and Esteem.'

For the moment, there were no more fortunes to be made by the English merchants at Leghorn. The war had interrupted the steady prosperity of that honest community. 'Poor Leghorn is quite undone,' says Mann; 'no ship dares venture out, so many Privateers from Corsica watch them. The Great Duke now sees the prejudice which arises from the Court of Vienna not joyning with England to oppose the French in taking that Island.'

The Minister was sadly harassed, too, by his countrymen and women in Florence, who, as soon as they read in the French and Italian journals details of the calamity which had fallen upon England, crowded his saloon, to know how far such details were trustworthy. When a French Courier brought letters and papers into Florence, with circumstantial intelligence of the destruction of our 'great fleet in a storm,' of which 'thirty,' they said, foundered in sight of their ports, thirty more were driven on their coasts, and that they saw many more wrecks floating to them, insomuch that they wept for the distress even of their enemies who became their prisoners,—this account was literally translated in the Italian Gazettes ; and Mann says, ' it was credited by everybody till they were undeceived by the accounts from England ;—which in truth were bad enough, without such exaggeration.'

The wildest reports were circulated and believed, especially as to the fortune of war by sea. Five mails were due in Florence from England, and the English in Tuscany were in the greatest perplexity. They did not know whether Admiral Byron had defeated d'Estaing, or that victory had gone the other way ; whether the French Admiral had been killed or had killed himself, or had killed Byron, and whether Martinique now belonged to France or England. The English believed in a triumph on their side. ' People have flocked to me this morning, to endeavour to persuade ' (now first spelt correctly) ' me of the certainty of it, and I feel myself quite disposed to believe it; but still I am impatient for a confirmation ; though 24 tedious hours must pass before the arrival of the post, and even then it is uncertain if he may bring the mails from England, till when we must live upon hope.'

But not Florence alone, all Italy was deeply interested in another matter, far more than it was as to which way the balance of victory would incline between the English and the French. Mount Vesuvius was in as agitated a state as the world itself ; and Florence received bulletins of the fiery eruption more frequently than she did trustworthy information touching contending hosts. Sir William Hamilton sent to Mann a painting which represented the volcano in one of its most furious outbursts (' in the compass of a card, excellently done ') ;

with some descriptive details. Mann forwarded
painting and letter to Walpole. ' Sir William,' writes
Sir Horace, ' does not speak of the Mob, though all
other letters do. They say that it was appeased by an
artful Friar, who told the mob that it was not decent
to carry out San Genuaro, with such links as they
had in their hands; but that next morning, wax
torches should be provided. This pleased them, and
they retired home. . . . An old woman that passes
for that Saint's relation harangued the people when
he ' (the figure of St. Januarius) ' was on the Ponte
della Madalena, in sight of the mountain, exhorting
them " to pray to Xt. to beg San Genuaro to make
the mountain be quiet." This is certainly true ! '
Mann's nephew said of the frenzied insurrection
of the people and the fury of the eruption, that it
was a ' wonderful picture of nature and human
nature in convulsion.' Walpole notices three eccentric
Englishwomen who were in Naples at this time.
' Lady Maynard' (the once notorious Nancy Parsons),
' who has always some fascinating powder, has established herself at the Court of Naples, by dispensing
James's. They say she is universally visited, except
by those English prudes the Countesses of Berkeley
and Orford. I should not wonder if the former was
to dethrone Lady Maynard, by distributing Keyser's
pills.'

Among those who had left Florence this year was
Zoffany, the painter, with the picture which he had
been commissioned to paint by the King (or Queen)
of England. ' I am glad,' Mann writes to Walpole,
' that you have seen Zoffany and his Portrait of the

Tribune.  So then it is not true that he was hanged
for bigamy, as was reported among the Italians, in
spite of all I could say to convince them that with us,
though he has two wives, it is not a hanging matter.
Your opinion of his laborious performance in all the
parts you mention agrees with that of our best judges
here ; but they found great fault with the perspective
which, they say, is all wrong.   I know that Zoffany
was sensible of it himself, and used to get assistance
to correct it ; but it was found impossible, and he
carried it away as it was.   How, or whether, it has
been done elsewhere, I know not.   I told him of the
impropriety of sticking so many figures in it, and
pointed out to him, the Great Duke and Dutchess,
one or two of their children, if he thought the variety
were pictoresk, and Lord Cowper.   He told me that
the King had expressly ordered my portrait to be
there, which I did not believe, but did not object
to it ; but he made the same merit with all the young
travellers then at Florence, some of whom he afterwards rubbed out, such as old Felton Harvey and one
of the Queen's Chaplains with a broad black ribbon
across his forehead, and filled up their places elsewhere.   If what he said is true, that the Queen sent
him to Florence to do that picture, and gave him
a large sum for his journey, the impropriety of
crowding in so many unknown figures was still
greater.   But is it true that it is for the Queen's
Closet, and that she is to give him three thousand
pounds for it ?   This he asserted, and it got him the
name of Her Majesty's Painter ; and in that quality
he had leave to have any Picture in the Gallery or

Palace taken down ; for you must have observed that
he has transported some from the latter place into *his*
Tribune.   I should think too the naked Venus which
is the principal figure, will not please Her Majesty
so much as it did the young men to whom it was
shewed.   As to the question you make me of my own
personage, I can only say that everybody thought it
like me, but I suppose Zoffany took pains to lessen
my pot-belly and the clumsiness of my figure, and
to make me stand in a posture which I never kept to,
but then, I remember, that I was sadly tired when I
was tortured by him to appear before their Majesties
in my best shape and looks.'

Walpole says of the above picture :—' The first
thing I looked for was *you*, and I could not find you.
" Pray, who is that Knight of the Bath?"—"Sir Horace
Mann."—"Impossible!" said I.   My dear sir, how you
have left me in the lurch !   You are grown fat, jolly,
young, while I am become the skeleton of Methusclah.
The idea I always thought an absurd one.   It is
rendered more so by being crowded by a flock of
travelling boys, and one does not know nor care
whom.   You and Sir John Dick, as Envoy and
Consul, are very proper.   The Grand Ducal family
would have been so too.   Most of the rest are as
impertinent as the names of churchwardens stuck up
in parishes, whenever a country church is repaired and
whitewashed . . . I do allow Earl Cowper a place in
the Tribune ; an Englishman who has never seen his
earldom, who takes root and bears fruit in Florence,
and is proud of a pinchbeck principality in a third
country, is as great a curiosity as any in the Tuscan

collection.'   In one paragraph, Walpole admirably
criticises this famous picture.   'The execution is good ;
most of the styles of painters happily imitated, the
labour and finishing infinite ; and no confusion,
though such a multiplicity of objects and colours.
The Titian's Venus, as the principal object, is the
worst finished ; the absence of the Venus of Medici
is surprising ; but the greatest fault is in the statues.
To distinguish them he has made them all of a colour;
not imitating the different hues of their marbles, and
thus they all look alike, like casts in plaster of Paris ;
however, it is a great and curious work,—though
Zoffani might have been better employed.   His talent
is representing natural humour.   I look upon him as
a Dutch painter polished or civilized.'

It was not astonishing that Mann, after living so
long abroad, should change in more than outward
looks, or that he occasionally used a foreign word, or
misused one in ordinary English even.   He complains
of the 'retardure' of the post, and speaks of a house
that would 'convene' him.   He is aware of how he is
breaking loose from his mother-tongue.   'You perceive,' he writes, 'that I have forgot my English and
I am sensible of it.   Lord Huntingdon told me, some
years ago, that, for a foreigner, I spoke it better than
any he had ever heard.   Nevertheless, in my sense of
the word, I still say, "I love and adore you."'   Walpole
had taken objection to this form of compliment, com-
paring himself at the same time with an old monkey,
which probably had the advantage of him, both outside and inside.   Mann frankly owned that age had
brought him to a like condition.   Half the year he

was engaged in attempts to bring the gout from his
distracted head into his already gout-crippled feet.
Walpole warned him not to suppose he could keep it
out of his stomach, by converting the latter into a
furnace, raging hot with strong wines.　Mann was ill
in bed, at Florence, with the gout, when his nephew
left him for England.　Walpole was ill in bed in
Arlington Street, with the gout, when he received the
nephew's visit ; and that nephew was unable to
stand in the room, as he was suffering acutely from
an incipient attack of the same disease, which spared
few people in 1779.

# CHAPTER XVI.

## 1780.

MANN opens the year 1780 with a reference to an earlier date. ' I shall ever remember,' he says, ' the year 1739 as the happiest of my life, as it procured me the greatest consolation I have ever since had, in your most inestimable friendship ; my only consolation and chief care shall be to preserve the continuance of it for the few years that may be allotted to me. Orestes and Pylades were nothing to us. They cultivated their friendship personally, but our separation has been so long that perhaps we should not know each other where we accidentally to meet ; for my part, however, I think I should, as I have a print of you constantly in my sight,' (it hung between the portraits in pastel of Chute and Whithed) ' and my nephew told me it was a perfect resemblance.' Sir Horace was then anxiously expecting news of our having punished Spain for not remaining neutral in our quarrel with other powers, as his Catholic Majesty had assured his daughter, the Grand Duchess, he intended to do. ' I have charged the Consul at Leghorn to send me an Express, with the first good news that can be depended upon, and the Porter is to

open the door to him at any hour of the night.  Oh !
how I should triumph over the Spanish Envoy if he
were alive.   However, I can teaze Barbantane' (the
French ambassador) 'and that will give me more
pleasure, for he is insufferably saucy ; but the Court
and the whole Town revenge me upon him.—My hand
shakes so much that I cannot force it to do more than
to tell you how anxious I am to hear that you are
free from the gout, and perfectly well.'

*February* 12*th.* — 'The Courier from Leghorn
arrived on Wednesday, and brought an account that
Admiral Rodney had defeated a small squadron of five
Spanish ships of the line and two frigates, on the 26th
past, that were cruising off Cape St. Vincent, to join
the French fleet from Brest that was to prevent any
succour getting into the Bay of Gibraltar.   When our
Admiral perceived the above squadron, he sent all his
transports and most of the frigates into that port, and
gave chace to the Enemy with his whole fleet, and
took four of their large ships, with their Admiral
Langara.   One of their ships blew up during the
combat, and two, it is said, escaped, which are supposed to be the frigates.   This little victory may
have great consequences, that of saving Gibraltar is
achieved, but we hope that our fleet will attack the
French coming from Brest, which must have been
near. . . .  This part of Italy rejoices much in it, and
in the hopes of seeing the freedom of the navigation
of the Mediterranean restored, without which every
State in it would become a Bankrupt.—To supply the
want of fish for the Lent food, the Pope has been
obliged to give the Catholics leave to eat flesh five

days in the week; but what they gain one way they will lose by another, as by this extraordinary consumption, meat will be dearer the rest of the year.'

*March 11th.*—' I immediately communicated the news of Rodney's victory to the Great Duke, by which attention I gained great applause, and to Barbantane' (French ambassador) 'who would not believe a word of it, of which he was ashamed afterwards. . . . It caught like wild fire about the town, and I received a *mi rallegro* from all I met. I sent it to the Pope, too. He was glad of it, in hopes that his markets would soon be supplied with salt fish, by the passage into the Mediterranean being opened; and so, in some measure it has happened; many ships arrived soon after at Leghorn and Civita Vecchia. . . . The Spanish Admiral Langara has been greatly rewarded for his bravery; he fought well, and would have deserved it on any other occasion, but he ought to be hanged for his temerity in resisting so much superior a force; by which 900 poor sailors were blown up in that ship, which was lost in the action, and I have not heard that there was a Corpo Santo on board to save their souls !'

*March 31st.*—' Sir George Rodney and his colleague Digby have raised a jealousy between our enemies. France is outrageous with Spain; the Spaniards are discontented with their Monarch; and *he* is so deceived that he actually writes to the Great Duchess, his daughter, that all goes on well; at the same time, her brother, in Spain, tells her quite the contrary; and both bewail the misfortune of their father in being so ill-advised. I have much to say on that subject, but not to be entrusted to the Post, without figures ' (cyphers).

The life of the British Resident was much embittered this year by news from America, which the French ambassador circulated in Florence, and which occasionally drove Sir Horace to despair. This feeling was a little relieved by Court gaieties, such as the following :—' The arrival here of the Arch-Duke (Ferdinand Governor of Austrian Lombardy), and Duchess (Maria Beatrix, of Modena), from Milan, has revived the Florentines by the amusements that have been, and that are still making for them. Every Saturday there is a publick Drawing-room at Court, in Gala ; three great Balls in Mask have been given at the Theater, *Gratis;* and the same number at Prince Corsini's, Riccardi's, and at the Casino dei Nobili. The foreign Ministers dined at Court, the first Great Dinner, and, by turn, had the honour to play at Ombre with the Great Dutchess and her Sister-in-law.' The latter was the daughter of Hercules Rinaldo, Duke of Modena. Her husband gained, by their marriage, the reversion of the Duchies of Modena, Mirandola, and Reggio.

There was, however, (previous and subsequently) in Florence a visitor whose announced coming had created more interest in Mann than that of the Arch-Duke and Duchess. ' It is a young Mr. Windham, a gentleman of Norfolk, of a very considerable estate, who is in a bad state of health and travels for it. I am not so much acquainted with him as with his character, which is excellent ; and then, he is a twig of the stump that was current in our country in my father's time.'

So wrote Walpole in October, 1779, adding:—'I do not always send you a tally to the letters of recommendation I am sometimes forced to give; but that which he carries to you, I confirm by this, in all points. I advise you to be intimate with him, I will warrant the safety of the connection, and I beg you to assist him with recommendations wherever you can. He is a particular friend of my great nephew, Lord Cholmondeley's cousin; but one I should have liked for my own friend, if the disparity of our ages would have allowed it; or if it were a time for me to make friends, when I could only leave them behind me.'

This 'gentleman of Norfolk' was Mr. Windham of Felbrigg, the last of the line that had held that estate from the year 1461. 'Young Mr. Windham,' as Walpole calls him, was, in 1780, thirty years of age, was addicted to mathematics and pugilism, and had but a faint idea of becoming the great statesman he afterwards proved to be. Mann was ready to give him a warm reception early in January, when the mountains round Florence were covered with snow, and the Grand Duke and Duchess were wading through it on the Bologna road to conduct the brother of the former, the Archduke Ferdinand, and the Archduchess, to Florence, on their way to Naples, for the Carnival; for whom the former city was made brilliantly gay in the spring. 'I have had the pleasure to see Mr. Windham, who, I am very sure, will answer the great expectations I had conceived of him from your letter. We are already as intimate as our short acquaintance can admit of; but two people so exactly well-disposed make a great progress in that article in a little time. He seems already convinced of my desire to give him and you every proof of my ambition to cultivate his friendship.' Later, Mann was somewhat disappointed with the gentleman from Norfolk. 'I am not so intimate,' he writes in March, 'with your recommandé, Mr. Windham, as I expected and could wish. He seldom calls upon me, but never refuses an invitation. He is very retired and applies to the two languages, the want of which has made him decline being presented at Court, or associating with the Italians. We wait for a croud, for the first. The latter will never tempt him to be more than a spectator, as he is at my Dinners and Conversaziones ; at both which I see him. On these occasions, he selects the few English who are here, and is with them communicative, but severe on publick affairs, which is the occasion, perhaps, that he is less so with me. His great good sense and politeness refrain (*sic*) him here on this subject. I shall now see him oftener as the Theaters are open and that the season will permit me to meet him in my Boxes there.'

In May, Mann says, on the text, ' Moderation in politicks is totally incompatible with modern Patriotism:'—'This was only what I complained of in Mr. Windham, who had imitated the most morose notions of his Spartan Teachers; but pray observe that I did not complain of his want of civility to me ; nay, the contrary was obvious from the constant constraint he laid himself under, when we met, to conceal his sentiments, which he broached in all other places. Every fortunate event to our Fleet or Armies was a dagger to him. He was sorry that Langara' (the

Spanish Admiral) 'had not destroyed our Fleets that
saved Gibraltar and Mahon, only because the loss
of them would have distressed the present Government. The Sowerness of his temper manifested itself
in every thing. Nothing pleased him. Even the
Italian language appeared so harsh to him that it hurt
his Ear ; but, with all these additions, he is a man of
sense, and what is called of strong reflection ; but not
a pleasant companion, though I am confident that he
will not complain of my want of any attention for him.
If I am not mistaken, he will go grumbling through
Italy, for want of amusement.'

A letter in reference to some dispute between Mr.
Windham and another Englishman appears to have
been lost. On June 16th, Mann alludes to it:—'I told
you by a late letter that I despaired of turning the
affair of Mr. Windham and Bagnal to any good, but I
hear now some hopes of success. They are become
much more tractable of late by the interposition of
our good friend here, who has convinced his Relation
that he is quite in the wrong, though he is still so
obstinate that he will not be the first to own it publickly. This was his last message. I cannot as yet
judge if others will waive this Punctiglio. I have
represented this affair honestly, and both my good
friends here, and I wait impatiently for their answer.'

In August, Mr. Windham was at Brussels, on his
return home. ' I am peevish with him,' says Walpole,
'for having looked on you through our ill-humoured,
foggy eyes. I have almost always been out of luck
with my recommendations ; but I assure you I do you
ample justice, and have always been convinced that

they have been in fault.   Your temper and flowing
benevolence for forty years, have been always uniform ;
and it is least of all likely that you should grow sour
only to those I interfere for.   I know you and my
countrymen better.   The latter have retained few of
their virtues, but I do not find they have exchanged
them for urbanity.   Mr. Windham, I believe, is a
worthy man, but I wish he had been less morose.'   It
was Mann's opinion that, ' in all stations of life,
our country produces more extravagant characters
and more mad-men than any other we know or
have heard of.'

Mr. Windham was in London in November, and
Walpole saw him.   ' He is wonderfully recovered and
looks robust again.   He said ten thousand fine things
in your praise.   Oh ! thought I, but said nothing.'

Of another Englishman, but more Italian than
English, there is this notice :—' Lord Cowper has
received the news of the death of his mother in law
(step-mother).   Her jointure of 1500*l.* a year and
5000*l.* worth of family Jewels fall into him, of course ;
and an abundance of other fine things which she has
left him, the particulars of which he is to be informed
of by a copy of the Will, the next Post.   There will
be a fine addition to the Jewels they have already
between them, which exceed twenty thousand pounds.'

There was this year a Russian squadron at Leghorn, although there was not a Russian merchantman
in the Mediterranean requiring protection.   Florence
could not account for the presence of the fleet.   ' I am
still considered here as Il Protettore dei Russi who
pass here, though I never got the Diamond Snuff-box

which their Empress is supposed to have destined for
me, and of which my nephew was persuaded I was
choused.   Count Czernichoff lately recommended an
officer of his nation to me, and last week I presented the Count's Son to the Great Duke and
Dutchess, by his desire.   I cannot enumerate what all
these Russi have cost me in Banquets, and after all, I
fear, that both my Superiors and I shall be the dupes
of our past good offices.'

While the Florentines were discussing the likeli-
hood of a Russian attack on the Crescent, a quarrel
arose nearer home.   'There is a great Bustle at
Bologna,' says Mann, 'between the Senat there and
the Pope's Legat, personally, and also with the Pope,
who refuses to hear the complaints which two members of the Senat have been sent to make to him.
The Bolognese talk high, and threaten to apply to the
Emperor and the Duke of Modena, as Guarantors of
their Privileges.   The Populace take part in it, and
have posted up the Emperor's arms.   His Holyness has
no other offensive weapons to send among them, but
the Horns of his Bulls, which have much blunted of
late.'

In other quarters the Pontiff was being circum-
vented.   Mann does not often concern himself with
literary subjects, but Walpole having expressed a
desire to see a history of the Medici family, the
Envoy informed him that one was being secretly
prepared, ' by a man who is very capable of executing
it,—Abbé Galuzzi, who is keeper of the Archivi
Segreti.   It is far advanced, but it will not be published till completed, lest Rome—which will not be

pleased—should make any opposition to the Progress of it, or terrify the authors; but *he* is as bold as a lion, and is protected by his Master (the Grand Duke) who sees every Quire of it before it is printed under his own Roof.'

*August* 16*th.*—'I announce to you the hopes of receiving in a few months the work you wished to see —the History of the Medici Family, of which the two first volumes, containing the Introduction, and the Lives of Cosmo and Francisco I., are already printed; but have been communicated to very few, lest the Court of Rome should get at the knowledge of them, that Court foreseeing that the iniquities of the Popes of these times may be disclosed, and so discredit the Tiara. The Emissaries of that Court are employed, and there is no doubt that every means would be used to prevent the publication of the work. The bigotry of the Empress' (Maria Theresa) 'is not less to be feared than the clamours from Rome, and might have greater weight, though those would make greater impression on her Piety, where her interest is not concerned. Had the Pope known as much as I do even of the two first volumes (and much more, I am assured, will appear in the others) I question much if He would not have made the suppressing of the work a condition for his Dispensation for the Simony by which Her son is to be a Chauvine of Munster, and a powerful Prince in Germany, in defiance of the King of Prussia. The Coadjutorship of Cologne is over, and that of Munster is expected to-morrow. I have seen a letter from that scrupulous King to the Elector, to tell him that he was too *young* to chuse a successor, (he is but 72!)

and another letter to the Chapter of Munster, declaring that he will not suffer an *Intru.*

'But, I have deviated from my History. The publication of it will do honour to the Great Duke, who hitherto has been suspected to have some tincture of his family-piety, notwithstanding his suppression of all the power of the Inquisition, and other opposition to the Dictates of Rome. He has seen every sheet before it was printed, which, for greater safety, has been and is doing in his Palace, and he has promised Protection to the author, against any future Resentment. For the reasons before mentioned, secrecy is to be observed till the day of publication and publick sale at all Booksellers' shops in the Town ; nor are the *Avvisi* to be published yet in Italy. At the request of the author and his associates, I send you a packet of them to be distributed to the Booksellers and others. I have advised them to get the work translated into French, to be published at the same time or before it could be done in France or elsewhere. They highly approve of the advice, but cannot find a proper Person whom they could trust.'

*October* 24*th.*—'I am glad to see that you are pleased with the Prospect of seeing the History of the *Famiglia Estinta,* which you shall have as soon as possible, on *Carta Cerulea,* which is no other than this on which I now write '—(which is not *cerulean,* and *is* very like tea-paper). ' Why it is called so, nobody here can tell me. The memory of the Family would be *estinta* even here, had they not left such lasting monuments of their protection of the Fine Arts which are totally lost here at present. Here is neither

Painter, Engraver, nor Sculptor above the most common class. The best of the latter sort is a drunken Englishman, whose whole employment is to make chimney pieces for the Palace, and some for Russia, whose Empress buys everything, good or bad, that her emissaries can find in Italy.'

'I am afraid that another Great Prince' (George the Third) 'was as ill-served in these parts; witness the collection bought of Smith at Venice, which I believe cost $\frac{m}{20}$ £. I never heard what was become of the Statues which *I* bought, many years ago, by Lord Melcombe's order, for the late Prince of Wales. Perhaps they still remain under a shed at Kew, where they were first placed, though they are worthy of a better habitation. Lord Bute told me that the King had offered them to him, but that he had refused to accept of them. I took the liberty to blame him, and I hope he has grown more complaisant since, that they may be at least brought to light somewhere. But—to return to the History—I think that I should send it to be presented to the King, but I cannot get it well bound here. I must therefore send it to my nephew, to have it done there.'

To the last, Mann continued to be profuse in his gifts to Walpole, who, in his turn, professed to be as much ashamed as he was grateful. Among the presents recently made were a valuable cameo and a crystal globe, or as Mann describes it,—'the greatest trifle, a Bit of Rock cristal which was sold publickly, among many other such pieces of *Rubbish* in the *Scaffali* of the *Tribuna*, after Bianchi, who set fire to the Gallery, had stript it of a gold foot that the

Medici had adorned it with, but they were profuse
People, and did not know what to do with their
money.' When Walpole acknowledged the safe
arrival of the cameo at Strawberry, with its handsome
young God, Apollo or Amazon, he knew not which
(it is an intaglio, on Cornelian, of Apollo), he alluded
to the other objects which Mann had sent to him from
Florence. ' My gem arrived like the lost sheep. You
cannot imagine how the Caligula, and the Bianca
Capello, and Benvenuto's coffer, and the Castiglione
and all your presents, embraced, and hugged it, and
inquired after you. The new-comer is lodged in a glass
case in *my Tribune*, over against Caligula.' As to
the bit of rock-crystal, Walpole says, in thanking the
donor :—' What you spoke of so irreverently, proves
a beautiful sculptured vase of rock-crystal. There is
no end of your gifts, but there must be. Remember,
reflect, how little time I may have to enjoy them. . . .
How sad is the thought that you are *never* to see your
presents arranged and displayed *here*, with all the
little honour I can confer on them.'

Walpole also makes an allusion to the death of the
Empress-Queen, Maria Theresa, in answer to a now
lost letter from Mann :—'I was with you just forty
years ago, when the departed Empress came to the
crown. What a tide of events that era occasioned!
You and I shall not see much of what this may
produce, and therefore I will not guess at a history
that is in the cradle for me, and that I shall not be
acquainted with when it is come to years of discretion.'
To this Mann replies :—' We have heard nothing
yet, in consequence of the Empress's death, excepting

that her successor' (her son Joseph) 'has confirmed
all her Ministers, and that she has loaded him with
enormous debts. It is said that her Will is very
favourable for the Great Duke. The Florentines only
weep for the loss of their Carnival, during which
all publick and private amusements are prohibited.'

The year ends with a notice of the revolution in
the family of the Count Albany, by his wife suddenly
and secretly leaving him. 'The mould,' says Mann,
December 30th, 'for any more casts of Royal Stuarts
has been broke, or what is equivalent to it, is now
shut up in a Convent of Nuns, under the double
lock and key of the Pope and Cardinal York, out of
the reach of any Dabbler who might foister in any
spurious copy. Historians may now close the Lives
of that family, unless the Cardinal should become
Pope, and that would only produce a short scene of
ridicule. The Countess Albanie, after a short stay
in the Convent here, was invited to Rome, by the
Pope and her Brother-in-law, to reside in the Convent of the *Orsolene*, and is to inhabit the same
appartment in which the Princess Sobieska frequently
took refuge from the Tyranny of her Husband. But,
Devotion had a great share in *that* retirement, and
probably, a view of being *Sainted*, in time, when her
bare bone knees and the Miracles she has since performed, which have been registered, cannot be dis-
proved.'

'The present Lady has more merit. During her
nine years' martyrdom, she has applied to cultivating
her mind, by studying Mathematicks, and reading
History and Poetry, at a time when one may well

suppose that she had a great struggle with her constitution to resist the temptation of her Master, the renowned Count Alfieri, without the least blemish to her character. I think she deserves a handsome pension from England, on that account. At present, she is to have half the Pension of twelve thousand crowns which the Pope gave her husband. This will affect him more than the loss of his wife, of whom he could make no other use than that of tormenting her ; but she must sacrifize her liberty during the Count Albany's life ; as she will not be permitted to go out, excepting on some urgent occasion, when the Cardinal is to lend her a Coach.'

Soon after, France was kind to this lady, less out of pity for her, than of spite against England. ' The Queen of France has lately wrote a very gracious letter to the Countess Albany, that her Royal Consort, the King of France, taking compassion of the Countess's past Sufferings, had assigned for her a pension of Twenty thousand Roman Crowns a year, for her life. You will easily judge how much the Countess applauds herself for having eloped from her nautious Tyrant. The Cardinal gives her four thousand, and maintains her sumptuously in a fine appartment, with Servants and Equipage.'

## CHAPTER XVII.

### 1781.

THE letters of Mann during this year are laden
with much circumstantiality of detail in reference to
the war in which England, America, France, Spain,
and Holland took part.    There are many reports
and many denials of what was previously reported;
but there is nothing either new or of interest now,
except an incident in connection with Minorca and
General Murray, who was defending it against Crillon
and a formidable force of besiegers.    'Murray wrote
to me, long ago, that if he had but two thousand
men more, he desired no fleet to assist him, and
would defy the Devil.    *That* would be an easy
task; but I, who am not a soldier, may fear that
so powerful an enemy may be more dangerous to
cope with.    The Duc de Crillon wrote a private
letter to General Murray, to offer him a million of
dollars to let him take the Castle, indicating to him
the means of doing it with safety to his honour.
The brave old General immediately summoned his
officers, to whom he read the treacherous letter
aloud, and sent an abusive answer to Crillon, saying, he would never have any other intercourse

with him but by the mouths of his cannon. That
was well said . . . The first onset is to be made by
4,000 *âmes damnées* collected from all the prisons
in Spain and Ceuta. If any survive, they are to
be pardoned, but most people think they have a
bad chance for their lives . . . Spain is resolved to
have it.' This resolution was rather ignobly expressed by Spain. '. . . A most scurrilous performance,' says Mann; 'it makes H. C. Majesty say
that,—that Island was a nest of Jews, and of the
*Canaille* of all countries, Pirates, who without distinction robbed the subjects of all nations, and that
the Court of Admiralty there, by the most unjust
sentences, justified their Piracy, which sentences were
always confirmed by the Court of Admiralty in England; that therefore, H. C. M. had determined to
root out such an infamous nest of Pirates.' An
united French and Spanish force contrived to land,
much to old Murray's surprize, and they captured
live stock and magazines, which capture caused a
serious loss to the English garrison. ' Mrs. Murray,
with all the English females, embarked the very day
the Enemy landed, and in twelve days got safe to
Leghorn . . . . *Te Deums* were sung, both at Madrid
and Port Mahon, for their success in landing,—without any opposition.' Murray did defend the place
like a Lion, and Minorca was not taken till 1782.

With much more lengthened circumstance of detail
does Mann recount the illness, the death, and the
testamentary troubles following the death of the ill-
regulated Countess of Orford. As Walpole's letters
contain replies which equally narrate the whole family

story, it is only necessary to submit here such incidents as refer to the life and death of this eccentric woman in Italy, and which are not to be found in Walpole. After referring to the asthma and erysipelas, which had rendered this once saucy beauty miserable to herself and to all others, save the Cavalier Mozzi, who may be called the last of her friends, but he was not one of either her husbands or lovers, and who was a thoroughly honest man, doing the old Countess service, according to Italian custom—after reference to the above-named afflictions, Mann writes, January 16th: 'I prepared you three days ago for the event which I have now to impart to you. Lady Orford died at Pisa on the 13th at noon . . . She gave orders to be buryed at Leghorn, which is to be performed to-day or to-morrow. Her original Will was deposited in the publick Archivi here, in 1773 ; but Mozzi brought me her writing-box the next day, which I opened in his presence, and of a lawyer's, in which I found a paper sealed with her seal and, wrote on the cover by her, "a copy of my last will.". . . She has left everything she was possessed of to Mozzi, of which he will take formal possession, according to the laws of this country, as soon as a certificate of her death can be procured from Pisa, by which he will be authorized to demand the original will deposited in the *Archivio*. The whole inheritance will be very considerable, reckoning only what she had here and at Naples.'

*February* 24th.—'Neither she nor Mozzi had the least apprehension of the approach of death, till the 10th January, and she died on the 13th. She had indeed been in a declining state for some time, yet she dined and went about as usual, but never complained. It is very certain that no courier was sent to England, either before or after her death. Mozzi has often assured me that Lady Orford never confided to him anything relating to her affairs in England; neither do I believe that she knew the detail of them herself; for it was her known custom, never, at least very seldom, to open any letter from her agents there; but threw them into a drawer, where many have been found sealed, as they came; all complaining of her silence and of the prejudice her affairs suffered by it. In one of Sharp's, he threatened to stop the money for his appointments, as she would not send him an order for it, which he had so often asked. That too was thrown into the drawer,—and yet she was very attentive to small expenses. . . . '

'I never heard of her having had two daughters by Richecourt, nor do I believe it. You seem to be mistaken about Mozzi. He is of one of the most antient families among the nobiltà here, and not poor for this country. She, to be sure, chose him for his beauty, which was then great and in its prime, but she wished it to be thought that his learning (for which he was distinguished, and he has published some approved works on the Mathematicks) biassed her choice. Richecourt was nothing but what his place here made him, not young and of a very common figure. Mozzi's attention has been greatly rewarded, but his mother and his family, or I should better say, his friends, always abused Lady Orford for being the obstacle to his marrying and raising issue to his own family, of which he is the only male.

You know that the Italians consider the extinction of
their name of the first importance and misfortune.
A Corsini and a Strozzi and a number of other of the
first young ladies have been offered to him, but he does
not seem disposed to forfeit his liberty a second time.'

Mrs. Damer, an English lady of another quality
than that which distinguished Lady Orford, passed
through Florence this year, on her way to Naples,
in order, as Walpole put it, 'to confirm a weak constitution.' He warmly recommended to Mann this
daughter of his heart, and Mann writes, in November:
'. . . The amiable Mrs. Damer arrived here a few
days ago. I fled to her the moment I was informed
of it, and she received me with a kindness which you
must have inspired her with. She had just got out of
her coach and was at supper. Few ladies would have
received a stranger at such a moment ; but her great
ease and affability made me flatter myself that I did
not appear such to her; and she has continued to treat
me as one inviolably attached to you, and as one who
respects and esteems her father. There are great
merits with her, but I have endeavoured to convince
her how ambitious I am of being useful to her, during
her stay here ; and she accepts with great goodness,
every mark of attention and respect which I attempt
to show her. She has declined being presented to the
Great Dutchess. . . She frequents the Gallery very
assiduously, where she has given great proofs of her
taste and judgment, particularly in Sculpture. She
will tell you how all the Niobe family are placed.
*Pajono tanti pazzi*, says Febroni, who has wrote their
story.'

The allusion to Niobe receives this illustration, in another letter:—'You would not know the Gallery, in the present transformation of it.  The entrance to it is by the stairs you so often went up to old Madame Suares's rooms, to which stairs a new flight is carried up to that part which was a narrow passage, where John Gaston' (the last of the Medici Dukes) 'in his enormous wig, stood.  From this one enters into a suite of rooms, parallel to the Corridor, down to the Cabinet de Madame.  By this means the Tribuna is perforated, the octagon table is removed (and not replaced) and only a few pictures and statues remain in it.  All the hidden *Scaffali* are taken away.  The Armoury is converted into bad rooms and are ill furnished with middling pictures.  The part a-cross, near the River, remains as it was, with the addition of the famous Torso of Gaddi, which the Great Duke bought, with many other good busts and pictures, of that family.  On that side of the Gallery, the China has been removed, and the rooms are appropriated for Modern Painters' heads, and will soon be crouded with them, as all kinds of Daubings are admitted.  The Medals remain as before, antient and modern Bronzi fill other rooms ; then you come to a very large, long, and most costly room, ornamented with stucco gilt, which has been many years about and looks like an appurtenance to a Church, in which the G. Duke has been ill-advised to place the Family of Niobe, with every figure detatched, so that they mean nothing and totally destroy the merit they had in a Group.  This tawdry room is near the Laocoon.  The Corridors are the same, excepting that the walls between the Statues

and the Busts are covered with bad pictures, and
strike one with the idea of a magazine or an uphol-
sterer's shop.   This tour of the Gallery has tired both
my hands, almost as much as I was in walking over
it, though I was carried up and down the stairs, and
sat down in every room.'

Subsequently, Sir Horace adds :—'There have been
annual sales out of the Palace (not out of the Gallery,
which has been respected and encreased by the present
G. Duke) since the beginning of the late Emperor's
reign.   The sales of late years have consisted of old
pictures, tables, chairs, and stools ; but there was
likewise much blue and white china, no setts, but
some pieces, old, and estimable on that account.   It
was impossible to attend the sales, for the croud of
Jews and upholders.   But what will you say to what
the Grand Maitre told me, that with the gold lace
and fringe that adorned the hangings, chairs, and
stools, he made three setts of Plate for the Table, of
36 covers each, with three dozen of gold knives, forks,
and spoons, for the use of the Princes.'   For Walpole's
stinging remarks on the detaching the figures in the
group of Niobe, his Letters may be consulted with
profit.   In the same collection he finds fault with
what he considers offences against good taste in parts
of Galuzzi's History of the Medici, the suggestion for
writing which he is less inclined to attribute to the
Grand Duke, Leopold, than to the Emperor Joseph,
who was undoubtedly first a German, and then, if you
please, a Catholic.   Mann replies :—

' The author is a young man and might be betrayed to make use of a harsh term by the horror of

the subject.   Every Quinterne was perused in manuscript by the G. Duke, as the author went on.   The
G. Duke positively ordered him to *Buttar giu Buffa*
and spare nobody.   To this you may reply that
German delicacy is not so great as that of English
and French modern authors.   Voltaire had views of
interest or fear to pass over the family squabble; but
how will Posterity learn what he means by it ?'

On the day Galuzzi's History was published in
Florence, a hundred copies were sold, which was a
great sale for a city not given much to reading.
Mann himself appears to have been an author.   'I
have a print of Camilla Martelli, Cosmo's second wife.
It is in the set of all their wives, which I sent to
England in 1768, with a manuscript descriptive of
Tuscany, which I drew up, by Lord Holderness's
order, for the King's instruction, though I do not
suppose that He ever cast an eye upon it; nor was
the receipt of it ever acknowledged.'

Leghorn lost this year one of those English
merchants whose dealings made the name honoured
abroad.   It was in the days before anything was
known of accommodation bills, or open credits, or sham
firms, or banks helping them to look like substantial
realities, and becoming virtuously indignant when the
bubble burst.   His name was Terney; a monument
was being erected to his memory in the English ceme-
tery at Leghorn.   Mann alludes thus to one of his
weaknesses:—'Mr. Terney was a splendid English
merchant, who acquired a large fortune at Leghorn,
and having no Relations, he left the greatest part of
his fortune to a God-son, a son of Commissary Proby,

whom he has never seen or heard of since he christened
him, but he was really at a loss how to dispose of his
wealth, as you will be persuaded when I tell you that
he has left a thousand zecchins to Lord Tylney,
because he was my Lord's Banker; and six hundred
to Lord Cowper, because he is a Prince, and that such
names, with the addition of his "noble friends,"
sound well in his Will. To poor me, he has left two
hundred zecchins for a ring, because the Countess of
Orford did, and to imitate a Countess. I have not
disposed of her legacy yet. Marquis Barbentane was
to send me a snuff-box, with her cypher, from Paris,
which possibly he may have forgotten, as very probably Lord Orford (her son) has the ring, he told you
he would send me.'

Greater folk were making more splendid presents
than these. 'The Emperor has made a present to the
Great Dutchess of the *Grande Maitresse* of the Lady's
Order, called "La Croix Etoilée," the last of which the
Empress gave to Mrs. Swinburne. The Emperor has
likewise sent the G. Dutchess, by the same Courier,
the Ensigns of a male Order, St. Stephen of Hungary,
which the Empress alone wore as Roy d'Hungarie,
and which the G. Dutchess (without that title) is now
alone (the only lady) to wear. She might have had
too that of St. Catherine of Russia, which some years
ago I was commissioned by Her Imperial Majesty to
offer her; but it was not accepted. Such a Star and
such a Badge, which were sent (not expecting a refusal) I never saw; but a great Lady then called
H. I. M., her *villaine sœur* all this is a great secret.
Who could foresee that the present connection would

be brought about, and there is still a probability that it will in a few years be still greater, when a young Plant here comes to maturity.'

Meanwhile, there was one of the drollest of revolutions making itself felt in the Grand Duke's dominion.

' You used to say,' writes Mann, ' that the dress of our Ladies was a Caricatura of the French. It has much encreased since your time. This Summer, they have made the most whimsical of Dresses to walk in, at night, on the Bridge ; which made quite a Patagonian Puppet-show ! Such a tumble of feathers and gauze to heighten their heads ! Such a swelling out of Polonaises, Circasiennes, and Levites, and a mixture of all according to the Ingenuity of the Lady who wished to give the Ton and attract applause and admirers. This folly was humbly imitated by all inferior ranks, even to the use of Cocks' and Hens' feathers, and a heap of washed Ribbons and Tinsel. The Cavalieri ammogliati and the poor honest Padri di famiglie are supposed to have privately presented memorials to the Great Duke—the first, the married Cavaliers, to complain of the expense and debts of their wives; the latter, the Fathers of families, to tell him that their Daughters lay upon their hands, as the young men were deterred from marrying, on account of the expense in decking out a wife, or the fear of her letting others do it. In short, the Great Duke, moved by such cogent reasons, *and* to put a stop to the *exit* of the great sums of money paid for such foreign *chiffonage,* put an end to all this by a printed Letter (from the Great Duke's Secretary) which

was sent to the Casino, on Monday, and ordered to be
read in a full assembly, exhorting the Nobility of both
Sexes to set the example of moderation and *Decency*
in their Dress.' This singular ducal expostulation
with the Ladies runs thus :—

'His Royal Highness sees, with the greatest
concern, the excessive luxury which has, for some
time, been introduced into Costume, and especially in
that of the Ladies ; and apprehends the very worst
consequences that may arise from it.

'Those Ladies, who from their own means, or
from the compliance and means of their husbands, are
possessed of ample incomes, in place of employing
them in many more useful and more noble objects
have the weakness to squander their money in the
most ridiculous display of variety. Many Ladies,
equal to others in rank, but not in substance, fancy
themselves bound by a false point of honour, to appear
in everything on an equality with ladies of greater
wealth. The ladies of every other rank, in consequence of the emulation which distinguishes the whole
sex, make ruinous efforts to imitate those who are
above them. And this extravagantly expensive taste
which Fashion introduces into the Capital City
rapidly extends itself throughout the Provincial towns,
and also, in proportion, but with more ruinous consequences, through country villages.'

' Thence arises the greatest difficulty in married life;
failure of means for properly educating the sons and for
establishing the daughters ; insufficiency of savings on
the part of those in business, their debts, and sometimes their frauds ; scarcity of capital in trade, dimin-

ution of help to the labouring classes; falling off of
land cultivation, family disaster, family dissension,
and evil life.'

'And this excess of vanity, which in some few
Ladies would only be a contemptible weakness, becomes in the greater part of the rest, in which that
excess is propagated, a serious crime; since, to satisfy
the vanity, they must either employ means not their
own, or devote to that purpose sums necessary to
accomplish the most essential duties of a Father or
of a Mother of a Family.'

'His Royal Highness, in the system of his government, formed to put the smallest possible constraint
on the liberty of action of his subjects, has not desired
to make any special law against luxury. Besides, he
well understands how difficult it is to regulate by laws
a matter so subject to assume diverse aspects, especially where female adornment is concerned, the extravagance of which very often, as in the fashion of
the present time, consists less in quality than in quantity and in the abuse of it; and he will always consider as repugnant to His Clemency those laws which
give too great facility alike to transgressions and to
merely vexatious matters.'

'But he has such confidence in the respect of his
subjects as to leave no doubt that they, knowing his
paternal affliction, will make no delay in seconding
him, and thus acquiring his Sovereign approval.'

'It being necessary that reform should begin with
the Nobility and through their example extend itself
to other ranks, your Lordship . . . will learn at the
Casino of the Nobles our Royal intentions.'

'In confirmation of the same, Their Royal Highnesses will be best pleased if, on Court receptions, and
on Gala days, and on any other occasions, the Nobility
will present themselves,—as well Men as Ladies,—in
plain costume, black by preference, and with that
supreme simplicity of ornament which is more suitable
to decency and to the propriety of plain costume than
excessive theatrical adornment.'

'Their Royal Highnesses' subjects must necessarily
be persuaded That their Royal Highnesses have too
much good sense to esteem the Nobility by their
richness of costume, rather than to value them for
their honourable sentiments, their good conduct, the
wise use of their substance, and their usefully directed
generosity.'

'On the contrary, His Royal Highness the Great
Duke will take moderation or excess in the costume of
all ranks of men, as well as in that of their wives and
daughters, as affording the strongest grounds of presumption of their good or bad conduct, of their good
sense or of their mental weakness : And this presumption will have much influence in the dispensing of the
Sovereign kindnesses and especially in that of official
employments, in all which judgment is required, and
a freedom from disorder in domestic economy.'

'And with the usual distinguished obsequiousness.
I declare myself, your —— most devoted and most
obliged Servant,

'VINCENZIO DEGLI ALBERTI.

'Florence, 10th August, 1781.'

Mann says :—'From the instant of the publication

of this letter a total reformation ensued ; no fantastical apparel, nor feathers are to be seen ; by which, the women are reduced to their natural size ;—of which, however, they appear to be ashamed.'

## 1782.

The happiest day to Mann, of the year 1782, was that on which he received the news of Rodney's victory over the Count de Grasse, which compensated for many a disaster that had sorely afflicted our Minister Plenipotentiary—for that was Sir Horace's new title.  'I immediately made the Victory known to all the town, who flocked to my house soon after, to compliment me upon that occasion.   Even the eldest Prince, not reflecting on his father's neutrality, or the attention due to his French uncle, meeting one of my servants out of the gates, called to him and bid him make me his compliments on the great news I had received.   The servant came running home, thinking himself as much honoured as I was pleased with his message.'

'The method of this young Prince's education ought to be followed, I mean adopted, for all children of his and a more inferior rank.   He was taken from the care of women before he could form any ideas, or they instil any foolish prejudices into his mind ; and he has ever since been attended by men of sense without the least tincture of pedantry ; they succeed each other.   His amusements even tend to his instruction.   He played at Geography by the dissected maps that I was desired to get from England, and in all his walks and rides he is accompanied by people who amuse and instruct him. He has learnt the principal modern languages as the natives do, having attendants of the different nations who always speak their own language to him, by which means they are all familiar to him. By the whole plan of his education, it is evident what progress a youth may make at the age of fifteen.'

During this year the Pope visited Vienna, in order to induce the Emperor Joseph to restore the convents he had suppressed, and to make amends for other offences against the Church. 'After the Tragedy of War,' Mann says, 'the Pope's excursion serves for the Farce. He has satisfied his family, has distributed millions of blessings with a better grace than any of his predecessors; by which he has gained applause and nothing else; but it is very dubious whether he will be received with as much on his return to Rome. The Emperor has acted his part in the Comedy extremely well; but even the Pope's presence did not interrupt the execution of his plan. The same will be adopted here in Florence in an inferior degree and by slower steps. Some convents, both of men and women, have been suppressed, but the individuals have been turned over to other convents; and it is now said that two male Orders have been forbidden to receive any more.'

When these great personages travelled, they interrupted the progress of the post, by taking the horses intended for the mails or couriers, if no others were to be had. Such a personage was Maria Amelia, wife of Don Ferdinand, Duke of Parma, and sister of

the Grand Duke of Tuscany. 'I told you that the
Dutchess of Parma is here. She calculated her arrival
to see Florence in Gala, and the spectacle of a horse-
race which she likes better than any other. She is
a perfect Amazon. The next day, she visited the
Great Duke's stables, as preferable to the Gallery or
Palazzo Pitti,—for she is lodged at the Imperiale,
where the Court resides. There is to be a great
Appartement this evening in Gala, but the Great
Dutchess, who is in danger of a Miscarriage, will not
assist at it. I wish I could be excused, for nothing
hurts me so much as standing long on my legs;
though perhaps I may have the honour of playing
with her at Ombre.'

Mann agrees with Walpole as to the co-operation
by which the history of the Medici was completed.
'I am much pleased with your thought that part of it
may have originated from Caesar, for, while Galuzzi
was writing it, he consulted Caesar's Brother here,
about the propriety, or I should rather say the Danger,
to which the author might be exposed by publishing
to the world all the Papal Infamy which he found in
the Archivio. The Great Duke replyed : "Tirate
giu la Buffa ; io vi guardero le Spalli "—(away with
all modesty ; I will guard you from being attacked)
'and away Galuzzi went exulting, for two reasons ;—
the first arising from the gratification of his own
inclinations ; the other, from the discovery of less
hereditary piety' (in the sons of Maria Theresa) 'than
he expected. It is not improbable that the Brothers
agreed on the great Plan, the execution of which was
reserved till the great obstacle' (the Empress-Queen)

'was removed; and indeed, when one considers how
much has been done in so short a time since, and in
the hurry of a thousand other important occupations,
one must conclude that the whole was digested while
the Emperor Joseph was a Pupil.    Maria Theresa
must shudder in her grave at such impiety!'

General Murray, the gallant but unsuccessful de-
fender of Minorca against the French and Spaniards,
under De Crillon, was a guest of Mann's; and many
of Murray's officers were in Florence.    There was
much division of opinion among them as to Murray's
quality as a soldier.    'The form and terms of the
capitulation are criticized by military people, and the
cordiality which passed between him and the Duc de
Crillon—after what had passed before'—(De Crillon's
offer of a bribe to Murray for the surrender of the
place), 'by accepting of an appartment in the house
of his quondam enemy, seemed odd, though they
quarrelled there, and he left it.'

Altogether, it was a dull and a sickly year in
Florence.    The court was much at Pisa.    The weather
was successively too cold, too hot, and too wet;
scarcity prevailed; famine threatened.    Mann was
bored by ladies of all nations who were recommended
to him for presentation at court, and who, if they
were bold enough to leave Italy by sea, ran the
risk of being snapped up by Algerine corsairs, and
being added to the seraglio of his Exaltedness, the
Dey.    The Plenipotentiary's dearly beloved country-
folk troubled him considerably.    'The English have,
by custom, a right to my dinners.    An omission of
that kind, to a very insignificant man, once drew upon

me almost a challenge (though he had often dined here
before), because he had heard that other English had
been invited and not he ! But, in general, I have
been free from quarrelling with my countrymen.' To
one of them, the modest English artist, Patch, Mann
was much attached. Sir Joshua's old fellow-traveller
in Italy first made Masaccio known to England by
his engravings after that great master. Mann lost
poor Patch in the spring of the year. 'This very
worthy man was most friendly attached to me. He
was attacked yesterday morning with an apoplexy in
my house, but finding himself ill, he went across the
street to his own, and threw himself on his bed. I was
sent for, but found him speechless. He languished
for a few hours, and expired this morning, April
30th.'

The great event of the year was the siege of
Gibraltar. In Florence, or at Pisa, the Spanish
ambassador every week solemnly delivered to the
Grand Duchess letters from her father the King of
Spain, with details of the triumphant progress of the
siege. 'I believe,' says Mann, 'that he neither writes
nor knows the truth. An Italian, high in rank, in their
service at Gibraltar, says in his last letter to a principal man here, that there is not a word of truth in all
the pompous account of the progress of the Siege, and
that they are no further advanced than they were the
first day ; though, not long ago, they had so much
confidence in their floating batteries, that great preparations were made at Cadiz to receive Count d'Artois '
(brother of Louis XVI., and afterwards Charles X.),
'and to celebrate the conquest of Gibraltar in his

presence. The Italians say that he will return to
Paris, *colle trombe nel sacco!* '

The Count not only returned—the Duke de Bourbon
in his company—with his trumpet in his carpet-bag, as
the Italians said, but to encounter a storm of Paris
wit. When Darçon's floating batteries were destroyed
by our red-hot shot, it was remembered that the
English fire was so 'infernal' that the Count was
unable to display his petulant bravery. His time was
passed in gay promenades on the beach within the
Spanish lines, and in giving magnificent fêtes and
banquets. Accordingly, on his return in November to
Paris, which he had left in the previous July, the
Paris epigrammatists said, among other things, that, as
far as the combined forces of France and Spain were
concerned, the only battery which had produced any
effect was the *batterie de cuisine* of the Count
d'Artois.

# CHAPTER XVIII.

## 1783.

IN what way the postal service was carried on at this period may be seen in Mann's letter dated February 16th :—' I might have received your letter of the 23rd January, with the joyfull news of Peace, last week, had not the Courier left the English Mail behind; his successor brought it on, on Wednesday, but forgot his own, so that there is still one in arrear.'

The replies from Florence, often thus delayed, are chiefly concerned with English politics and family affairs. As regards Mann himself, he begins the year in this fashion :—' I write from a couch, with the smallest touch of the gout I ever had in one foot, which only hinders me from going to the Opera, to see the Siege of Vienna, extremely well represented in a Dance.'

The most important figure in this year's correspondence is that of the Pope. Italy had been terribly excited by fear and sympathy at the news of the destructive earthquake which had devastated Messina, and swept with fatal effect through Calabria. 'The details of the destruction are horrible.' So Mann writes, March 8th, and adds:—' When the news of it

arrived at Rome, the Governour proposed to the Pope
to shut up the Theaters, and to prohibit the diversions
of the Carnival; but his Holiness would not hear of it.
He has a trite expression, which he frequently makes
use of : " *Digitus Dei, hic est!* " he applyed it on this
occasion, and seemed to think that it was a very
proper Chastisement for the Suppression of the Inquisition in Sicily ! His insensibility on this occasion is
shocking to humanity. He is held in the utmost
contempt at Rome. All his undertakings, by which
he has totally exhausted the publick Treasure, have
either failed or been disapproved of. The draining the
Pontine Marshes has failed, and has been discontinued.
The Sacristy of St. Peter's is a costly useless blemish
to that Church. The Pope's journey to Vienna was
expensive, humiliating, and totally useless. But, at
the expense of his reputation and Dignity, he has
found the means of enriching his family, by availing
himself of the weakness of a devout, simple, but a
very rich old Priest, to make him a Donation of all his
Wealth, which amounts to two Millions of crowns,
besides many family jewels, and great quantity of
Plate, etc., of all which the Pope's nephew is in actual
Possession ; the Donor having only reserved for his
own Maintenance six thousand crowns a year during
his life, which sum is paid to him by the Pope who,
both in the publick writings and that of his acceptance,
is only named,—Angelo Braschi.'

' The Priest I am speaking of is Marquis Lepri, the
elder Brother of him who, with his wife, was some
years ago in England. The Priest having been persuaded that the Intail of the Estate finished in him,

has given it to Angelo Braschi in prejudice of a niece and many near and very poor Relations. But the niece, who is the daughter of the beautiful Marquise Lepri, has great Protectors, and (though but ten years old) has been betrothed to Prince Sforza Cesarini, who will dispute the whole inheritance with Angelo Braschi, who is condemned by all Rome for this shameful transaction; and the Lawyers are divided as to the validity of it.'

While this affair was being discussed, the Royal Stuart in Florence was ignobly decaying amid ignoble family circumstances. 'I have told you' (April 5th) 'how dangerously ill the Count Albani has been. His Physicians sent to inform me that a mortification had begun in his Legs, that his Body was swelled; that the *affanno* was great, so that he thought Him to be in the most imminent danger. This account was sent Post to Rome to his Brother and his Countess. The former set out on his way hither, but being dubious if he should find him alive, stopped at Siena and sent a Courier to get Intelligence, which encouraged him to come on, when he found that the mortification had disappeared, and that other circumstances began to take a favourable turn. Count Albani has continued to grow better ever since, and is now said to be out of immediate danger; but his Physicians apprehend that he will fall into a chronical disease of a Dropsy in his Breast. He made a Will in a hurry; and it has been said, in joke, that he has bequeathed his three kingdoms to a third son of the Great Duke, in example of what King Theodore did, by leaving his crown to his creditors.'

*April* 26*th*.—' I formerly gave you an account of
the *fracas* in the Pretender's family, by the Elopement of his wife, whom everybody then pitied and
applauded. The tables are now turned. The cat, at
last, is out of the bag. The Cardinal of York's visit
to his Brother gave the latter an opportunity to un-
deceive him, by proving to him that the complaints
laid to his charge, of ill-using her, were invented to
cover a Plot formed by Count Alfieri who, (by working
up Tragedies, of which he has wrote many, is most
expert, though he always kept behind the curtain,)
had imposed upon the Great Duke, the Pope, and the
Cardinal, and all those who took her part. All he
said on that subject, at a time that he thought himself
and was supposed by everybody to be in the most
imminent danger, made a great impression on his
Brother, who, on his return to Rome, exposed the
whole to the Pope, and obtained an order from him
to Count Alfieri, to leave the Pope's State, in fifteen
days. Not content with that satisfaction, the impru-
dent Cardinal (for a more silly mortal never existed)
published the whole of the Countess's intrigues with
Alfieri. This has exasperated all the Roman Nobility
against the Cardinal, insomuch that, instead of con-
sidering the delinquencies of the Parties, their wrath
is turned against the Publisher of the Scandal ; and
they compassionate the situation of the disconsolate
Lady who, I really believe, will marry the Count, a
week after she becomes a widow.'

Our Minister Plenipotentiary speaks thus of his
own bodily weakness. August 2nd :—' I hobble
strangely, and can neither walk or stand on my legs

long.   They are frequently put to a severe trial when
I have strangers to present to the Great Duke ; he
loves to talk with them, to show his great affability
and hear their stories.   At the audience he gave to
Sir William Hamilton, he kept us standing an hour
and three quarters.   I could with difficulty, afterwards, hobble to a stool in the Ante-chamber, from
whence I was led down stairs, and remained a cripple
for three days.   These audiences will soon be at an
end.   H. R. H. does not love Florence or its inhabitants who, he thinks, do not love him ; so that he
will remove to Pisa the beginning of the next month,
and fix his residence there, for the whole winter.
Neither his own nor the foreign ministers are to
attend him there.   The Great Dutchess vyes with our
Gracious Queen in fertility, and is to lay in at Pisa
in October.'

' I shall be glad to see your nephew, Mr. Cholmondeley.   If he comes soon and is musical, he may
hear Marchesi, who is the most pleasing singer I have
ever heard, though some prefer Paccherotti to him,—
whom I have not heard.'

Mann ended the year in good company—that of
Gustavus the Third, King of Sweden, who, nine years
later, was slain by Ankarstroem at a masked ball.
On December 13th, Mann says:—'The King of Sweden
is still here, and as he has thrown himself upon Lord
Cowper and me, we go on treating him as we began.
He comes to one of our houses every evening ; and as
that, especially on me, draws great Invasions, they are
very expensive as well as troublesome.   He defers his
departure from one post day to another, in expecta-

tion of hearing that the Emperor has fixed a day for
his arrival at Pisa; but this is quite uncertain at
present; and it has been whispered that the Emperor
does not wish to see him. The King probably does
not know this; but he told me here yesterday evening,
that he would wait for the letters of to-morrow, and
then would decide. It is certain that neither the
Emperor nor the Empress of Russia is satisfied with
him; and even the very cool reception and treatment
of him at Pisa is a confirmation of it. They wish to
get him out of the hands of France, but he seems to
be too well-fixed in that alliance, and thence proceeds
this coldness towards him . . . I have lately received
a Letter from Lord Hardwicke, with a printed copy
of some Anecdotes of your Father. I never had
the honour of any connection with His Lordship,
excepting a few years ago, when he wrote to me
about the correspondence between the Jesuits at Rome
and those in England, which was found in their college
at Rome, relating to Gunpowder Plot, of which I had
given notice by my official letters to Government.'

## 1784.

The poor Pretender is the subject of eight of
Mann's letters of this year, and it is clear from these
that the same subject was to be found in other of
the Plenipotentiary's letters, which have been lost.

*January 24th.*—' Yesterday afternoon, I received
a message from Count Albany's Physician, to inform
me that he had been suddenly taken very ill, and
that he thought him to be in great danger. I had

seen him at the Theatre' (for the first time so spelt
in this correspondence) 'the evening before, when he
appeared as usual.  The company he invited to dinner,
went to his House at two o'clock, not having received
any message to forbid them.  In the course of the
day he grew worse, and soon became both speechless
and insensible.  His Physician, who at first thought
He had had a stroke of Apoplexy, declared in the
evening, that it was an Inflamation in his Brain, and
thought there could be no remedy.  A Courier was
despatched to his Brother at Rome, who probably will
not move from thence, with so little hopes of finding
him alive ; besides, they quarrelled so much the last
time the Cardinal came here that the Count cannot
wish to see him again.  It will be a singular circumstance to see a King-Cardinal.  The Emperor Maxi-
milian wanted to be one, in order to become Pope,
and then a Saint, that His Daughter might pray to
Him ; but His ambition was disappointed by His not
getting money enough to bribe His Holyness and his
Sacred College.'

' 12 o'clock.  The Count grows worse every hour,
and has had the Extreme Unction.  This is the last
account I can give you of him, before the departure of
the Post, which is already on horseback.'

*January* 31*st.*—'At the departure of my last
letter, Count Albany was thought to be at the last
period of his life.  He remained so for two days, both
speechless and insensible ; he then, for a short time,
recovered his senses, but not his speech.  The next
day he recovered the latter, for a few hours only.
Yesterday evening, he was again thought to be ex-

piring, but in the night, less unfavourable symptoms
appeared. I shall receive further accounts before the
departure of this Letter, to which I will add a Postscript. The passage between this place and Rome is
totally stopt by the snow ; so that no answer has
been received from Cardinal York to the letters that
were sent to him by a Courier last week.'

' P.S.—In the course of the last night, very favour-
able symptoms have appeared in Count Albany's illness.
He has recovered his senses and, in some degree, his
Speech.'

*February* 14*th*.—' Count Albany has got over the
danger he was threatened with. He wants only some
strength to recover that feeble state he had been
in for years before. There is a strange hitch in the
execution of the great and generous promises that the
King of Sweden made him ; but his Majesty has,
since that, seen the Countess of Albany and Cardinal
Bernis, at Rome, who have told him that the Count
was very rich, and neither wanted his money nor
deserved his compassion. I believe that it suited well
with His Majesty's Finances, to give them full credit
on both points. The poor Count does not yet know
this, and his friends fear the effect, when it must be
revealed to him. He would have done better to dye
when he was so near it.'

Charles Edward was of a different opinion. He
lived yet with a purpose in view. In July, there was
a thorough change imminent in the little court of the
Stuart, through the abandonment of him on the part
of his wife, the *amie* of the poet, Count Alfieri. July
24th.—' Count Albany has, by solemn Deed, acknow-

ledged his natural Daughter, by a Mrs. Walsingham,'
(Walkinshaw). 'She has been educated in a Convent
at Paris, and still resides *en Pension,* by the name
of Lady Charlotte Stuart, to which (and by his Will
appointing her sole-heiress to all he may be possessed
of at his death) he has added the Title of Dutchess of
Albany; and has wrote to M. de Vergennes to get
that deed registered in the Parliament of Paris. *He*
will smile probably both at the Title and the Request.
The young Lady is about thirty years of age, and, it
is said, often quits her Convent to visit Prince Rohan,
Archbishop of Bordeaux, whose Society (the Archbishop's nephew, who was lately here, says) she prefers much to that of Les Dames de S$^{te}$ Marie. With
the above Deeds, Stewart, Count Albany's old faithful
servant, was despatched to Paris, by the last French
Courier, with orders to the Count's Daughter to come
to live with him at Florence, where he proposes to
marry her to a Florentine Cavalier, if one good
enough can be found. This is his Plan, but he decays
so fast that it seems dubious if he should live to see
the Completion of it, or that he may have understanding enough left to enjoy it.'

*September* 11*th.*—' I have not heard anything
more relating to the Daughter of Count Albany and
Mrs. Walkinshaw ; but, it is said in his family that she
is expected here soon, and that the retardure is owing
to the preparations necessary to equip her out properly, to appear, first at Paris, and then here, under
the new Title her Father has given her of Dutchess
d'Albany. She is not to be accompanied by her
Mother, who would disgrace her, but by some great

Lady, who must ask that honour as *Dame de Compa-gnie* (as the discarded Countess has—a Lady who is a Chanoinesse and sister of a Prince Malsan).    It will require time to settle all these matters ; and after all there may be some difficulty in the Etiquette.    If the Count has not erred in his calculations, the family of Fitzjames need not be under any apprehension of their *Cousine* being a future expense to them ; for the Count proposes to marry her, not indeed to one of the Arch-Dukes, but to a Florentine nobleman, and to leave her twelve thousand crowns a year, a sum which would tempt any of them, more than the tinc-ture of Royalty.'

*September* 18*th.*—' The affair relating to Count Albany and his natural Daughter is drawing to a conclusion.    Lady Charlotte Stuart, Dutchess of Albany, is supposed to be on the road hither, at-tended by two Ladies and two Gentlemen, and is ex-pected in the beginning of next month.    The Count is very busy in furnishing his House with all the *meubles* he has lately received from Rome, and that his Father left.    They are numerous and costly.    Besides those, he has received a large quantity of Plate, and a share of his Mother's jewels, excepting the Great Ruby, and one lesser, that were pawned by the Repub-lick of Poland, for a very large sum, to his Grand-father, Sobieski, with a power, it is said, of reclaiming them in the space of one hundred years—which are nearly elapsed.    These, therefore, the Cardinal would not trust to his Brother, being persuaded that if he could find a Purchaser, he would sell them, or even part with them, for a large *Rente viagere*, to an

Empress of Russia, or some other Court; but it is not probable he will ever have the Disposal of them, and that when they fall to the Cardinal, he will rather give them to the Madonna di Loreto than to his Niece, with whose adoption he is not pleased, nor was consulted about it.'

'Nobody can foresee what the Cardinal will do with his Crown, after his Brother's Death. The Pope cannot permit him to wear it, as he never acknowledged or permitted the Elder Brother to assume it. You may remember the struggle which I then had with the Marquis D'Aubeterre, the French Ambassador at Rome, and my victory over him, which he never forgave. Some years after, he expressed himself to Marquis de Barbantane, who questioned him about it, in these words:—"Ha! Monsieur le Marquis, je croyois faire le plus beau Coup possible; mais, je ne fis qu'un pas de Clerc. Ce diable de M. Mann m'avoit prevenu et gâté mon projet,"—which was, to take the Pope by surprize; but, in my letters to old Cardinal Albani, which were read in the Consistory held on that subject, I asserted that the French Ambassador could not have received orders from his Court, whose engagements with that of England made it inconsistent with its honor to insist upon it; and that the Ambassador had laid a snare for the Pope, which he might avoid by only waiting for an answer from Paris, which I was very sure would bring a disavowal of the Ambassador's conduct. This encouraged the Pope to tell D'Aubeterre, that if his master would be the first, he (the Pope) would be the second to acknowledge the Pretender, under the titles the latter contended for.

The answer from France was such as I foretold, and General Conway, who was then Secretary of State, conveyed to me the King's approbation of what I had done. From all this I conclude that no future Pope will permit Cardinal York to install himself—King of England.'

*October* 18*th*.—'The arrival of Lady Charlotte Stuart, Dutchess of Albany, has occasioned some little bustle in the Town. A French Lady, who for thirty years had been totally neglected, but who, on a sudden, was transformed into a Dutchess, was an object that excited the curiosity of both Sexes—of the Men, to see her figure ;—of the Ladies, to scrupulously examine *that*, and the new *Modes* she has brought from Paris. The result of all which is that she is allowed to be of a good figure, tall, and well made, but that the features of her face resemble too much those of her father to be handsome. She is gay, lively, very affable, and has the behaviour of a well-bred Frenchwoman, without assuming the least distinction among our Ladies on account of her new dignity. They flock to her doors, to leave their cards, visits which she is to return, though the Countess of Albany, her step-mother did *not*, and therefore, or perhaps for another reason, she lived alone with Count Alfieri who, as a writer of tragedies, formed the Plot of her Elopement ; on which the acknowledgment of this natural Daughter, all the honours she has received, and all the future advantages she will have, by being Heiress to all her Father can leave her, depend. Perhaps, neither the Countess nor her lover foresaw all this, and it is very probable that she will repent of it, and consequently detest her adviser.'

' The Countess renounced everything to obtain her Liberty ; gave up her Pin money, which was 3000 crowns a year, and could not obtain anything for a separate maintenance, so that she does not receive a shilling from the Stuart family ; and is only to receive a jointure of 6000 crowns after her husband's death— a poor equivalent for what she has lost.  However, she obtained a Pension from the Court of France soon after her separation (when her complaints were listened to with compassion) of twenty thousand *petits Ecus,* which she now lives upon.'

' The new Dutchess has appeared at the Theatres (which were crowded on her account) with all her father's jewels, which are very fine.  He asked leave of the Great Duke to put a *Baldachino,* or *Dais,* over his boxes in each Theatre, and a velvet carpet to hang before it, which was refused, but he had permission to line the Boxes as he pleased.  That in the Great Theatre is hung with Crimson Damask; the cushion, velvet, with gold Lace.  In the other Theatre it is yellow Damask.  The Count is much pleased with this distinction.  The Dutchess brought with her, as Dame de Compagnie, a French woman (who married an Irish officer, named O'Donnel), and an Ecuyer named Nairn, a Scotchman, whom they call My Lord. We have heard that the King of France has legiti-mated her so far as to enable her to inherit what her father possesses in France ; and (it is said) she was received in quality of Duchesse at that Court, and had the Tabouret.  An attempt has been made to have her presented to the Great Duchesse, but excuses have been made under various pretences.'

*December* 18*th.*—'Poor Count Albany decays every day, visibly. The disorder inhis legs encreases. His Daughter did well to come in time to reap his succession, for which she will not wait long. The faculties of his mind are as weak as his body. They are always employed, when awake, in abusing his Brother, the Cardinal, for refusing to adopt his Niece, to whose letter, on her arrival here, he made no answer, though the Pope *did*, and congratulated her upon it.'

Mann chronicles, among other court news, the removal of the young Archduke, Francis, the youth who congratulated him on Rodney's victory, to Vienna, to go in training to act that part of Emperor which he ultimately played under circumstances of sorrow and humiliation. 'Tuscany,' said Mann, 'is to become an Appendix to Austria, like Milan and Brussels.' A story which amused the court, and an incident which amused the town, Mann tells in these words:—

'One of the King of Prussia's soldiers stole, out of a Catholick Church, the jewels that adorned a Madonna. He owned possession, but denyed the theft, saying that the Madonna had given them to him. There were no witnesses to disprove him. The King, therefore, sent for some Romish priests, and asked them if there was anything impossible for a Madonna. They were shocked at the question, and affirmed her Omnipotence. . . . "In that case," replied the King, "I cannot condemn the soldier, but I will forbid him ever to receive any more presents from a Madonna." '

The hero of the incident that amused the town was Lady Orford's old Cicisbeo, Cavaliere Mozzi. 'Mozzi was married last Saturday. To convince the world that it was not a youthful Passion that had induced him, at past fifty, to take that step, he deferred carrying the Bride to his own house till the Monday following, where, as usual, a sumptuous Banquet was prepared, at which I was invited to assist, but I excused myself on account of my health.'

In fact, the Minister Plenipotentiary was decaying faster than Count Albany. 'You must observe,' he says towards the close of the year, 'what strange omissions I frequently make in my letters. I can only account for it by my hands not being able to keep pace with my head, from the weakness of my nerves, which obliges me to make use of both hands to push on my pen. You have too much Humanity and Indulgence not to excuse such Infirmities of Age.'

## CHAPTER XIX.

### 1785.

THE remaining record consists of fragmentary details,
of letters written not off hand, with the post waiting
in the street on horseback, as was often the case in
former days, but painfully, one letter taking up all
the feeble efforts of many days, and sometimes despatched unfinished after all.   The old Plenipotentiary,
now nearly eighty years of age, expresses in one letter
indifference with regard to life, and earnest depreca-
tion of a lingering death.   Occasionally he wakes up
to discuss with Walpole the very dryest of political
questions in his old dry way ; and there is, amid this
mere dust of detail, a *flash* like the following :—

*March* 15*th.*—' You probably have heard of the
numerous promotions of Cardinals.   The Pope had
protracted it to accumulate riches for his family ; and
then he sold the State for the same purpose ; by
which, it is positively asserted, that in ready money
and Presents (for these are made publickly) he has got
200,000 crowns.   But that sum won't do to establish
an inheritance that would put his nephew on a par
with other Papal families, especially if the Donation of

Lepri should be decided to be invalid, as there is great reason to suppose will be the case, even during his reign, but not doubted of under that of his successor.'

The decision came at the earlier date. 'Madame Lepri,' says Mann, June 7th, 'has gained her great cause against the Pope. Six Auditors of the Rota had the courage to give sentence in her favour, in defiance of the frowns of a reigning Pope, whose mortification for the loss of such an important acquisition to his family has been aggravated by the exultation of all Rome. Thousands of people waited in the court-yard of the Palace, and with shouts of applause communicated their joy to the whole town. They accompanied the six Judges in triumph to their houses. Thus, the whole donation to the Pope has become null and illicit. Ten thousand copies of the sentence and the motives for it were ordered to be printed. The Pope, if he pleases, can apply for a revision (not an appeal), but it will then depend on the same six Judges to grant it, and even if they do, they themselves are to determine whether their own Sentence is right or not. This judgment only regards the entailed estate, which the foolish priest, the uncle, imagined ended in him. He consequently made a Donation of it to the Pope. It amounted to seven hundred thousand crowns ; but doubts arising, an attempt at accommodation was set on foot. The Pope offered to give Madame Lepri 250,000 crowns ; she insisted on 300,000, which being refused, the treaty broke off, and a few days after the donation was declared illicit. The Donor is still living, and has publickly declared

his repentance of what he had done; saying, that he
was not in his true senses at the time, and that he was
over-persuaded by artful people. This adds great
prejudice to the Pope's honour, which his subjects
personally manifest by their behaviour to him when he
appears abroad.'

Florence was divided between the Pope and the
King and Queen of Naples, who were received with a
prodigality of festivity, which so exhausted the Grand
Ducal and Municipal treasuries, that when those royal
personages returned from Milan to Florence, on their
way back to their own dominions, no notice was taken
of them at all. In August, Mann refers to visitors
in whom he took much more interest. 'Sometime
ago, Mr. King, a Jew, the author of the letters signed
"Neptune," and of a most scurrilous libel against
Mr. Fox, arrived at Leghorn, with his wife, Lady
Lanesborough. He wrote likewise another severe
libel against the Duke and Dutchess of Cumberland,
and tried to get it printed at Leghorn, but was
refused. He says that he abjured Judaism; by which
he got rid of his first wife (who is daughter of Lara,
a noted Jew, in London), and three children he had
by her. He then married Lady Lanesborough,'
(widow of the second Earl, and daughter of Robert
Rochfort, Earl of Belvedere). 'They have resided
some time at Leghorn; but when their story was
sent from England, with advice from Lara that his
daughter, with two children, was set out for Leghorn,
in search of her husband, the principal English
merchants then grew shy of them. Nevertheless, in
compassion to Lady Lanesborough and her two

children by her late Lord, they most humanely
offered her every assistance, to enable her to go to
England, upon condition that she would separate
from King,—as they could not look on her marriage
with him to be valid.    Those kind offers she refused
with disdain.    In the meantime, that is to say, three
days ago, the first wife arrived at Leghorn. . . .
King, in hopes of securing himself, has taken out
what is called the Priviledges of the free Port of
Leghorn, which protect him against any Prosecution
for all crimes committed before, out of this State.'

One incident in the Grand Ducal family, this year,
serves to show that the annual Giuoco, called the
Battle of the Bridge, at Pisa, was very serious sport
indeed :—' The Pisans are attached to it with an
enthusiasm that cannot be described ; and it is performed with all the pomp of a regular battle.    Two
of the young Arch-Dukes have taken opposite parts
in it ; and, in their disputes, one of them, who is
a Hussar, drew his Hanger, and wounded his Brother
in the face ; for which they were both put under
arrest for some days.'    One would like to know if
this impetuous young Hussar was the Archduke
Charles who, in succeeding days, drew his Hanger
(so to speak) with such effect on France, and saved
the Imperial Austrian dynasty from ruin.

### 1786.

The letters of this year are written with a trem-
bling hand ; occasionally the Minister Plenipotentiary,
unable to write at all, dictates his rather confused

chronicles, week after week, from bed.    Several brief
notes from Sir Horace's nephew express the fears of
the writer, that his uncle's career is painfully closing.
In February, Mann says :—'Though I am not vehemently attached to this world, I must do it the justice
to own that I have no right to complain of my lot
in it, during a very decent course of time, and with
more comfort than I had any pretensions to, at the
beginning of it.    Upon the whole, therefore, I am
perfectly well satisfied, and look forward with a total
indifference as to myself, though to the last hour of
my existence, I shall be anxious to hear of your
welfare.'

Unable to leave his couch to escort Mrs. Damer,
who was again in Florence, Mann writes to Walpole :—
' My nephews ' (two were now with him) ' obtained
leave to be her *Cavalieri Serventi*, which, you know,
is a post of dignity here, among the Italian Dames.'

Rather a journal than a letter, the following is
one of the records worth noting :—' The Albany family
has determined to fix its residence at Rome.    Last
week, the Count was seized with an epileptick fit, the
duration of which gave it the semblance of an
apoplexy.    The Cardinal, his Brother, was sent for
from Frascati, and administered the *Viaticum* to him ;
but by the last letter, he is supposed to be out of
immediate danger, though the fever continued.'

The Dukes of Cumberland and Gloucester, with
their respective Duchesses, were then travelling in
Italy, each couple carefully avoiding the other.    ' The
Duke and Dss. of Gloucester are at Milan.    My
Nephew attempted to pay his duty to them, at Genoa,

to receive their commands for England ; but he was
made to wait, and was then dismissed by a message
that gave him no inducement to return. The other
Royal Duke and Dss. are at Naples, which will probably prevent the former from proceeding further that
way.'

In May, the Minister writes the following bulletin
of himself :—' My weakness, which daily increases, has
reduced me to a most disagreeable situation. I am
frequently forced to sit silent, in the midst of the small
company that surrounds me, in the evening ; but the
Tête à Têtes in the morning are more fatiguing, as
they succeed each other, and the weaker one appears
to be, the more necessary they think it incumbent
upon them to stay to keep up one's spirits till they are
relieved by other tedious visitors.' At a later period
he adds :—' The Duke and Dss. of Cumberland arrived
here late on Tuesday night. I was a little apprehensive that I should be obliged to break through my
rules ; and I asked leave to pay my duty on condition
of being permitted to be carried up and down their
stairs ; but this was prohibited, and the Duke immediately came to me, as the Dutchess did, in the
evening, and put me quite at my ease. They eat Ices,
and then went to the Theatre, in each of which my
Boxes have been a little decorated on this occasion.
My cook dresses *their* dinner, at their inn, and my
Credenzier ' (butler) ' sends *my* Ices every day from
hence, for the *dessert ;* and they make use of my
Coaches. With these attentions, I avoid, or make up
for, my incapacity of any personal attendance.'

' We have another curious being hovering about

Tuscany, but has not yet been here, the Episcopal
Earl of Bristol (Bishop of Derry, and the third of the
three sons of "sweet Molly Lepel," Lady Hervey, who
succeeded to the Earldom.)   ' He moves from place to
place, to avoid his eldest son, whom he leaves in absolute distress, at a time when he himself squanders vast
sums in what he calls the Beaux Arts, though he only
purchases the dregs of them.   Lord Hervey, who,
with his Lady and a numerous family, had resided at
Naples for some time, made frequent trips to Rome,
to implore his father's assistance.   He was often
refused admittance, and when he did obtain it, always
met with a denial.   The young Lord, when his father
escaped from Rome, unknown to any of his family,
went back to Naples, to quit his creditors.'

*July 8th.*—' I am reduced to a state of the most
irksome languor ; but when I recollect, which I often
do, that so long ago as when I had the happiness to
see you here, you used to resemble me to a sheet of
wet brown paper, I ought rather to wonder that a
frame, so weak then could be propt up to the age of
eighty, which I think the next month will compleat—
for I have not any precise memorandum about it.'
Mann, however, was not so much affected by languor
as not to exert himself to serve an Earl-Bishop. When
the news reached Florence, that ' fighting Fitzgerald,'
who had fought in six and twenty duels, was hanged,
for a brutal and cowardly murder at last, Mann
says:—' I prevented the publication of it in the Italian
Gazettes, knowing the prejudices of all Italy on such
a subject, besides, that a first Cousin of his was then
here, and that the Bishop, Fitzgerald's Uncle, is in

the neighbourhood. Lady Killmurray did not so ;
for when her nephew, Lord Ferrers, was executed, she
wrote circular letters to her friends here, to notify
the event, and added, how terrible it was to have
a nephew hanged.'

A letter, dated September 5th, 1786, is the last of
a series amounting to ' thousands,' for Mann wrote
one, and often two, a week, during forty years. ' I
creep on,' he says, ' and have been very diligent in
dictating (from my bed) and underwriting my letters
to the office, which is all that a foreign Minister, in
perfect health, is required to do. . . . I have for some
time suspected that a noble Earl here has turned all
his views, either to supplant me or to succeed me. If
he is to take possession while I am living, you will
easily imagine the mortification and disturbance it
must give me, whatever *Douceur* it may be accompanied with to make it palatable.' After a few more
lines on the same subject, the aged writer suddenly
ends with the words :—' Adieu, my Dear Sir, I am
quite exhausted. Y's H. M.'

Mann's nephew took up the theme, as it were,
where his uncle left it. On the 25th September, he
writes to Walpole :—' Nature seems nearly exhausted.
. . . I have given him your Letter ; he read it, and
wept over it.' On the 6th November, the nephew
says: 'I have not had the courage to write to you during
the last month, for I could only have described to you
a state of suffering which would have hurt your
affectionate heart. At this instant, though the breath of
Life remains, the weakness has totally overcome his
feelings, and his friends can only be glad that he is in-

sensible.'  November 17th.—'After a state of delirium
for many days, which I mentioned to you, as a state
even of consolation, he died last night, without a pang.
. . . His Will mentions you with the greatest respect
and esteem, and he has desired your acceptance
of five pictures of Poussin, as a small token of his
friendship.  He has ordered his funeral to be at Leghorn.  Am I culpable in counteracting those orders,
and in having given others to have his body embalmed
and sent to Linton ?  He wished there should be a
sepulchral Urn placed there. . . . To whose Taste
and Sense,' says the nephew (December 12th), 'can I
apply for the Urn and proper inscription, than to
your's ?  In delegating this office to his dearest friend,
I gratify my own mind, and trust I do an act grateful
to yourself. . . . His legacies here and his annuities to
his servants are very great ; they show his unlimited
humanity. . . . From the sovereigns of the country I
have received every mark of respect to the memory of
a man dear to every one. . . . The Great Duke has
exempted his servants from the duties payable on their
legacies, of eight per cent.'

*December 24th.*—'It seemed to me I could make
my uncle's liberality really beneficial to his servants.
I dreaded the accession of large sums to an extravagant
race, in a country notorious for inattention to wives
and children.  I ordered a Deed to be drawn up
privately, by which they bound themselves to secure
to their families two-thirds of the sum they would
respectively have from their Patron's legacy.  I was
derided for the attempt, but the Deed was drawn by a
Notary, who also derided it. I called them all together,

and tho' never possessed of the gift of eloquence or persuasion, yet my sincerity, even in a foreign language, operated powerfully. With tears and every expression of gratitude they pressed forward to sign the instrument that secured to their wives and families a future maintenance,—for the value of the Legacy is very great. . . . I have had the honour of receiving from the Great Duke the most distinct thanks for having diverted into the channel of Humanity what would otherwise have been food for debauchery and ruin. I knew my departure would otherwise have been a signal for plunder. . . . I have totally forbid all Theatres, all Balls, all cursed Carnival riots as unbecoming the dress they wear, and the disposition they ought to have. . . .'

Young Sir Horace Mann was offered by his government, if he would perform his uncle's ministerial duties till a successor was appointed, the magnificent sum of two pounds per day, which would not have paid the cost of entertaining half the wandering English who visited Florence with letters to their minister. 'This paltry, ignominious offer,' he says, ' I refused with indignation.' He declared that he would prefer serving his Majesty for nothing ; and for six months his Majesty's ministers took him at his word, never answered his letters, at last named a ' Mr. Fawkener ' as British envoy, and neither ever paid a farthing of the expenses to which Mann's nephew had been put, nor gave him the coldest word of thanks for the trouble he had taken during six or seven months.

In two of the letters addressed by the nephew of the deceased Plenipotentiary to Walpole, there are the

following sketches of the way of life of the Duke and
Duchess of Gloucester. The younger Mann met them
in Rome, where their graciousness made ample amends
for old incivility at Genoa. 'He is very seriously ill
indeed, and from all appearances, has but a very short
period of remaining existence. . . . I shall not comment upon the state of his mind and body. . . . The
Duke and Duchess are unhappy. From the conversation I had with you when I last saw you, that is
easily accounted for ; but mutual discontent is so
obvious that it cannot be concealed from the most
superficial eye. I stayed two hours with them. The
contest was, who should shew me the greatest civilities ;
but in this contest there was a great degree of mutual
ill-will too discernible. Would it were otherwise !
We, however, know full well the cause of it, and that
cause will not be removed. It is fixed and will operate
with full effect.'

Sir Horace Mann's body was duly deposited at
Linton (Kent). His age at his death, according to
Walpole, was eighty-five. He had hoped that Linton
would never lack a master of the old line of Mann,
and he looked to his nephew as a means to that end.
But that younger Horace did not again marry. Linton,
however, has continued in the family ' by the distaff.'
Catherine, daughter of Galfridus Mann, in 1771
became the wife of James Cornwallis, fourth Earl
Cornwallis, and subsequently Bishop of Lichfield and
Coventry. Their son James, the fifth and last Earl
inheriting Linton, dropped his family name, and took
that of Mann only. This last Earl's only surviving
daughter, Lady Julia Mann, married in August, 1862,
William Archer Amherst, Viscount Holmesdale, eldest

son of Earl Amherst.    'The House is fine,' said
Walpole, in 1757, 'and stands like the Citadel of
Kent.   The whole county is its garden.   So rich a
prospect scarce wants my Thames.'   The house is
occupied by Lord and Lady Holmesdale, and Mann's
old home could hardly be in better keeping.


THE END.


LONDON: PRINTED BY WILLIAM CLOWES AND SONS, STAMFORD STREET
AND CHARING CROSS.

1120212R0

Printed in Great Britain by
Amazon.co.uk, Ltd.,
Marston Gate.